Doing Research

Doing Research

The Hows and Whys of Applied Research

Nel Verhoeven

LYCEUM
BOOKS, INC.

Chicago, Illinois

Published in North America By

LYCEUM BOOKS, INC.

5758 S Blackstone Avenue

Chicago, Illinois 60637

773-643-1902 (Phone)

773-643-1903 (Fax)

lyceum@lyceumbooks.com

www.lyceumbooks.com

6 5 4 3 2 1   12 13 14 15 16

ISBN 978-1-935871-11-8

Copyright Nel Verhoeven 2011. This revised third edition originally published in The Netherlands by Eleven International Publishing, www.elevenpub.com.

Printed in the United States of America.

Translated by Barbara Reed, Harare, Zimbabwe.

For Jan Willem, Sharon and Sander

Library of Congress Cataloging-in-Publication Data

Verhoeven, Pieternella Susanna, 1961-
[Wat is onderzoek? English]
Doing research : the hows and whys of applied research / Nel Verhoeven. -- 3rd ed.
    p. cm.
"This revised third edition originally published in The Netherlands by Eleven International Publishing, www.elevenpub.com. Translated by Barbara Reed, Harare, Zimbabwe."
    Includes bibliographical references and index.
    ISBN 978-1-935871-11-8 (pbk. : alk. paper)
1. Social sciences--Research 2. Social sciences--Research--Methodology. 3. Research--Methodology--Handbooks, manuals, etc. 4. Report writing--Handbooks, manuals, etc. I. Title.
    H62.V39413 2012
    001.4--dc23   2011044077

Preface

When developing and teaching research methods, those in the business generally have to resort to using more than one book. I noticed this when I became involved in the subject at college and university level. Alongside standard textbooks, students are given readers containing chapters from other books, articles and examples. Moreover, lecturers at colleges often use books meant for university level to draw material for their lessons. In brief, there is no all-in-one, clearly laid out introduction to research methods and techniques for colleges. With *Doing Research*, I hope to fill this gap.

Subjects such as research methods and statistics are not the most popular among students. Often they dread these courses: they are afraid that they won't understand the subject matter, let alone be able to apply it. They tremble at the very thought of using formulas, and in their opinion they will never (again) have to put research into practice. When I wrote the first edition of *Doing Research*, I tried to lower this threshold to carrying out research and getting to know stats. From the numerous reactions that I received I could tell that I had succeeded in my intentions. I also received many comments and remarks from other lecturers to do with ways to improve and supplement the text. In 2006, we used these suggestions in the new edition, to change the order of the book so that it matches the various research phases. The second edition also contained new material and the website was changed accordingly.

Learning research skills
This book contains an introduction to research methods and techniques for students at college level. It is practice-oriented, using current examples and case studies, and it teaches students research skills step by step, from the simple to the more complicated. The aim is to let students become acquainted with the research process in all its facets, using a clear, easy-to-grasp method. This is done in such a way that students do not lose sight of the big picture – i.e., that research as a whole is a cyclic procedure – by emphasizing the position that each phase has in the overall research process.

The third edition
When working on the third edition, I was careful to pay attention to all the reactions to *Doing Research* that I have had over the years. I would like to

thank all those who have taken the trouble to respond and provide me with all their valuable suggestions. The result of this lies before you: the third edition. This edition comprises a thorough revision of its predecessors, without departing from the original intention: to convey research (and statistics) in a clear and lucid fashion to those who need to use them.

This edition contains many new exercises. As usual, solutions to these can be found on the website. We also looked at the order of the subjects and adapted it where necessary. There is a clear division in the book between qualitative and quantitative research. I have tried to do justice to both in equal measure, and to show, more so than in previous editions, that these two methods often complement each other well and as such ought to be used alongside each other where appropriate. I have included a wide array of new (and up to date) examples and cases to illustrate how methods and instruments are used in practice, thus demonstrating the link between research and reality. At the end of every chapter there is a summary listing the key terms and definitions contained in that particular chapter. In addition, the reference list has been updated and adjusted to take into account the latest APA guidelines. Methods used for researching source material have been adapted to allow for the latest Internet developments. Finally, the website has been redone, updated and extended. For instance, it now houses a library of assignments and exercises.

Many people were involved in the compiling of previous editions of this book. When I wrote the first edition, Bob Bouhuijs of Windesheim Christian University, Annete Bogstra of University College Utrecht and Jan van Leeuwen of Fontys University Eindhoven all gave me advice. Jan Willem Zeijseink advised me on Chapter 6 and Rika Verhoef did the same for parts of Chapter 7. Peter Swanborn, Siep van der Werf of the University of Applied Sciences Amsterdam, and Anya Luscombe all went through the text thoroughly and put forward their suggestions for changes. I am grateful to Kip Coggins, University of Manitoba and John McNutt, University of Delaware for reviewing the book. For the current edition, Mirca Groenen gave detailed editorial comments and went through the words for the index register with a fine-toothed comb. Finally I would like to thank Rianne de Klerk for all her advice and her quick response to all my questions and comments.

It took six months to put this edition together, a period in which my partner Jan Willem was seconded to Bosnia. I had to work without his advice, patience and care. Whenever he could, he thought it through with me, motivated me and stimulated me, all at long distance. For this reason, I dedicate this edition to him.

Curricula for research methods and statistics develop continuously. Books used in these subjects do that too, and this is why I am a grateful recipient of any remarks and suggestions that you may have. Enjoy the read!

Middelburg, September 2011
Nel Verhoeven

Table of Contents

Introduction

This textbook is intended for use in colleges and universities. It is a general introduction to the methods and techniques that you will use to set up and conduct – normal practice-oriented – research, in other words: getting answers to research questions from the field.

Which field? These days, research is carried out in virtually every field or profession. Clients and employers want to be able to substantiate and assess the policies they have drafted properly; they want to see their returns expressed in figures; they want to be able to make the correct diagnosis. Carrying out research in the field correctly is growing in importance.

Practice makes perfect! You learn about research by doing it! But also by reading about it, and by doing practice-based exercises and assignments. During your studies, you will come across research in its various manifestations.

This book is about designing and setting up research, gathering and analyzing information and evaluating the results, all of these from a practical point of view.

Transfer problems
During the course of your study, you'll come across a lot of questions that need answering. For instance:
- How can I best structure my research?
- Which methods should I use?
- How can I formulate the problem properly?
- What would be a good time schedule?
- How do I find information about a subject and where do I find reliable sources?
- How do I gather data? Which methods would be best for my purposes?
- Which analyses do I need to carry out?
- How can I draw good conclusions?
- What is the best way to present my research results?

In your first year, you'll do stats, often in combination with a crash course in SPSS. Then you will be taught about qualitative and quantitative research, methodology that is, as separate subjects.

By the time you get to structuring your own research project, in your final year, the assumption will be that you know about the various methods and techniques. Due to the fragmented nature of your exposure to research thus far, this is where you will encounter problems, problems that may well render you unable to put what you have learned about research into practice. You've never had a bird's eye view of the subject. It's difficult for you to combine the bits and pieces of knowledge that you have picked up over the years, to integrate them into a well-formulated research design, one that will stand you in good stead during your research project.

The information in this book will allow you to tackle this problem of transference (Pieters & Jochems, 2003). It will not only give you tips and hints, but also a lot of exercise material, practical examples, and prompts to research things yourself, in such a way that bit by bit you will be able to bring the separate pieces of 'doing research' together, and all the different aspects will fall neatly into place. Once again: You don't talk about research, you do it!

The goal of this book

The *main objective* of this book is to equip you with enough tools so that you can train yourself to design, execute and assess a simple research project. The objective is that you learn to integrate and co-ordinate the knowledge, skills and attitude that you have acquired in such a way that you can adequately answer a well-formulated research question.

Bear in mind that 'doing research well' does not necessarily mean that you arrive at the right answer, it means that you can ask the right questions! In short: learn to be curious!

The book's structure

The book is divided into four parts that correspond to the *phases* of a research project, as illustrated in Figure 1 (see also Section 1.6).

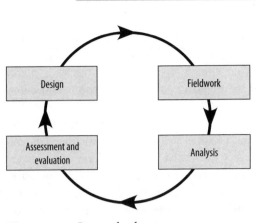

Figure 1   *Research phases*

Before you start actually practicing research, you get to know the underlying   *before you* principles of 'doing research', i.e., the theory. The introduction includes the   *begin* theory of *the science of methodology*. This requires an explanation. By 'methodology' we mean a number of basic research principles, i.e., 'norms'. Even though this book is mainly about how to set up and carry out research in the field, it is important that you know about a few of these basic principles. These research norms (and methodologies) are particularly important when it comes to fundamental research (more to do with theory than with practice). Fundamental research is mainly done at universities. There they develop the basic principles that give research in the field the necessary theoretical depth and ensure that you tackle research with the right attitude. Knowing about these basic research norms is crucial for a good understanding of the function of research.

'Methodology' should not be confused with its meaning as it is used in   *methodology* research practice. There it has a more practical meaning to do with research procedures as in 'methods and techniques'. According to Swanborn (1987, p.41), the use of the word 'methods' is more general and broader. In this book we'll be using Swanborn's definition.
The questions we'll be answering in this chapter are: what does 'doing research' mean? How do you start, what are your basic assumptions, which steps do you have to take as a researcher? You'll be given an introduction to all these aspects in the form of an overview of the more theoretical principles of research. Chapter 1 is therefore the least 'practice oriented' chapter in the book. It deals with the more general principles and concepts of research, rather than any one specific aspect.

Part I
Design

Part 1 deals with all the aspects that have to do with demarcating your research, as well as research design and planning. Chapter 2 is about the background to your research, your choice of subject, briefings with clients and so on. Chapter 3 discusses the objectives, theoretical aspects and defining the research problem.

Part II
Fieldwork

Part II is all about gathering data. Chapter 4 discusses quantitative data collection methods while in Chapter 5 qualitative data collection methods are explained. Operationalization of concept to instruments is discussed in Chapter 6, and this includes introducing concepts that determine the 'quality of research'. Chapter 7 deals with all those aspects to do with the practical side of your research, such as determining the size of the sample and approaching research participants. We will be dealing with research surveys as well as in-depth interviews.

Part III
Analysis

Chapters 8 and 9 handle aspects of quantitative and qualitative analysis. These chapters also contain information about the software that you require for analysis, and the literature that has been written about this software. For the statistically minded, this book's website has additional information about stats.

Part IV
Assessment
and evalua-
tion

Part IV describes how you arrive at conclusions, how you review your research, how you evaluate it and how you report your findings. Chapter 10 discusses concepts such as validity and reliability (the quality of research) and Chapter 11 shows you how to evaluate and report on your findings. Having said that, research quality is a topic that is discussed from Chapter 6 onwards.

learning
objectives

The learning objectives for each chapter are given at the beginning of each chapter. They may look easy, but you will understand that you will have to apply the knowledge found in the chapters in order to reach these objectives. You will have had to practice a lot before you are capable of actually setting up a good research project.

section
structure

The chapters are structured as follows. Per section, the necessary information is presented in short paragraphs. Words in the margin sometimes clarify the text, sometimes they give a short précis. Most of the figures are there to illustrate the text, making it easier to understand. In the yellow boxes you will find examples to do with the research design, planning, problem definitions, research schedules, analyses, results and conclusions.

Each chapter closes with a summary in the shape of a table containing a   *summary*
glossary of the most important terms used in that chapter and their meaning.

At the end of each chapter you will find a number of assignments. These   *assignments*
contain questions about what you have learned and how to apply this
knowledge. Sometimes the assignments will be ordered according to difficulty (ascending). This means that you must complete the assignments consecutively. Make sure that when you have group assignments, you divide the
tasks properly.

The Internet is in a constant state of flux, which means that information   *the website*
about interesting and relevant sites becomes outdated very quickly. URLs
change, changes become out of date and, before you know it, the information you have presented can no longer be found, even though it remains
relevant.
For this reason we have set up a website where teachers and other users can
access new material, examples and current sites (www.doingresearch.nl). The
site also contains Power Point presentations for each chapter, as well as extra
material and the solutions for all the assignments and cases. Teachers will
also find tips for assisting their students in carrying out the design cases
and other assignments in the book, and where necessary course oriented
background information (such as additional analysis techniques, specific
examples, assignments and so on). The site also contains a library with
assignments and their solutions. Finally, an introduction to SPSS is also
available on this site.

On the website you will find two ongoing *design cases*: these are the red   *design cases*
thread in the *assignments* in the book. Practice makes perfect: you learn
research by doing it over and over again, by going through the cycle again
and again, and by not only looking forward during your research, but by
looking back too.
By carrying out the assignments with the help of the design cases you can
practice these skills.
The cases start with a fictitious question about a client. In each section, the
assignments confront you with the choices you have to make, the steps that
you can and must take, and the techniques that are relevant at that point.
The cases are extended during each research phase. Having undertaken all
the assignments, you will have a research design, database, analysis, evaluation and report to call your own.

The cases are structured from various points of view, corresponding to the structure of the research type under discussion. One of the cases, for instance, gives you the opportunity to design a plan for open interviews; in another you will design the questionnaire to be used for a large group of respondents.

logbook The choices and progress that you make during your research journey can be recorded in a 'research log'. With each assignment, you will be given instructions on how to set up this logbook. The logbook enables you to integrate all the separate parts of the research project into one design, as well as provide you with an overview of your research. We will talk about this later when we discuss research design for the first time in Chapter 2.

reading If research is new to you, then start at the beginning of the book and work
guide your way through. Hone your research skills by undertaking the assignments in phases, in ascending degree of difficulty.

If you have some research experience, then it will suffice to go through specific chapters in the book, such as the chapters on interviewing techniques, qualitative analysis or reporting. The index is a quick reference guide to finding the places in the book where a specific term is discussed. In any event, it is prudent to read Chapter 3, specifically where it discusses the information that you need for setting up a research plan. A good plan is the ultimate basis for a thorough research project.

1

The Purpose of Research

Think of research as a journey. Along the way – from the start of your journey until the end (your report) – you come across several forks, crossroads and side roads. These represent the choices that you'll have to make during the research process. Bill Trochim brings this route to life in his 'research road' (see Figure 1.1). Research design, execution and evaluation, according to Trochim, are all interlinked, they are not independent of each other. This road is a dual carriageway. By this he means that you must look at your research with a critical eye, not only during the project, but once it is completed as well. You should also assess research carried out by your colleagues and fellow students: by studying one another's methods you can learn from each other.

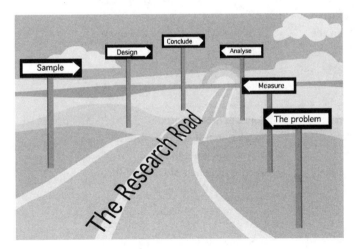

Figure 1.1   Research routes according to Trochim

Without a good foundation, without departure points, your research will be a bumpy dirt road full of potholes, mud and rocks. The road will be uneven, you'll get bogged down. The foundation of research, the tarmac as it were, consists of the departure points, the topic, the objectives, and the methods. Without the structure that these departure points provide (call them road signs and the highway code) the project will become bogged down and you won't be able to proceed (Trochim 2006). Starting a project from scratch is a dangerous business, as illustrated in Text box 1.1.

Look before you leap ...

Mary-Anne has just finished college where she completed a diploma course in Human Resources and Labor Relations. Her first project for a big accounting firm involves tackling the high staff turnover problem that they are experiencing, i.e., an intervention is called for. Mary-Anne is keen: it's her first big assignment. She gets to work straight away. She talks to the people in the human resources (HR) department. They know what the problem is: high staff turnover. It's because the staff aren't given enough financial incentive to carry on working for the firm – that's according to HR. incentives, good leave conditions, study breaks, a decent pension scheme and extra bonuses: all of these together will bring staff turnover down to an acceptable level, Mary-Anne is assured. Mary-Anne draws up her plan of action and comes up with several financial incentives. The presentation of her plan to the board goes well and she's given the go-ahead to put her plan to the test for one year. It will be evaluated every three months (how's it going, has turnover dropped, how much has it cost so far?).

After six months it becomes clear that her measures are costing an awful lot of money and staff turnover has not really dropped. The measures are not working. The board decides to call it a day. Had Mary-Anne done some thorough research, it would have helped. Mary-Anne shouldn't have just adopted the objectives of the organization. She should have spoken to the departments concerned and carried out interviews with the staff involved. Had she done research, she could have reduced the problem to its proper proportions and gotten answers to the following questions:

- Is there really a staff turnover problem?
- If so, to what extent?
- What are the factors underlying this turnover?
- How can it be reduced?
- To what extent will it be reduced if measures are put in place?
- Over what period of time can they expect to see results?

Had she adopted an independent frame of mind, she would not have been swayed by the subjective opinions of the HR department. Instead she could have compared these opinions with the views of the others who were involved. Mary-Anne may then have discovered that money played no role in poor staff motivation, that it was all to do with a bad working atmosphere. She would have realized that effective measures had nothing to do with throwing more money at people; instead something needed to be done about staff relations. The problem should have been tackled by using coaching, team building and, where necessary, changing staff round.

In brief, Mary-Anne should have researched things properly, put together a thorough research plan, and presented it to the board. It may have cost more time and money in the beginning, but it would have paid in the end. Now Mary-Anne has no choice but to walk away, disappointed and with her tail between her legs.

Box 1.1

This situation may seem like a 'worst case scenario'. But in practice it happens far too often that action is undertaken or changes are made without good reason, which is not only costly but bad news for the organization too. All too often it emerges that the root of the problem is something altogether different (see Text box 1.2).

Unrest

During a period of problems with labor, the trade unions organize a strike to try and force a pay rise. After a day of striking, the parties involved (employer, employees and the union) once again sit down and agree to a small monthly increase of 2.5%. But it becomes clear in the months that follow that people are still leaving the company. Had they

researched the reasons for the unrest, they would have discovered that the real reasons had nothing to do with low wages, instead the problem involved the company manager. The hope was that he would go because of the strike. When that didn't happen, several members of staff left anyway.

Box 1.2

Learning objectives

At the end of this chapter, you will be familiar with several basic research principles, you will be able to tell the difference between the various types of research and you will know what is required for a proper scientific

approach. In addition, you will able to recognize the various phases in a research project and you will know what the requirements are for good scientific research.

Box 1.3

1.1   You Have to Learn to Do Research

Learning how to do research involves much more than merely acquiring knowledge. This book can teach you how to set up a plan, design a research project, and define a problem. It can also teach you how to analyze your results, write a report and present the findings. When it comes to actually *conducting* research, there's a lot more to it. You have to be able to combine the knowledge and skills that you've acquired; you have to develop a kind of helicopter view of your research. Doing research has much more to do with skill than with knowledge. In brief, you have to get experience. You learn research by doing it!

Queues at ticket sales

A big name band is coming to town. They're playing at Madison Square Garden. You and your friends go down to the box office to buy tickets. The queue is around the block! What if the tickets sell out! You check out the lines and take the shortest one.

Box 1.4

Maybe you don't realize it, but when you have a problem or a question, you often use research techniques to find the answer. Look at the example in Text box 1.4:

- Your question is: how can I get to the till in the shortest space of time?
- To answer your question, you look at the queues. You count how many people are in each.
- Your conclusion is that the shortest queue will mean the shortest wait.
- You go to the queue with the fewest people.

Train trip

You've made a date to have dinner with a friend downtown. You arrange to meet at Central Station at 7:30 in the evening. It's busy and the trains are delayed. You check the board and it says the trains going downtown are delayed by ten minutes. You see a conductor walking around, maybe he has the latest information. He reassures you, the trains are only running 5 minutes late. You go to the platform where you see other travelers looking worried. You ask again, and they mumble '... there's a fifteen minute delay ...' You call your friend and let her know about the delay.

Box 1.5

For the example in Text box 1.5, you've taken the following steps:

- The question is: when can you expect to arrive at Central Station?
- To solve the problem, you use the following methods:
  - You look at the board (ten minutes delay).
  - You ask the conductor (five minutes delay).
  - You ask the other passengers (fifteen minute delay).
- The answer to your question is that the expected time of arrival is probably ten minutes after your planned time of arrival.

Both before and during the train journey, you carried out research: you formulated your question and you came up with a research method (you made observations, and asked questions), you gathered information, you formulated an answer to your question and drew your conclusions.

The fact of the matter is that we all carry out research activities, even when we do so subconsciously. By using this book you will get experience in the logical order of research, you will become acquainted with the steps that need to be taken for any research project. These steps are the same regardless of whether you're trying to predict the time the train will arrive (as dicey as that may be) or whether you're setting up a complicated research project into the causes of a particular disease.

These examples are very simple. When you're involved in research for a client, practical research that is, it is much more complicated. The research project is normally big, and a lot of people may be involved, you carry out extensive and complex analysis, you write a long report and present it to the client. Still, whether research projects are complex or simple, they all follow the same pattern.

Reflections on a vacation

The weather is great, it's the end of August and you're on vacation. You're visiting London and it seems like an excellent day for a boat trip on the Thames. Once on the boat you see a group of young Oriental people. Complete with cameras and strange shoes, they're jabbering in what sounds like Japanese, but then it would, wouldn't it? Must be Japanese tourists, you think to yourself. Are they really? What you're looking at is a group of first year students who have come to study at the London School of Economics. It's their introduction week.

Box 1.6

Is anyone who makes a casual observation automatically a proper researcher? No, not quite. As you can see from Text box 1.6, you observe things and then you draw conclusions. Because you yourself are on vacation, you automatically assume that the young Japanese people are too. You use your own frame of reference to draw your conclusions.

Researchers have three characteristics or attributes that distinguish them from non-researchers. They are: attitude, knowledge and skills.

attitude   The first thing that sets researchers apart is their *attitude*. This ought to be objective – we know this from Mary-Anne's example. By this we mean that your own personal preferences should play no role in your research. But that is not all. As a researcher you strive for openness in your research, you are open to comments from your peers. You are accountable for your findings. If the findings of your research are contradicted by other research, then it is not because your research was inferior, it's because the findings have been 'refuted'. This means that your research project may be the first in a series of thorough scientific analyses. It is the start of a scientific investigation; the research is ongoing, developing. This 'scientific attitude' is important because it will reinforce your research findings.

knowledge   Obviously you can't apply research methods if you don't know what they are. *Knowledge* of methods is and always will be an important part of doing research. Even this book will expose you to it. Alongside knowledge about methods, you will also need to know about the subject you intend to research. This is the kind of knowledge that you have to polish up on each time. You can look for information on the subject; you can read about it. Knowledge about research methods, on the other hand, is consistent: you always need to know what research methods exist, what criteria they use and what the pros and cons are of applying a particular one.

skills   Besides acquiring knowledge about how to set up and structure a research project, you polish the skills you need for research by actively going out and doing it. As a student, you become familiar with all the aspects of research, step by step, through examples and cases, and then you learn how to apply this knowledge. The methods that you use for this not only give you the background information that you need, they also contain a whole lot of 'recipes' that you can use when it comes to stats, software and so on.

Highlands Sports Club

Every year, Highlands Sports Club organizes a cross country meet. Cross country involves running, not only on the roads, tracks and paths, but also across fields and streams. The distances and age categories vary. During a study for Highlands, a question is raised about the average age of the participants. The reason for this is that they need to know which age group shows the most interest in Highlands' cross country meet so that they can focus their advertising more effectively. To answer the question, a researcher asks all the participants what their age is (in years). The researcher then works out the average age. To do this, he has a choice:

1   Either add all the ages together and divide the result by the number of participants that answered; in other words 'do it by hand' (generally using a calculator);

2   or enter all the age groups into a computer and one push on the button and the average age pops up, a trick of the trade!

The result: he lets the client, Highlands Sports Club, know what the average age of the participants is.

Box 1.7

Sometimes when you're doing research it's important to know a few 'tricks of the trade'. Some examples: selecting the research group, entering data in a software package, devising a test, and crunching the numbers. See Text box 1.7 for an example.

tricks of the trade

1.2   Research Approaches

You don't do research in a vacuum. First you draft a research plan; you define the problem; you check whether anyone else has researched the problem and what their conclusion was; you set a deadline and you draw up a budget to see what is necessary (and available) for carrying out the study; you consult your supervisor, your client, and your co-researchers. These are the practical aspects of research. Besides these, there are other, underlying approaches that can be used to classify research. For instance, there's a difference between fundamental and practical research, between qualitative and quantitative. You can also follow a particular research school of thought, also known as a 'paradigm'.

funda-
mental or
applied
research?

In principle, and according to the science of methodology, there are two main types of research: *fundamental* (empirical) research and *applied research*. University students are more often than not confronted with fundamental research, while college students mainly carry out applied research. The main difference between these two approaches is the type of problem to be solved. The questions raised in fundamental research are generally not primarily concerned with practical application. Applied research however is all about solving problems that have a practical application.

A theoretical problem questions scientific theory, and the solution is sought using fundamental research. A practical problem is normally one that arises in daily life, from the world outside the scientific one. Applied research, therefore, often has social relevance. Fundamental research tends to have scientific relevance. This does not detract from the fact that both fundamental and applied research can address theoretical questions.

Equally, fundamental research can test theories so that social problems can be solved. Scientific research into the effects of earthquakes, for instance, may well have far-reaching social relevance for those living in earthquake prone areas.

Text box 1.8 contains an example of fundamental research. The topic under investigation is not a practical one. The researcher wants to test a theory's validity by carrying out a newly developed experiment.

Arachnophobia

Between 1995 and 2000, Birgit Mayer (2000) investigated phobias. A phobia is an irrational fear of certain objects (for example spiders) or situations. Mayer wanted to test the hypothesis that the person's body reacts to the object or situation before the person is consciously aware of it. Your body prepares itself automatically, as it were, before you spot the spider. She didn't come up with this hypothesis herself; it came from a Swedish researcher, Ohrman. Mayer carried out a number of experiments in the Netherlands to assess whether Orhman's theory was correct. The findings of her experiments did not confirm the prediction that the body reacts before you actually see the spider.

Box 1.8

If the topic originates in society, as is the case with Highlands Sports Club (Text box 1.9), then the research is 'applied'. The question is about practical knowledge that can be applied. The objective, for example, is to change or improve a situation.

Highlands Sports Club (2)

For many years, Highlands Sports Club has held an international cross country event. Every year, lots of volunteers are involved in the event, and the race is broadcast on television. At the annual evaluation meeting that follows, the question is always raised about what the participants, staff and spectators thought of the race. The board wants to see the answer in figures. This will allow them to keep the sponsors happy and perhaps even attract new sponsors. Not only that, the results of this evaluation can be used to improve the organizational aspects of the event. Research into the satisfaction of the three groups of people is carried out.

There are two distinct types of research: qualitative and quantitative. There is an important distinction between the two when it comes to choosing the research method you are going to use. *qualitative or quantitative?*

Quantitative research is based on numerical information, figures that represent objects, organizations and people. Statistics are then used to describe the results and to test the assumptions that the figures represent. Statistical techniques are the tools used in quantitative methods. The researcher takes a step back from the objects or units (people) that are being researched by assigning figures to these various attributes and then ordering them as illustrated in Text box 1.10. Some researchers favor quantitative methods because they prefer to rely on numbers: figures lend them a feeling of security in the sense that they feel quantitative research is 'more accurate' than qualitative research.

Highlands Sports Club (3)

A research plan is drawn up to assess the level of satisfaction among the cross country participants (i.e., the athletes). To gather the information, they decide carry out a survey in which about 20% of the 2,500 athletes will be interviewed. They will assess levels of satisfaction for a number of aspects (in other words 'parts') by 'rating' them. The characteristics of the athletes themselves will also be recorded (gender, age etc.). Their responses will be analyzed numerically (quantitatively), by comparing the various ratings. Differences between the ratings will be compared according the various groups as well (i.e., young versus old, men versus women and so on).

When *qualitative* methods are used, hardly any reference is made to numbers. The researcher carries out research in the 'field' – in 'reality' – and is mainly interested in the meaning that a person attaches to a situation or experience. The 'research subjects' (people being researched) are studied in their environment as a whole. This is also known as *holism*. This means that the experience is seen as a part of the whole system in which the person lives, and not as a separate, independent entity. Some researchers view qualitative research results as less reliable than those based on quantitative research. By the same token, qualitative researchers believe that figures do not offer enough insight into the issues at hand because the figures cannot reveal the information underlying them. For this reason, qualitative researchers make a case for methods that not only focus on the figures, but also listen to what the people have to say (Wester, 1991). In Text boxes 1.11 and 1.12 you will see examples of qualitative research: in-depth interviews with experts and observational research.

Parliamentary Enquiry Committee

Since the 1980s, the Commons has often put into practice their right to hold enquiries. Interviewing experts and other concerned parties, and holding hearings (under oath) with ministers and civil servants, allows them to not only reveal the detailed facts underlying certain events, but also to find out what the interviewees think about the situation and their experience of it. There have been several enquiries, the most notable being the Parliamentary Enquiry into the Iraq conflict. 'Enquiry Committee' is a misnomer because investigations of this type are actually qualitative research: open interviews with a restricted number of respondents.

Box 1.11

Non-verbal aggression

Imagine that you want to investigate whether there is any difference between non-verbal aggression shown by children aged 6 and those aged 10 when they're playing. You may decide to observe the behavior of children in Grade 2 and those in Grade 5 during break time, on two consecutive days. You make a note of what you see on an observation form and then you compare what you have noted. This is qualitative research.

Box 1.12

When you gather information for qualitative research, the methods you use are open and flexible, and you can intervene when the unexpected happens. The information is not recorded in numbers, but in every day language (Maso & Smaling, 1998). The most important aspect of qualitative research is the value and meaning that people (research participants) attach to situations and issues. These days various kinds of qualitative and quantitative methods are often combined in one research design. This is known as *triangulation*. It enhances the validity of the research results. This concept will be discussed in Chapter 5.

1.3   Schools of Thought in Research

We have seen that researchers use various approaches when conducting research. Although this book deals with applied research, it is important to describe a number of fundamental approaches to research, in other words paradigms. Why? Because in applied research, too, there are a number of underlying principles. In order to understand these principles, you need to know something about the theory. Besides the divide relating to qualitative – quantitative and fundamental – applied, we will describe three paradigms, or 'schools of thought'. Certain data collection methods are linked to these three research paradigms. This means that within each paradigm, certain research methods are preferred and the researchers belonging to that group share the same basic assumptions used in scientific research.

Empirical-analytical
Akin to the sciences, the first school of research takes its distance from the research units (or respondents), in the same way as an objective research approach does. By research units, we mean all the elements involved in the research (people, situations, objects and so on).
Empirical means that the research is conducted using systems to assess what takes place in a certain setting. Another word used to describe the 'setting' is 'reality'. Empirical means using 'experience as the source of knowledge'. This school of research is 'analytical' because they view their results with a critical and rational eye: research findings remain 'valid' until they are refuted. This is why the results of earlier research are not inferior in quality. It is simply a matter of new information becoming available that leads to different results. This is what is known as scientific progress.
Researchers that belong to this school of thought strive to carry out objective research and like to control the research situation as far as possible. They

leave nothing to chance; their research, by its design, can be *replicated* and *verified*. This means that if the study is conducted again, using the same design, it will produce similar results. They view all the processes in their research rationally and logically; it is well deliberated. They don't use their gut feelings in their research. Before they start, they predict the results of their research questions on the basis of existing hypotheses. They then test whether the answers correspond to their data. They do so by studying the reality (of everyday life). You could, for instance, test a notion that you have about how people behave by observing as many people as possible and then analyzing the data you have gathered. The more frequently you observe certain behavior among a group of people, the more likely it is that your claims are correct.

A great deal of fundamental research is carried out using this type of research. Their preferred methods of gathering information are experiments and surveys. The attributes of people, groups and organizations are analyzed numerically, in the same way as Birgit Mayer (2000) did in her research into fear of spiders.

Interpretative

Are you interested in the way people (research participants) experience things? Do you want to explore what it is that underlies what people think and feel? Are you using texts, observations and stories to support your research approach? Then you are part of the *interpretative* school of scientific research. The word says it all: 'interpretative' means that you a looking for an interpretation, the way people perceive situations and circumstances, the meat on the bones of the numbers. This kind of research is mainly qualitative in nature and focuses on people and groups of people.

Interpretative research is very popular among anthropologists (scientists who study and describe human culture). They often go and live with tribes so that they can study their every day lives and customs. It's important that the researchers live among the people so that they can investigate why it is that people within the group behave in certain ways (by asking them, for instance) or to observe which habits prevail within the group. This kind of 'field research' is also called 'participatory observation' because the researchers mingle with the people they are observing, and take part in their daily lives. This kind of research also takes place in First World countries. Social scientists, for instance, go and live in poorer neighborhoods of large cities, suburbs with high unemployment, so that they can study the daily lives of people living on the edge of society. In Europe, Godfried Engbersen and his colleagues carried out this kind of research in the '80s (Engbersen, 1991).

Some institutes, such as the Huygens Institute in the Netherlands (www.huygensinstituut.knaw.nl), also carry out interpretative research on historical documents dating back to the Middle Ages so that they can make this literature accessible to the general public.

Critical-emancipatory

The third school of research, *critical research*, is neither particularly quantitative nor qualitative. Any information gathering method can be used, except for experiments. The word 'critical' describes this movement's approach: concern with society. Proponents of critical research not only study society with a critical eye, but also their own research findings. Researchers who follow this school of thought strive to contribute to those social processes that lead to greater emancipation among certain groups (equal rights for men and women), which is why the word *emancipatory* is included.

While this movement is no longer as strong as it once was (Karl Marx was an important source of inspiration for them), elements of their ideas are still applied in research today (Boeije, 't Hart & Hox, 2009; Van Dijk, 1984). The emphasis of their research lies in observation and intervention. The researcher, together with those commissioning the project, endeavour to get processes of change underway. A lot of this type of research is found in organizations and sometimes within society (see Text box 1.13).

Generation without boundaries

A recent example of a critical-emancipatory study is the 'mentality research' that Martijn Lampert and Frits Spangenberg carried out over a period of 25 years among the Dutch population. They presented their results at the beginning of 2010. They carried out an attitudes and opinions study among today's 'generation without boundaries': how they deal with rules in light of all the flexibility and freedom with which they have been brought up in the Netherlands of today. The findings show that today's young people do indeed enjoy a lot of freedom, that they have the means to build a future and that they are positive about their lot. But it's a double-edged sword, both researchers confirmed. Obesity, alcohol abuse, school drop out levels and aggression are a few of the negative tendencies that the researchers mention. A lot of counselors are involved in helping these young people who have been brought up with freedom and independence instead of guidance and boundaries, and it doesn't always turn out for the best. In brief, this is a critical study, focusing on the parameters of change (Spangenberg & Lampert, 2010; Lampert, Haveman, Zuur & Sahin, 2005).

Box 1.13

1.4   Assessing the Quality of Research

This section could easily be entitled 'The rules of research' or 'Research objectives'. There are a number of criteria in scientific research that every researcher must stick to, and they are the criteria that determine the scientific quality of the research. These criteria are relevant to applied research too. Researchers doing applied research must also bear a few rules in mind. Yet it will not suffice to say: 'Stick to the rules and then your research will be good.' As noted in Section 1.1, you also have to have the right scientific attitude, knowledge and skills for your research to be of good quality.

Independence
Research is first and foremost *independent*: unbiased as far as the preferences and opinions of those involved are concerned (i.e., the client or tutor). It could be that those in charge of an organization will benefit if the interventions lead in a certain direction, so that the organization is distracted from the true problems. This may not be the result of conscious decisions; often organizations have no idea where the real root of the problem lies. Independent research can throw light on the real issues, ensure that good solutions are developed to address them and that these solutions are effective.

Objectivity also includes being free from the influence of the researcher. We discussed this unbiased attitude in Section 1.1. What was the story again? The story is this: when you do research, you keep your distance from the subject, you don't allow your personal preferences to influence you (at least, as far as possible). Your own personal opinion of the situation is not what it's about. This kind of *objectivity* is not always possible. After all, researchers are people too, with their own views and opinions. This is why *intersubjectivity* is often used as a criterion: researchers agree with one another as far as the results are concerned. This means that if the research is conducted again, by another researcher using the same methods, it should lead to the same results. It can be *replicated* as it were, and the researchers are in *agreement* about the results.

Falsifiability of statements
One objective of research is to get results about things that are observable in 'reality'. A subject, question or assertion must be *falsifiable*. This means that you can't make claims like 'angels exist' or 'Manchester United is the best'. These are assertions that cannot be proven, that cannot be verified through testing. They are speculative and normative. The point of research is to make claims that can be tested.

All research needs to be *refutable*. This means that an idea or expectation should be able to be *confirmed* or *refuted* (rejected). This has consequences for the way in which you formulate the subject, question or expectation of your research. There can be no confusion about the people or objects under discussion, about the time and place that are relevant to the research or about the terms and concepts that you use to describe them. In short, the subject must be unambiguous. It must also be *public*. A statement cannot be confirmed or refuted if you keep it to yourself and are not prepared to listen to feedback on the subject from others. Making assertions in public means that they can be tested, that research based on the same design can repeated in another situation. This means that research can be *replicated*.

Reliability

Research is generally judged by the *reliability* of its results. Research results are often used to make important decisions, not only in organizations, but also for policy making. It must therefore be of good quality. *Random errors* in the design and execution of research can affect the reliability. If you carry out the research under different circumstances, at some other point in time, then it should lead to the same results. This *replicability* of research is therefore crucial when it comes to assessing the reliability of research, and it is consequently closely linked to the criteria of falsifiability and independence. The reliability of research has to do with the extent to which it is free of *random errors*. In Chapter 6 we'll discuss this criterion at length.

Informativity

The *information content* of your statements must be optimal. This is another aspect that is linked to the falsifiability of your claims. To be able to verify a statement (verifiability criterion), it needs to be accurately formulated, you need to know what it is you are about to research, when and with whom. This is why it is important that you describe your subject *accurately* (Boeije, 't Hart & Hox 2009; Swanborn, 2010, p. 243-244, 1987, p. 35 onwards). You have to very carefully indicate:

- the situation that you are referring to;
- the boundaries within which your research applies;
- the groups involved;
- the period that is relevant to your research;
- the '*domain*' of your research: i.e., the whole 'area' that is relevant to your research, and all the elements that your research involves. The larger the domain, the more informative your statements will be.

Generalizability

What would happen if we went about making statements about situations without researching them? What if we made rules without evaluating them? If the shops stocked things without finding out beforehand if they sell? What if people were given medicine without investigating what the effects might be and whether they are the right drugs for the sickness that ails them? Imagine if we went by what they have to say in the papers about certain groups of people, and dealt with these people harshly without investigating the facts of the matter first. What if we don't verify these assumptions, we don't take into account the background to our observations and/or conclusions?

Based on their results, researchers want to be able to make claims about as many people or situations as they can. They analyze a specific part of 'reality' and make their statements based on that. If these statements have been verified accurately, and according to all the criteria for this, then they can be considered valid for a larger group or other situations: they are generalizable.

By *statistical generalization*, we mean that statistical tests are used to assess whether results are generalizable or not. It is more important in some kinds of research (quantitative) than it is in others (qualitative). When statistical generalization is not relevant, researchers will try to get results that are comparable to results from similar situations, i.e., *theoretical generalization* (Boeije et al., 2009, p.280). An example of this is when applied research is carried out within one department of an organization. It is not necessary to apply the results to the whole organization, but they may be relevant to similar departments, even though the study was not conducted in those departments.

Validity

Validity has to do with the accuracy of the research results. Simply put: we need to be sure that we are 'measuring what we intend to measure' and that the research doesn't have any *systematic errors*. If your research is *internally valid*, then you will be able to draw the correct conclusions from your results.

As we have seen, if you can apply your research to a large group of people (larger, that is, than the group directly involved in the research project), then your results will be generalizable. That has to do with the *external validity*, in other words the statistical generalization that we discussed above. Chapter 6 will tell you more about this important research criterion.

Practical criteria

Finally, there are a number of practical criteria that research must meet. Text box 1.14 gives an example of this. Research must be *efficient*. This means that the costs should be in proportion with the results, and the schedule should be feasible. A general consideration that is particularly relevant to applied research is that it should be *usable*. Many of the criteria mentioned are open to discussion, usability is not one of them. There is no point at all in doing research that has no practical application, whether it's done for universities or clients alike. No-one needs research that goes straight into the dustbin. This may seem obvious. But when it comes to discussing concepts such as reliability and validity, we will see that usability is a valid criterion for research. We will come back to this in Section 6.5.

Highlands Sports Club (4)

In follow-up research among the participants of the cross country event, the board of Highlands Sports Club commissions research into the experiences and motivation of the voluntary staff. There are 130 in all. A written questionnaire is distributed to all of them, and 39 are completed and returned. That is a response rate of 30%. Are these results valid? Yes!

Statistic generalization is a tough requirement. The club wants to use this research to optimize the camaraderie among the staff and the organization. Even though the researchers are independent, a repeat of this research will probably produce different results. The timing of the research is crucial (the questionnaire was distributed in the fall, during a quite period well before they started organizing the event), as is the setting (people filled in the questionnaire at home) and so on. For the client, these results are valuable because people were given the opportunity to give their opinion of things in open questions, there was plenty of room for suggestions and, finally, the respondents had the chance to talk to the board. In short, the results are very useful.

Box 1.14

1.5 Research Cycles

When you're designing and conducting research you are constantly asking questions, for example:

- What am I going to research?
- Why am I going to research it?
- Who am I going to research?

decision time

- How am I going to do my research?
- Where am I going to do my research?
- When am I going to do my research?

You don't only ask yourself these questions when you start researching, when you're busy designing your research. During the research, too, you continually ask yourself questions about its purpose, how it's going, the changes that need to be made. You stop in your tracks and look back, and then forwards. You keep going over the process, it's a cycle:

- Am I still on track?
- What changes must I make?
- What am I aiming at?
- What was the issue again?
- Is the schedule still feasible?

As you can see, during the research project there will be times when you have to make decisions. We saw this in the analogy of research as a journey at the beginning of this chapter. Research has a fixed structure made up of a number of so-called 'research phases'. At the end of each cycle (of phases) it often happens that not only the initial question has been answered, but that a whole lot of new research questions have emerged, ones that can be addressed in the next research project. In this section we'll be discussing two of these series (also known as *cycles*), after which we'll be looking at more practical tools for research phases.

empirical cycle During lectures about research methods you will often hear it said that research has been done properly if it raises more questions than it answers. In fundamental research, theories are tested or developed without necessarily being prompted by a social or practical problem. In this type of research, problems are often formulated (i.e., a specific question is posed) and then a theoretical solution is sought and provided by the scientist. Scientists hope to find solutions to questions using theories. They use research to test whether theories actually produce the answer they are looking for. They draw conclusions based on the results of their research: either the theory does provide an answer, or it doesn't. More research follows, with new questions, and so it goes on.

This process is like a spiral or cycle. In fundamental research it's called an *empirical cycle*. Its spiral shape indicates that most research leads to new questions because you keep repeating the same series over and over, but you don't start at exactly the same place each time. This empirical cycle can be given various shapes, but we'll keep it simple here.

Figure 1.2   Empirical cycle

It doesn't stop here: answers to theoretical questions prompt new questions, then you formulate a new theoretical answer and new research questions, and so on. The outline below shows how this process is structured; it's also known as the PTA outline (Chalmers, 1987; Swanborn, 1987; Ultee, Arts & Flap, 1992). PTA stands for Problem, Theory, Analysis.

Figure 1.3   PTA outline in spiral form

Applied research uses an adapted type of empirical cycle. Some call this cycle 'regulative' because it focuses more on decisions and/or changes (Van Strien 1975, 1986). There are a lot of models that are based on this spiral. The aim of an applied research cycle is to offer a framework that supports the search for solutions to practical problems. This cycle is a handy tool that you can use to give your research project shape. *applied research cycle*

1.6   Research Phases in Research

Applied research may well consist of the following phases (may well because there are so many different types of applied research cycles):

1 Problem analysis
When you do applied research, you have clients to contend with. There'll be a research question, a problem, and intervention or a diagnosis, that the client will want you to tackle. Often it is necessary to narrow the problem

down so that you can come up with a workable objective and question. This may happen for several reasons: either because the problem hasn't been refined at all; or because it was, but not correctly; or because it's not complete or clearly formulated. To do all this, you can do some preliminary research by speaking to experts within the organization, reading through material on the subject, attending meetings and so on. The most important goal of this phase of your research is to come up with a good demarcation of your research objective and question areas. If you don't, your research may well become completely unwieldy and you won't get the clear and usable conclusions that you are looking for.

2 Research design

The next step is to design your research, showing how you intend to address the question, which methods you will use to do so, how much time, what you'll need, and who will be involved in your research. You also specify which research instruments you'll be using.

In this phase you may suggest they opt for an intervention, for instance, and go on to develop instruments to assess whether your instruments worked. Equally, you may decide to assess the impact of measures afterwards. You may choose instead to research the causes of the problem within the organization thoroughly, leaving recommendations for interventions to your research. In short, there are so many different ways of approaching your research design. It may even be possible to include some fundamental research in your applied research project, by testing a theory or a method that has already been developed, like the study among the volunteers in Text box 1.15.

3 Fieldwork

After you finalized the design, you go on to conduct the research. This is when you go about collecting the information that you need to answer the research question or questions. There are so many strategies for this, depending on the number of subjects (people, objects, organizations) that you will be researching, the nature of the question (does it lend itself to qualitative or quantitative research?), and the time and budget available (see Text box 1.15).

Box 1.15

Highlands Sports Club (5)

The question for the staff of the sports club is as follows: 'As the organizer of an athletics meet, how can you motivate volunteers?' The researchers set up questionnaire-based research (also known as a survey) that includes some background questions about the respondents themselves, how they spend their time, their work and what motivates them. To assess what motivates these volunteers, they use a scale that has been developed for this purpose (Lindeman, 1996). The researchers compile a list of statements to do with social contacts, care for others, and actively promoting and investing in human capital (this entails actually using your contacts for specific goals, keeping contacts going and extending your network if necessary). The respondents (the volunteers) are asked to indicate to what extent they agree with the statements. The responses to these statements are then aggregated to show one motivational scale for volunteer work. (How you go about this is explained in Chapter 6.)

4 Analysis

You then go on to process and analyze the data that you have gathered. As is the case in Phases 2 and 3, there are several methods to choose from when it comes to analysis, both qualitative and quantitative, depending on the kind of data collected. This will be discussed later in the book.

5 Assessment and evaluation

At the reporting stage, you look all the way back to the beginning: what was it that we were researching, which methods were used, did we manage to answer all the questions using these methods, and if so, what are the answers? What recommendations can be made? Are there any other opportunities for research? How can we evaluate the research project? Is it good quality research? Are their issues to do with the content and/or research design? Although looking back on your research is an important final step, it is also crucial to stop along the way and check on its progress. Are things going according to plan? Are you on the right track when it comes to the content? Are you on schedule? Are you within the budget? Sometimes you have to stop in your tracks, reconsider your whole research project, talk to your client or go back to the drawing board. Most important, after all, are your findings because the organization you are doing the research for has to be able to use them. Generally research is complete once you've written the report and presented your findings. But these findings may also lead to follow-up research. In this case it may be that the questions that remained unanswered can be addressed in the new research project. Or your research may be the first in a series of projects, as part of a tracking study for example. (This is when information is collected over a period of time, to do with developments in the area under investigation. See Chapter 4.)

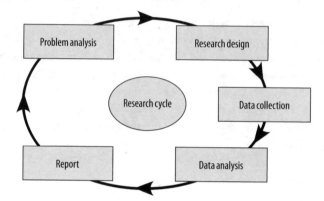

Figure 1.4   Applied research cycles

cycles   Earlier on we discussed empirical and regulative cycles. Figure 1.4 illustrates the research cycle for applied research. This cycle is based on the applied research phases that we have just discussed. It's a handy tool that you can use when you are setting up your research. This spiral is also known as the research work cycle because it gives *the broad outline* of the research set up and the sequence of research activities that will take place. Once again, this cycle can vary considerably depending on the question areas, the number of people involved and the changes that need to take place, but the sequence of events remains the same.

It is worth noting that Figure 1.4 shows the problem analysis and the research design as two different phases. Yet in Figure 1 in the introduction to these two 'sub-phases' were described as one, namely the design phase. Although both of these sub-phases do take place during the design process, in terms of content they are quite different. This is why we decided to show them as two separate phases. In Chapter 3 we will explain why.

Depending on your research question, you can approach this cycle in various ways. In policy research, for instance, you may be asked to chart the consequences of a particular policy measure. The measure may have been introduced some time ago: the intervention might have already taken effect. Your research plan will therefore be designed to carry out an investigation *after* the event, to report on the effectiveness of the intervention, and to formulate a proposal for changes if need be.

It could be that your research design is not completely fixed. For example, if you are investigating a problem in one department of an organization, it may be necessary for you to first find out what the problem is exactly (diagnosis). You may discover that poor communications lie at the root of the high staff turnover. You then put forward a proposal for changes (an intervention is developed: a communication plan that includes clear guidelines for progress meetings and so on). You go on to research whether this intervention is effective. Sometimes it's very clear what the problem is. Sometimes you have to find out first exactly what the problem is.

1.7   Glossary of Most Important Terms and Their Meaning

Scientific attitude	Having the correct independent attitude, knowledge and skills to be able to conduct research.
Domain	The whole 'area' that is relevant to your research.
Elements	All the elements, people and objects that you will make statements about as a result of your research.
Fundamental research	Research that addresses theoretical questions.
Applied research	Research that addresses practical questions.
Quantitative	Research based on numerical information.
Qualitative	Research that is not based on numerical information.
Holism	Research that studies research elements as part of the system to which they belong.
Paradigm	A type of research that uses a specific scientific approach and methods.
Empirical analytical approach	Measures behavior objectively, leaving nothing to chance and approaches processes rationally.
Interpretative approach	Explains behavior by analyzing underlying experience and focuses on the object of the research.
Critical-emancipatory	Looks at society and their own research findings critically; intent on facilitating change.

Independent attitude	Disregard the attitudes and opinions of those involved in the research; safeguard objectivity.
Intersubjectivity	Researchers among themselves agree about the research results.
Falsifiability	Statements can be tested for their validity.
Informativity	Statements are formulated accurately and specifically so that they can be tested for validity.
Generalizability	The scope of your research, both in terms of content and statistics.
PTA outline	Problem, Theory, Analysis: outline for solving theory related questions.
Empirical cycle	The cycle that covers all the phases of empirical research.
Regulative cycle	Cycle for applied research, based on decisions.
Work cycle	Cycle that covers all the phases of applied research.
Reliability	The extent to which research is free of random errors.
Validity	The extent to which research is free of system errors.

1.8   Assignments for Chapter 1

1 Which data collection methods were used:
   a for the Highlands Sports Club research;
   b the arachnophobia research;
   c the parliamentary enquiry;
   d the research into non-verbal aggression?
2 For each of the parts in Question 1, indicate:
   a whether it is qualitative or quantitative research;
   b whether it is fundamental or applied research.

3 For each of the following examples, indicate which type of research is applicable and why:
   - fundamental or applied;
   - qualitative or quantitative research.
   a Research into the impact that information about skin cancer has on the behavior of sunbathers;
   b Research into the lifestyle of Roma people in Northern Europe;
   c Research into the views of parents and children on the quality of education given at Southbank School Kensington;
   d Research into the profiles of visitors to an information website about Q fever;
   e Research into the regional identity of people living in Sri-Lanka;
   f Experimental research into the likelihood of a person changing their behavior when confronted with aggression on the street if the number of spectators increases;
   g Research into the factors that influence final exam results for statistics among college students on the East Coast;
   h Research into how professors spend their time once they have retired.

4 How would you categorize the research subjects in Question 3 in terms of approach (empirical, interpretative or critical) and why?

5 Study the example about non-verbal aggression (Text box 1.12) and the generation without boundaries (Text box 1.13).
   a Identify the domain.
   b What can you say about the statistical and theoretical generalizability?

6 Read through the example in Text box 1.1 again ('Look before you leap …'). How could Mary-Anne adopt a scientific attitude? How would you do this for the example 'Unrest' (Text box 1.2)? Indicate which type of generalizability would be the best for Mary-Anne to try to achieve in her research.

7 There are complaints in the student council about the canteen in the main building of your school. Students say the food is expensive and not good, and the service is not much better. The cutlery is often dirty and there is rubbish on the floor. The way the canteen is laid out is also an issue. What if you were asked to investigate the situation and put forward suggestions for improvement: how would you tackle the problem? Who would you interview for your research? What aspects need to be looked into, according to you? In what sequence would you tackle things? Discuss the answers in your study group. You've never done research before? That's not a problem. Use the material in Chapter 1 and your own experience to approach the problem.

8 In this chapter we discussed two cycles: the PTA outline and the research work cycle.

   a How would you plan the study on arachnophobia (Text box 1.8) using the PTA outline?

   b The research into arachnophobia can also answer social questions, i.e., practical questions. Think of a practical question and design a work cycle to tackle it.

   c Compare both cycles (the PTA outline and work cycle). What are the similarities and differences?

   d Design your own cycle. How would you do it? Talk about it with your fellow students.

9 Describe how you would approach the following situations. Before you start, think about which steps you would take and which questions you would ask based on your own experience. How do you get your information and what do you do with it? Divide the problems into parts.

   a You're about to start college and you need to get a season ticket for the subway. This should be simple, or maybe not?

   b It's your mother's birthday soon. She's expecting a special gift.

   c You're not feeling at all well. What's the problem?

   d You're going out tonight. Where to?

   e You really want to study at Yale. Why?

   f You can't concentrate because your neighbors are too noisy. Are you the only one who is bothered by it? What can you do about it?

Discuss your solutions with your study group.

Then propose a plan of action for one of the above.

10 Read the following pairs of statements and for each indicate which is the most informative and why.

   a I Most college students have a job to earn pocket money.

     II Most college students work in restaurants to earn pocket money.

   b I Recently the sales of hybrid cars have risen sharply.

     II During the past three months, sales of hybrid cars have risen sharply.

   c I Recently the sales of hybrid cars have risen sharply.

     II Recently the sales of hybrid cars have risen by 20%.

   d I Girls are more likely to go for communication sciences than boys.

     II Boys are more likely to go for information technology sciences than girls.

11 Read about the study into the generation without boundaries in Text box 1.13.

   a Discuss its reliability, how informative it is and the generalizability of the results.

   b How independent do you think the researchers are?

On www.doingresearch.nl you will find the solutions to the assignments given at the end of each chapter. You will find them by chapter under the tab 'Assignment solutions'. This icon indicates references to the assignments.

Part I
Design

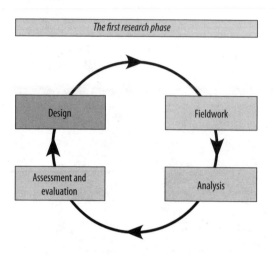

Part I of this book is about research design, a subject that some researchers call 'preliminary research'. This initial research phase addresses issues such as:

- What is to be researched?
- Why (with what objective) is it being researched?
- How will it be researched?
- When will it be researched?
- Who will be researched?

Chapter 2 is about the purpose of your research, the contacts that you have with the client (or tutor) about its purpose, the objective and the first steps on the path of the research design. Chapter 2 also discusses two methods for finding information, as well as how to set up your research logbook. The latter starts with a notebook in which you keep a record of the progress and content of your research project. A useful tool in all this is a computer: you can make a chart based on the various research phases that we will be discussing. You can then sort your notes into a time schedule, a work schedule and so on.

In Chapter 3, you will be demarcating your objective and question area as well as the concepts that you will be using for your research. You will be given information about a number of question types and you will be taught how best to go about designing a research model, how to describe concepts and how to structure a research plan. This chapter also deals with sub-questions and your research time schedule.

2

Reasons for Research

In this chapter we will discuss the reasons for doing research and you will learn how you can demarcate your research. Besides talking about dealings with clients, we will also discuss the various ways of looking for information. Seeking out information is a crucial aspect of research. It starts in your preliminary research, and it goes on throughout your research project. Good tools are therefore essential. You will also read about how you can record the information you collect in a research logbook.

In this chapter's assignments, we will start setting up a design case. This is done using the website. The design case is research that you will be designing throughout the course of this book. As a student, you will be designing and conducting research for Curiosa Research Bureau. On the website you will find two cases:

- a quantitative research case, Wal*Mart;
- a qualitative research case, Labor Union H.E.P.

It's advisable to read through the introduction to the cases on the website before you start working on the design cases. At the end of each chapter you'll be given instructions on how to develop the design, the decisions that need to be made and how to motivate them. Initially the instructions will be given for both cases. In the chapters on analysis, there'll be general instructions and instructions for one case. By the time you get to the end of the book, you will have set up your own research project (and perhaps conducted it too) and you will be able to report on it.

Learning objectives	
After going through this chapter, you will be able to delineate a research topic and give the reasons for doing the research project. You'll be able to	look up literature and other information in the library and on the Internet. You'll know what the objective is of setting up a logbook and how to go about it.

Box 2.1

2.1 Choosing Your Topic

It won't happen often that you will have to choose a topic for applied research. Normally it is the client who decides and you have nothing to say in the matter. At the very most, you may decide not to do the research.

choosing a There are several ways of going about choosing a topic for research.

topic 1 If the research project is part of your *degree or diploma*, you choose a suitable subject. There may be a list of subject areas from which to choose, to do with the topic you are interested in. You may be able to propose a subject to your lecturer or tutor. The subject will have to meet your course requirements.

2 A client may *request* research into a specific problem area. As noted before, your only option will be to do the research project or not. You have a choice, but it has nothing to do with the subject.

3 As a researcher, you may want to test a theory so that you can expand your knowledge. This would be *fundamental* research. This kind of research is mainly done at universities. You may be free to choose your subject, but normally the research is part of a program and, as a researcher, you choose a topic that is part of the program. Incidentally, it is not so that applied research only takes place outside the realm of universities. More and more often these days, clients commission research to be done by universities.

On the face of it, it doesn't look like you have much to choose from. Most topics are decided at the beginning of your research. It may seem this way, but don't be misled. Even if the research area is pretty much decided, you do have a say about the specific subject of your research. It will be do to with:

- your ideas about the research design;
- your interest in a specific subject (area);
- the process by which, together with the client, you define the subject so that there is an area to be researched;
- your ability to demarcate the area to be researched and to make the right decisions so that your research design addresses the critical issue or solves the problem.

Reason

There is always a reason to conduct research, particularly when it comes to applied research. The reasons may vary (see Figure 2.1). We'll look at a number of examples. The researcher may want to test a theory and use the research to expand existing knowledge of a certain area (Text box 2.2). The research into potential customers in Text box 2.3 is more practical in nature because it puts forward policy recommendations. Yet it is still fundamental research because it tests Ellen Lindeman's (1996, p.13) theory of art. However, in general applied research addresses problems that can be solved by research, such as the research into truancy and dropping out (Text box 2.4).

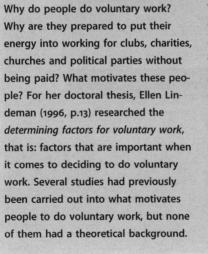

Figure 2.1   Reasons for doing research

Reasons for doing research I: The choice to do voluntary work

Why do people do voluntary work? Why are they prepared to put their energy into working for clubs, charities, churches and political parties without being paid? What motivates these people? For her doctoral thesis, Ellen Lindeman (1996, p.13) researched the *determining factors for voluntary work*, that is: factors that are important when it comes to deciding to do voluntary work. Several studies had previously been carried out into what motivates people to do voluntary work, but none of them had a theoretical background.

This meant that it was not clear how these factors interact and relate to each other. This was the theoretical basis, the objective of which was to expand and deepen knowledge about the way determinants influence the decision to do voluntary work.

One remark on the subject. The knowledge gleaned during this research also served a practical purpose: policy makers in government can use this fundamental research to decide and adjust policies to do with voluntary work.

Box 2.2

Reason for research II: New roads? New opportunities?

When the new highway opened in 2011, the Northern side of the city of Middletown became more accessible for visitors from the other side of town. A shopping center on the north side of town wanted to find out to what extent this opened opportunities for new clientele. So they asked a research agency to carry out research among residents from the south side of Middeltown, hoping it would indicate that a new customer base was awaiting them.

Box 2.3

Reasons for doing research III: truancy

Dropping out of school and playing truant can be very damaging for young people, for their futures, their chances in life and for their place in society later in life. It is important that the government has good insight into truancy behavior and that they put measures in place to stop this behavior. In brief, plenty of good reasons to research the issue, which is what happened on a grand scale. In 2010, the Institute of Education in Utrecht published the results of their research into truancy and dropping out under college students (Pauchli, 2010.) In his discussion of the findings, he puts forward recommendations for ways to reduce this absenteeism.

Box 2.4

Reasons for doing research IV: 'When I was on Ritalin, I was in less of a hurry'

Research needs to be done into the influence that Ritalin has on driving, was the advice a commission gave to the government. More and more adults are using Ritalin. They shouldn't be allowed to drive, but they're worse drivers without the pills.

She's spent around $4,000 on driving lessons and she's got a brand new car, but a month ago Angelique Kieft had to revert to using public transport to get to work. Kieft has ADHD and is on Ritalin. It's a stimulant and according to the law this means that she cannot get behind the wheel, even though research shows that ADHD sufferers, with their concentration problems and impulsive behavior, are a much greater danger on the road when they're off their meds than when they're on them. Kieft has lodged an objection to the Central Vehicle Department (CVD). This week the Ministry of Traffic will be looking into the issue. A specially formed committee, headed by child psychiatrist Prof. Jan Buitelaar, has advised that research needs to be done into the effects of Ritalin on driving. Until then, all those who want to drive

Continued

have to undergo a medical. Otherwise the 'strange consequence', according to Buitelaar, 'is that ADHD sufferers who stop taking their medicine are free to drive, with all the risks that this entails, while those who keep taking their pills to combat the symptoms are the victims'. Research shows that ADHD affects an estimated 160,000 adults in the Netherlands. Only a few thousand of these are on treatment. The ministry will decide this week whether to take the advice of the committee. They can also approach the National Health Council for further advice. After consultations the decision will be taken whether or not to change the Road Traffic Act.

The issues surrounding Ritalin are relatively new for the CVD. Until recently, it wasn't generally known that adults also suffer from ADHD and Ritalin was only used to treat children. Like cocaine, pharmaceutically Ritalin is categorized as a stimulant. According to medical regulations for driving, people taking it are unfit to drive. ADHD patients point out that their medication does not have the dreaded 'cocaine effect', instead it reduces their symptoms. Untreated ADHD sufferers are four times more likely to be involved in accidents than other road users.

ADHD sufferers protest against CVD driving ban

Hartman, who drives for a living, drove for four years without Ritalin, and four years on it, and he's noticed the difference. 'I wasn't in a hurry, I could concentrate.' Hartman took legal action against the CVD when they turned down his Class E driver's license. He'd passed previous driving tests, before he knew he had ADHD, and now he risked losing those licenses too. The courts in Alkmaar ruled that there was enough legal leeway to allow an individual assessment: even though stimulants can affect driving, it is not always the case. The Council of State upheld this ruling on appeal. Earlier this year, Hartman was granted his driver's license after all. He wants compensation from the CVD. He had to stop driving for a living. He now works in stores. Angelique Kieft knows she can drive: three years ago she passed her test without a hitch. Her license does, however, have a medical endorsement, which means she has to go for regular medical examinations. She passed the medical this year but her license was turned down anyway.

Source: De Visser, 2003

Box 2.5

Text box 2.5 describes a reason for research. This newspaper article prompts questions into the effect of Ritalin on driving fitness. People who suffer from ADHD who don't take Ritalin are allowed to take driving tests, even though they are more accident-prone. People who are on Ritalin are better drivers, but they aren't allowed to drive because Ritalin is a stimulant. What would be the wise thing to do? The answer is obvious: research thoroughly the effects of Ritalin on driving fitness. Before 2003, little had been researched. There were reasons aplenty for doing so (De Visser, 2003). This kind of research could be both fundamental and applied.

Measuring the effects of Ritalin on driving fitness

In recent years, a lot of (mainly applied) research has been done into the effects of Ritalin on fitness to drive among those with ADHD. A Dutch research group carried out research by way of a pure experiment in which the effects of methylphenidate (contained in Ritalin) were tested on an experimental group, while a control group was not given the drug. The results showed that Ritalin has a positive effect on the driving fitness of people with ADHD (Verster, Bekker, De Roos, Minova, Eijken, Kooij, et al., 2008).

Box 2.6

Ritalin use and driving fitness continued ...

In 2004 the Road Traffic Act was amended so that it is now possible to get your license even if you are on Ritalin. Normal licenses are now valid for three years, those for trucks and buses, for one year.

Box 2.7

2.2   Clients: You Can't Always Get What You Want

If you are invited to put forward a research proposal, then you are generally not alone. Clients often ask several firms to pitch for the job and then they choose the proposal that suits them best. This does not necessarily mean that they go for the cheapest, or that expensive is always 'good'. You normally have to do a lot of investigating and carry out an awful lot of leg and spade work before you're awarded a project and start your research,

what the   During the initial briefing with the client, you make a list of what it is they
client wants   want. Often there's a problem or a question, an objective and a reason. The objective may be that the client wants to optimize their service. The question is: how can they best go about this?

Sometimes there's a hidden agenda, an ulterior motive. Behind the issue you are presented with lies a completely different goal to the one you may see on

the surface. It's your job to get to the real objective and to formulate the relevant questions. This is crucial. If you launch into the project, without getting to the real objective of the research, you'll be talking at cross-purposes and the chances of you getting the job will be compromised. Apart from anything else, as the researcher you are supposed to be independent and objective. You are there to help solve a problem, you don't allow yourself to be used for any other purpose. Dealing with clients and what they want is sometimes difficult. You have to make the topic 'researchable', but at the same time you have to keep the client happy by doing what they want as far as possible.

Tips & tricks
- Make sure you know your client's organization and its profile.
- Be convincing.
- Listen carefully and ask questions: don't come up with 'the solution' at the drop of a hat.
- Make a note of how the first meeting went! Afterwards you can remind yourself of your first impressions.
- Don't argue the point, even if you're right.
- Don't get involved in the subject: be critical and objective.
- Know what the client expects of you.
- Know what you expect of the client.
- Make sure it is clear what is required (research objective).
- Use the right combination of what you've learned during your study and how to apply it in practice.
- During the briefing, make it very clear to the client what your intended procedure will be.
- Give serious thought to whether you can answer your client's question, and if so, how.
- Work on your proposal at home or in the office.

Once you know what your client's issues and objectives are, then you can set *demarcating* about demarcating the subject. You check whether you are familiar with the *your subject* subject, if you know something about it, or have read about it, whether research into the subject has already been done, or whether it's connected to projects you've done in the past. What problem will be solved by your research? The aim of this demarcation is to translate the client's question into a researchable question. This is also known as problem analysis.

possibilities and limitations Once you've established the main research question (more about this in Chapter 3 under formulating the central problem), you think of ways to address it. The answer depends on the nature of the question, but also on what is possible and the restrictions that the client may impose. The question may be about how happy passengers are with the price of train tickets. You could answer this by organizing a survey, but if the client has budget constraints, or time restrictions, then you'll have to adjust your proposal accordingly. Your research design may well have some very practical restrictions. The solution depends on:

- whether you can organize the research project in terms of time and money;
- whether it's possible to gather the information from the specified research group;
- what's possible and what's not in terms of the issue to be researched;
- what's possible in terms of the research area (you can't do interviews in a noisy factory, for instance).

After analyzing the problem, you choose the plan that you think offers the best solution to the problem, you put your research proposal to the client. In Figure 2.2 you'll find an outline of this.

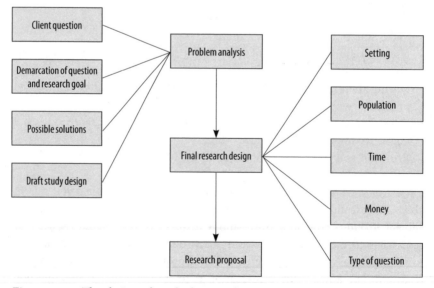

Figure 2.2   *The design of applied research*

After the briefing with the client and once you've demarcated your subject, *research*
you write a proposal. In it you describe the client's issue and the background *proposals*
to it, the objective, the concepts you'll use and the way you intend to answer
the question. Draw up a time schedule and a budget. Keep in mind the following aspects:
- Be comprehensive in your proposal, mention the client and the researchers by name, even if this seems obvious.
- Be clear and concise about the background, the problem demarcation and
  the design.
- Don't forget to mention who will be responsible for the various tasks.
- Make sure your work is correct, and is neat and tidy, even if it is just a
  proposal.
- Always be professional, in your appearance and behavior.
- Make sure the client knows what you're talking about, use the terminol-
  ogy that is familiar to the client, and don't use jargon that no one under-
  stands.
- Include an accompanying letter.

You can always use a different approach. Consider the following pitfalls that
lie in wait when it comes to putting together research proposals:
- Expensive means good.
- The client knows who we are, so why bother mentioning our names and
  so on.
- If I write screeds, there's bound to be something good in there.
- If I hardly write anything at all, I won't make many mistakes.
- My colleague wrote the proposal, so don't look at me! That's called divi-
  sion of labor and I'm all for it.

Scientific research must be objective and reliable. That's what researchers *indepen-*
aim for. How do you handle clients who are more interested in status and *dence*
making money? What do you do if you find out that the client has a hidden
agenda? What if the client wants to use the results to get rid of people
within the organization, to peddle products, and so on? Of course, pushing
products is not necessarily a bad thing. It may well be market research that
you're doing, with the specific aim of launching a product. But these days
research is often used to promote products, instead of actually researching
them. That is an example of a hidden agenda and dodgy to say the least.
It goes without saying that you don't amend your research design and findings for these kinds of goals. As a researcher you have to be *independent* and
objective. But all too often research is amended, results are taken from other

research projects, findings are ignored so that more positive conclusions can be drawn. Fiddling with the data happens too. Things like this happen throughout, at commercial firms and in the academic world. Delnooz (1996, p.111) discusses research done in the United States that revealed that 'half of the academics know about misconduct: from falsifying data to withholding information'.

(mis)inter-
pretation When reading research results, always be critical and careful when interpreting them. Not all research is objective and independent, and the way that results are reflected in the media is also not always correct. In the fall of 2002, for instance, an article in the newspapers (Van Vliet 2002) reported that every glass of alcohol that women drink (on average) increases their risk of breast cancer by 7%. Alarm and despondency! Did this mean that if you drank four glasses of wine, you would increase your risk by 28%? A closer inspection of the research findings revealed that the journalist had misinterpreted the results. Turns out the increase of 7% per additional glass was related to the *initial risk* of alcohol consumption! It boils down to a *general* increase in risk (given the other risk factors) of 0.7%! In Chapter 10, we'll be discussing the interpretation of this research in greater detail.

2.3 Data Collection

Normally research problems are defined broadly, such as 'research into sick leave', 'customer satisfaction research' or 'research into internal communication of a company'. When you are working on the design, you demarcate the question areas as best you can, but you also investigate the subject. Is there literature on the topic? Has research been done before? Is anyone else investigating the subject? Are there existing models that may offer solutions? This kind of information is gathered during the preliminary research phase. But you carry on gathering data throughout the whole process of your research:
a as part of the preliminary research;
b as part of your chosen method, for example during your literature search;
c as a way of gathering new information.

finding Where do you find the information that you need? The first place to look is
information in the client's archives or documentation center. You may find documents that clarify the reasons for the research, such as minutes of meetings, financial overviews, organograms, policy plans, financial indicators, and so on. You can find comparative material on the Internet. If you're looking for the

theoretical background (it may be your research objective) or you're looking for previous research on a specific subject, then you can also look in libraries, university libraries in particular.

In this age of information, you can find information on any subject you care to mention. These days the issue is not whether there is information on a specific topic, but rather where and how to find it and how to process it once you have it. Surfing the web or browsing in the library has not been made easier. More and more information has become available, especially on the Internet. Use a search engine and type in 'school'. You'll get more than 5,630,000,000 hits (or at least that's what came up on September 22, 2010)!

This is why it is important to define your search as specifically as you can. You'll find that this makes searching easier and that you'll be able to find usable information must faster. In recent years, a lot of tools have been developed to help make searching easier, especially on the web. We'll present two of them in this chapter. We'll also be introducing the logbook. A log-book not only supports your search for information, it also helps you to plan and conduct your research.

Another important aspect is the quality of the information that you find. *information quality* Look on Wikipedia, or on any one of the many online encyclopedias on the web. You will be able to find almost all the information that you are looking for. But you have to ask yourself whether this information is reliable. Is it accurate? You have no idea who put it there. If you are looking for reliable information, try to find out who the actual source is. Don't cite things indiscriminately, check instead whether it is correct by finding, for instance, another source that contains the same information. That will at least increase the reliability of your results.

2.3.1   Six Rules for When Searching for Information

The first method used for searching that we'll discuss is the Big6™ that was *Big6™* developed by Berkowitz among others (Eisenberg & Berkowitz, 1992; Canning, 2002). This method is fairly straightforward: it presents six rules that you use to describe your search, carry out the search and evaluate the results. This method can be used to look for all kinds of information sources, be they scientific literature, software manuals, newspaper articles or websites. Every time you search you follow the same six steps so that you end up with a sound result:

1 Task definition. This means that you have to define the information problem, that you investigate how much you yourself, and those around you,
   already know on the subject. You may well have books on the subject in
   your bookcase. In short, you establish what information you already have
   and what information you still need to find.

2 Choose the correct search strategy. This has to do with deciding how you
   are going to look up the information you need in the books, websites or
   documents that you have found. You may choose to use 'key words' to
   look up the information, or to go through the index, contents, executive
   summary and so on.

3 Decide *where* you're going to look. There are so many places to look, the
   most popular being the Internet, especially the online sources and libraries
   that are available (see Text box 2.8). The library is another option, provided they have the right books. Depending on the subject, you'll have to
   decide which is the right place for you to look for the information you
   need.

Online databases

There are lots of online databases where you can find information. One of the most reliable sources of information (about books and journals) is Scopus, now officially named SciVerse Scopus. SciVerse Scopus is the world's largest abstract and citation database of peer-reviewed literature and quality web sources, where you can find information on more than 18,000 titles from 5,000 publishers. Scopus also offers sophisti-cated tools to track, analyze and visua-lize research. Every university and most polytechnic colleges maintain their own knowledge center, such as the University of Nevada, Reno: http://knowledge-center.unr.edu, or Calpoly at California State University: http://lib.calpoly.edu/. You can login using a password and get access to millions of texts and other sources. This means you don't even have to leave your room to do your search.

Box 2.8

---

4 Study the information and select what you need. This may seem obvious
   but it is a step often overlooked. You don't just store the information: go
   through it. If you read through the various sources, you'll see whether
   there are any overlaps.

5 *Organize* your information in such a way that it answers your questions
   or solves the problem. You use the most relevant documents, sites or
   books to address the question. In other words: sort and classify the information in terms of relevance!

6 *Evaluate* the results. Have you collected enough information, or do you need to carry on searching? If necessary, repeat the steps until you have enough information to support a demarcated subject for the client or to address the research question.

Figure 2.3 outlines this search plan.

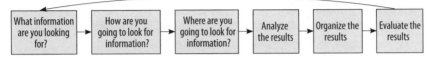

Figure 2.3   Information seeking rules

In Text box 2.9, you'll find an example of a search for information about the effects of Ritalin use on ADHD.

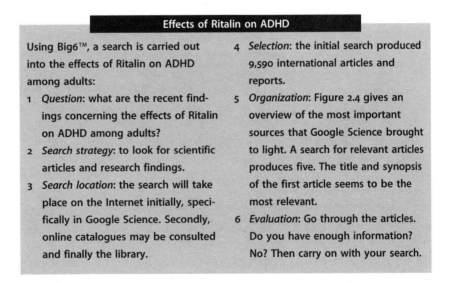

Effects of Ritalin on ADHD

Using Big6™, a search is carried out into the effects of Ritalin on ADHD among adults:

1 *Question*: what are the recent findings concerning the effects of Ritalin on ADHD among adults?

2 *Search strategy*: to look for scientific articles and research findings.

3 *Search location*: the search will take place on the Internet initially, specifically in Google Science. Secondly, online catalogues may be consulted and finally the library.

4 *Selection*: the initial search produced 9,590 international articles and reports.

5 *Organization*: Figure 2.4 gives an overview of the most important sources that Google Science brought to light. A search for relevant articles produces five. The title and synopsis of the first article seems to be the most relevant.

6 *Evaluation*: Go through the articles. Do you have enough information? No? Then carry on with your search.

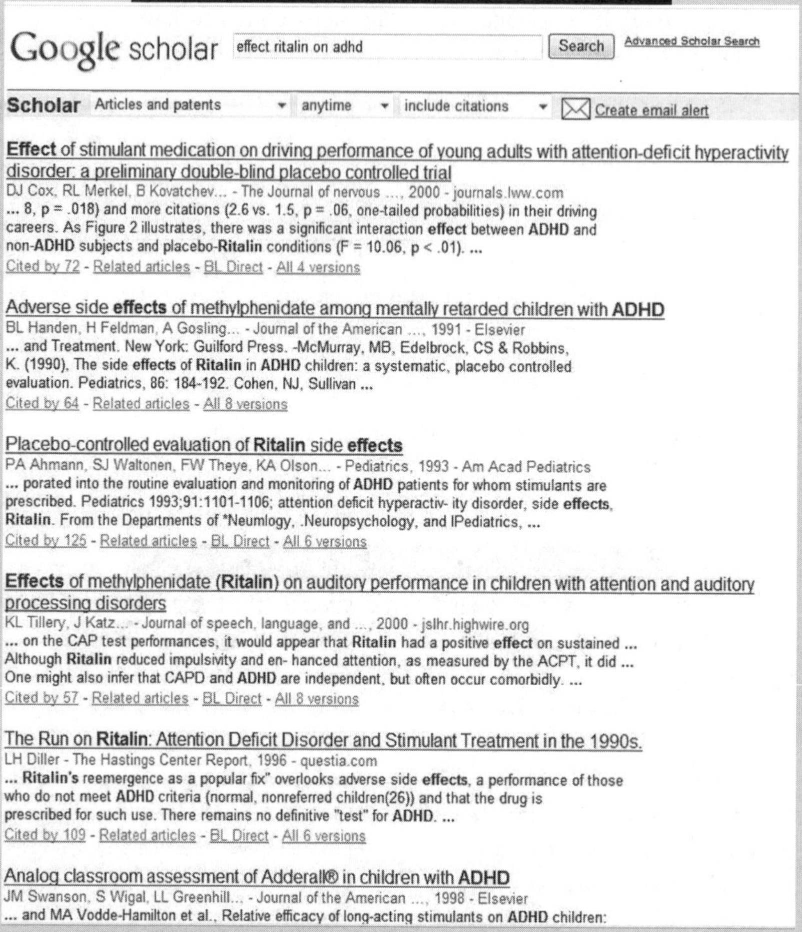

Google scholar   effect ritalin on adhd   [Search]   Advanced Scholar Search

Scholar   Articles and patents   ▼   anytime   ▼   include citations   ▼   ☒ Create email alert

Effect of stimulant medication on driving performance of young adults with attention-deficit hyperactivity
disorder: a preliminary double-blind placebo controlled trial
DJ Cox, RL Merkel, B Kovatchev... - The Journal of nervous ..., 2000 - journals.lww.com
... 8, p = .018) and more citations (2.6 vs. 1.5, p = .06, one-tailed probabilities) in their driving
careers. As Figure 2 illustrates, there was a significant interaction **effect** between ADHD and
non-**ADHD** subjects and placebo-**Ritalin** conditions (F = 10.06, p < .01). ...
Cited by 72 - Related articles - BL Direct - All 4 versions

Adverse side **effects** of methylphenidate among mentally retarded children with **ADHD**
BL Handen, H Feldman, A Gosling... - Journal of the American ..., 1991 - Elsevier
... and Treatment. New York: Guilford Press. -McMurray, MB, Edelbrock, CS & Robbins,
K. (1990), The side **effects** of **Ritalin** in **ADHD** children: a systematic, placebo controlled
evaluation. Pediatrics, 86: 184-192. Cohen, NJ, Sullivan ...
Cited by 64 - Related articles - All 8 versions

Placebo-controlled evaluation of **Ritalin** side **effects**
PA Ahmann, SJ Waltonen, FW Theye, KA Olson... - Pediatrics, 1993 - Am Acad Pediatrics
... porated into the routine evaluation and monitoring of **ADHD** patients are
prescribed. Pediatrics 1993;91:1101-1106; attention deficit hyperactiv- ity disorder, side **effects**,
Ritalin. From the Departments of *Neumlogy, .Neuropsychology, and lPediatrics, ...
Cited by 125 - Related articles - BL Direct - All 6 versions

Effects of methylphenidate (**Ritalin**) on auditory performance in children with attention and auditory
processing disorders
KL Tillery, J Katz... - Journal of speech, language, and ..., 2000 - jslhr.highwire.org
... on the CAP test performances, it would appear that **Ritalin** had a positive **effect** on sustained ...
Although **Ritalin** reduced impulsivity and en- hanced attention, as measured by the ACPT, it did ...
One might also infer that CAPD and **ADHD** are independent, but often occur comorbidly. ...
Cited by 57 - Related articles - BL Direct - All 8 versions

The Run on **Ritalin**: Attention Deficit Disorder and Stimulant Treatment in the 1990s.
LH Diller - The Hastings Center Report, 1996 - questia.com
... **Ritalin's** reemergence as a popular fix" overlooks adverse side **effects**, a performance of those
who do not meet **ADHD** criteria (normal, nonreferred children(26)) and that the drug is
prescribed for such use. There remains no definitive "test" for **ADHD**. ...
Cited by 109 - Related articles - BL Direct - All 6 versions

Analog classroom assessment of Adderall® in children with **ADHD**
JM Swanson, S Wigal, LL Greenhill... - Journal of the American ..., 1998 - Elsevier
... and MA Vodde-Hamilton et al., Relative efficacy of long-acting stimulants on **ADHD** children:

Figure 2.4 Search results for Google Science

Box 2.9

2.3.2   Searching on the Internet

Imagine you've got some leave due and
you want to plan a holiday. Where
could you go? You visit a travel agent
and ask for help. The agent asks you a
few questions:

- Where would you like to go? (Florida)
- When? (Spring break)
- What is your budget? ($500 per per-
son)
- How many of you are going? (Two)

Continued

- How would you get there: by car, plane, train, bike maybe? (Plane)

Depending on your answers, the agent will give you a pile of brochures (about hotels and other accommodation in Florida) that you can take home and leaf through to find something that suits you. Alternatively you can look for this information on the Internet. One evening you go online, open your search engine and type 'Florida'. You get 140,000,000 results! Yikes!

Box 2.10

Looking for information may seem easy, there's enough information to *search* choose from! Looking for the *correct* information, however, is not as easy as *engines* it seems. Take the Internet. There are several 'search engines' that you can use, such as Ilse, Alltheweb, Google, Yahoo, MSN, Vindex, AltaVista, to mention a few. For some time Google has been considered the best search engine in Europe and the States (see the figures in Text box 2.11). These figures date from 2005. In 2008 Google's market share rose slightly to 95% and in 2009, even further. A new verb was coined: to google. If you want to take it a step further when searching on the Internet, you can visit a so-called *metacrawler*, of which there are many, for example: Webcrawler, Webfetch, Infospace, Dogpile and Atnio. These metacrawlers compare the various search engines for the number of search results that they produce for the search terms that you enter.

A good search engine for scientific information is 'Google Scholar'. You can use it to look for scientific information, such as articles (mainly databases, theses, synopses, information about universities and so on. This engine is definitely recommended if it's reliable information you are looking for.

Figure 2.5   Search engines and metacrawlers on www.bovenaan.nl

Google rules the search engine world

Since 2002, Checkit, in collaboration with R&M Interactive Research Bureau, have been presenting the results of the National Search Engine Monitor (NSEM). Last October they did so again, this time presenting the results of a survey conducted among 1,185 Internet users. The research sample is representative of Dutch Internet users. The National Search Engine Monitor includes the following information about search engines:

- awareness;
- usage;
- perceptions;
- user characteristics.

The figure gives information about the awareness and usage of the six best-known search engines in the Netherlands. The figures between brackets indicate the rise or decrease in percentage points compared to the NSEM figures from February 2010.
The research shows that Google is the undisputed leader in search engine country. An astonishing 98% of Internet users in the Netherlands know this search engine, 90% use it, and in the Netherlands Google enjoys 74% of the market share. This is in sharp contrast to the figures for the best known Dutch search engine, Ilse. Name recognition for Ilse remains high at 92%, but only 33% of Dutch Internet users use this search engine. And Ilse only has 14% of the search engine market share in the Netherlands. A new addition to the NSEM is that they investigated usage and perception of toolbars. Sixty-six percent of Dutch Internet users have heard of toolbars, of these 70% know about the Google toolbar, 50% know the MSN toolbar and 25% know the Yahoo toolbar. Google is head and shoulders above their rivals in this respect too. Awareness of toolbars is higher than usage: 15% use the Google toolbar, while the MSN and Yahoo toolbars are used by 3% and 1% of Internet users respectively. Blocking pop-ups (48%) and searching (76%) are the most popular toolbar functions for Google and this toolbar scores an average rating of 7.6 among its users.

	Prompted awareness	Ever used	Used most
Google	98% (+1)	90% (+7)	74% (+6)
Ilse	92% (-4)	33% (-14)	14% (-3)
MSN	68% (-3)	16% (-5)	3% (-1)
Altavista	73% (-5)	13% (-3)	2% (0)
Yahoo	73% (-2)	10% (-2)	4% (+3)
Lycos	73% (-1)	5% (-5)	0% (-1)

Source: Checkit, 2010

Box 2.11

Even when you use a metacrawler, finding information on the web is not *tips for* that simple. But if you follow a few simple guidelines, you'll get results faster. *searching on* Van Ess (2002) has come up with a few tips for this. *the Internet*

1 Be as specific as possible: put your search term *between quotation marks.* Without quotation marks, a term such as 'cycling to California' will get too many results. The engine will show all the results (27,000,000 on April 3, 2011!) for 'cycling' and 'Ireland' using Google. The word 'to' is ignored because it is too general. If you put "cycling to California" between double quotation marks, then it will be seen as a whole and you'll be given far fewer results (763 on April, 3 2011). Using the same term on the same day, Yahoo produced 18,300,000 without quotation marks and 27 with! Some websites suggest using a plus sign, but it doesn't always narrow down the number of results. Try it! By the way, using quotes doesn't always work. It means that the same words need to appear in the title and on the page, and that is not always the case. Give it a go. But remember: we're talking about quality here, not quantity. Using a good search term does not always produce a huge number of results, but often the ones you get are of better quality.

2 You may be looking for a specific fact. You can try using an *incomplete sentence* (between double quotes), for example: "the unions are worried". The search produced 10,300 results compared to 34,600,000 without the quotation marks (Google, April 3, 2011).

3 If you're looking for a webpage with a specific name but you're not sure what it is exactly, then you can precede the search with *allintitle:* (not forgetting the ':'). The words following this will only produce results if they occur in the webpage title. If you enter 'environmental disaster sea', you'll get 1,010,000 (Google, April 3, 2011); for 'allintitle: environmental disaster sea', you'll get 817 pages with the words 'environmental disaster' and 'sea' in the title.

4 Using some search engines (such as Google), it is possible to search for documents generated in Word or Acrobat by typing '*filetype*:doc' or '*filetype*:pdf.

5 You may find a site that is no longer functional. When you try to open the site, you'll get an error message 'This page cannot be found'. It is the familiar http 404 error (File not found). Go to the web address with your cursor, take off the extension (.us or .com or .org) plus any information after the *domain* (the location on the web where a specific site under a specific name is to be found, the 'phone number' or 'address' of a site), and search again. You can also try 'refreshing' your search.

6　Are you looking for international information and you want to see results in various languages? Or are you looking for words that start with a specific syllable? Use an asterisk: Lond*n, Par*s, computer program*. This may not give you what you're looking for, though, because all possible prefixes, infixes, and suffixes will be shown. Try looking for all information using Rom* as a search word!

7　If you are looking for an abbreviation, then enter the reference word that you are looking for. For example ISI can mean a lot of things. If you add 'Statistics', then you'll get the website for International Statistical Institute.

8　The most important tip is about 'advanced search'. Many search engines have an 'advanced search' option. This is another way of making your search as specific as possible. You can enter groups of words, lists, incomplete search terms, operators and so on. It always works and it is a combination of all of the above.

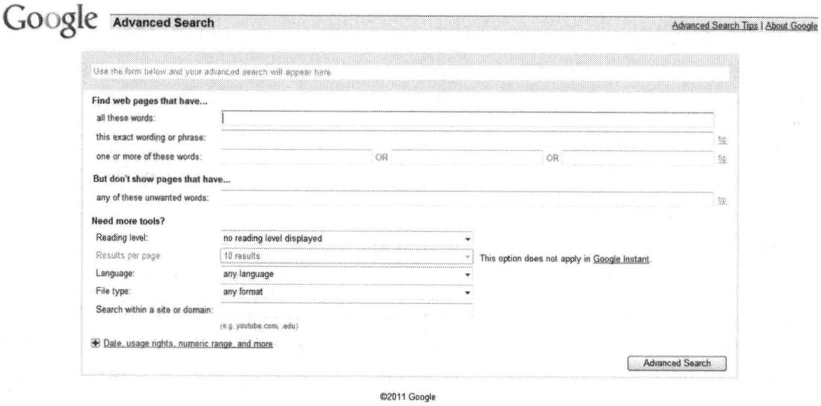

Figure 2.6　Google Advanced Search screen

In Chapter 11 we'll be talking about how you can integrate the information you have found into your report.

2.3.3　Logbook

sorting information During the course of your research you will often have to make decisions, about the process itself as well as about the content of the research. Research processes are cyclical. During and after your research, you will look back on the decisions you made. Maybe you'll want to know why you made a decision at a given moment, or whether you met your deadlines, and if not, why not. Also, from the beginning of your research you will start writing the report. If you don't do this in a structured way, then you'll end up at the end of your fieldwork with a huge pile of unsorted information ... and your head in your hands. This is why it is useful to keep a research logbook.

A research logbook is a kind of diary that you regularly write up (sometimes *logbook* even daily) and in which you make notes of all the processes and content to do with your research. You start by making notes daily in a notebook, just like a diary. There once was a professor who kept a logbook of all his research work, throughout his career. By the time he retired, he had dozens of notebooks, full of information. He was able to go back over research results from 25 years previously. It is an extremely valuable source of information, not only for the professor himself, but for many of his students.

You'll soon find out that your daily notes will not give your research the *file structure* structure that it needs. You'll only have a chronological record, without it being divided into processes, content and so on. That's why it's a good idea to process the notes on a computer and make a chart out of them. If you make 'draft notes', you'll be able to indicate the research phase that the remarks/notes belong to. If you process them on the computer, you'll quickly find the relevant spot.
Figure 2.7 shows that in the folder 'My research project' there are several subfolders, each containing part of your research. Under the subfolders, you can add more subfolders by subject, for example 'planning' (for your daily activities), 'theory', 'method', 'sample', 'response', 'data', 'analyses', and so on. In your 'planning' folder, you can put your notes in chronological order. You can put your notes into the other folders in alphabetical order, or by subject.

Useful programs to use for planning your project are Excel and MS Project. *planning* They make it easy to follow schedules that you can tick off once that part of the project is complete. They also give you space for notes and you can display your progress on a chart.

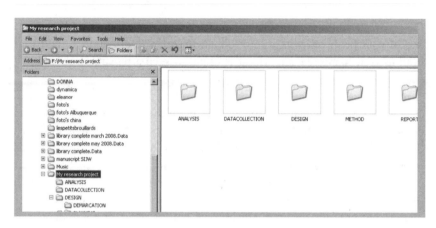

Figure 2.7   Folders for keeping a log on your computer

There are several ways to structure a logbook. Some researchers structure them according to the time schedule; others do so by research phases. The most important thing is that the logbook becomes a useful document for you, which means it can come in many forms. Figure 2.8, for instance, shows the start of a concept demarcation for an observation research project into teaching behavior, in the shape of a handwritten logbook. Table 2.1 shows that it can be a whole lot neater: here notes are processed for a preliminary study in an organization.

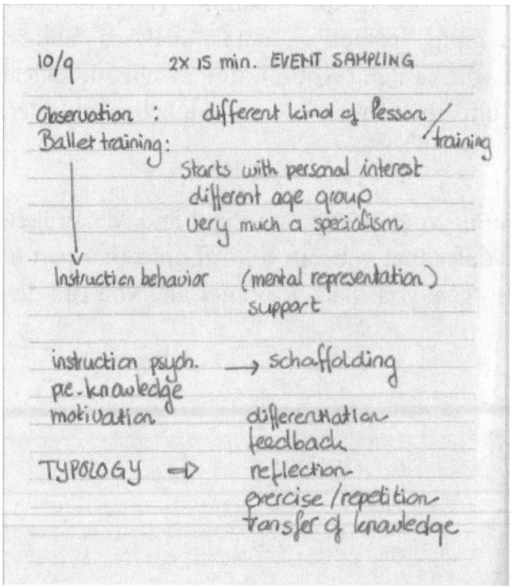

Figure 2.8   Example of a handwritten logbook

Table 2.1   *Processed logbook notes*

Date	Subject	Research phase	Remarks	Processes	Action	Deadline	Hours
2-1	Information search	Design	When searching for info on web, found following interesting sites:	INFO_search	Put into research plan	20-2	2
4-1	Appt. intake	Design	For demarcating subject, paid a visit to the head of the dept. The chat led to: 1. 2. 3.	Design rep. 1	Put into research plan	20-2	4

Besides the date, subject and remarks, the following are shown: the research phases, the document containing the notes, actions that may result, and the most important deadline for that particular subject. As noted, there are many ways to do this, as long as it is clear and easy for you, the researcher. Keep a note of your progress as often as you can, daily if necessary (see Baarda, De Goede & Teunissen, 2001, p. 350). Write down everything to do with your research and anything else that may be relevant, such as:

- decisions you make;
- discussion points, ideas;
- time (not only in milestones, but also: how many hours you've spent on your research);
- processes;
- content;
- method;
- population (research group) and sample (part of the group that you collected data about);
- things that you came across during the analysis;
- possible interpretations;
- links with the question;
- and so on

Group work: exchanging documents
Is there a group of you doing the research? Are you working together with   *Google Docs* other students? Then it's useful to exchange information: parts of the report, information that you've collected, notes, and logbook information as well.

Google Docs (docs.google.com) offers you a very useful (and free!) tool for this. After you've made a Google account, go to Docs. In Docs you can upload your documents and invite other people (your fellow students) to read or work on your documents. You can put your logbook there. If a member of your group does something for the project, then they can add this to the logbook using Google Docs and everyone that's been invited can see the changes.

2.4   Glossary of Most Important Terms and Their Meaning

Reason for research	Reasons why a research project is started.
Big6™	Search method, applicable for literature searches.
Information search tips	Tips to help you look for information efficiently.
Logbook	Research journal.
Milestone	Important point in time (target, decision moment) during your research.

2.5   Assignments for Chapter 2

1 Search methods.
   a Use six key words to describe the Big6™ method.
   b Use six key words to describe tips for searching on the web.
   c What is the difference between a metacrawler and a search engine?

2 Twitter is the latest social networking medium. During elections it's a really popular medium because most candidates post tweets. At the moment a lot of research is being carried out into Twitter's reach and the effect it is having on social contacts.
   The words 'Twitter' and 'research' are put into a search engine: 350,000,000 search results are produced. Next "Twittering research" is entered, with 62 results, as shown in Figure 2.9.

Google "twittering research"

Advanced search

Search   About 62 results (0,12 seconden)

Everything   AMR Research, **Twittering - Research** - Enterprise 2.0 - Egentia
Images   www.enterprise2news.com/.../2983-AMR-Researc... - Vertaal deze pagina
The next big thing: 'Control Towers' · IT Toolbox: Blogs 2011-07-05. Submitted by Trevor
Maps   Miles, director of thought leadership for Kinaxis, provider of the ...

Videos   IDC, **Twittering - Research** - Enterprise 2.0 - Egentia
www.enterprise2news.com/.../2986-IDC?...all - Vertaal deze pagina
News   Salesforce app could be tablet's enterprise 'trojan horse' · IT World Canada ...

Shopping   Gartner, **Twittering - Research** - Enterprise 2.0 - Egentia
More   www.enterprise2news.com/.../2985-Gartner?... - Vertaal deze pagina
The Rise of Ungoverned Data · Information Management - Blogs 2011-09-18. TM ...

Forrester Research, **Twittering - Research** - Enterprise 2.0 - Egentia
www.enterprise2news.com/.../2984-Forrester-Res... - Vertaal deze pagina
10+ items – Login · Sign Up · Create Your Own Portal. Portal ...
· Big Process Thinking" Will Power The Next Generation Of Business Transformation
· This Week Forrester Rates Social Business Platforms, SharePoint Ranks – CMSWire
· The ROI Of Next Best Action: Measuring The Lift From Improved Customer ...

Show more results from enterprise2news.com

Figure 2.9   *Results of a search on the Internet into "Twittering research"*

a Which research question is used in this search?

b What is the difference between the two search instructions?

c Which of the two gives the best results and why?

3 Holland is known as a cycling country. Bicycles are not only used to get to and from work, but also for vacations. Recently, long distance trips by bike have become increasingly popular: so-called 'NBRs' (National Bicycle Routes) have been plotted that cover the whole of Europe, and cycling holiday expos are more popular than ever before. Search the web for long distance cycling routes using the following criteria:

• not too many, but not too few, results

• usable information (informativity).

4 The National Institutes of Health (www.nih.gov) wants research to be done into the effects of obesity on health. They predict that an exercise program will have a more positive effect on obesity than simply following a diet. The subject is broad and needs to be demarcated by sub-questions. This can be done by exploring whether research into the subject has been done before. During the preliminary research, a search is done on the web for relevant pages on the subject. The first search (obesity, sport, health, diet on April 3, 2011) produces 9,050,000 results.

a What is a good search term for this preliminary research?

b Initially, the words 'obesity', 'sport', 'health' and 'diet' are used. Can this be improved, and if so, how?

c Carry out the search on the Internet.

d Select the five most relevant sites.

5 Recently, a lot of measures have been put in place to stimulate sustainable fishing. You want to know where things stand at the moment. Look for information about *research into sustainable fishing*. Search on the web or use the college library. Use the Big6™ method. Select the five most relevant information sources. Describe the search and present the results using the outline in Figure 2.3. How can you use the results?

6 In this chapter we gave an example about research into dropping out and truancy among college students. Check the Internet to see whether the same problem exists for grad school students.

a Come up with as many relevant search terms as possible to cover the research questions.

b Come up with combinations of these terms.

c Carry out searches until you get less that ten results. Use the tips given in Section 2.3.2.

d Choose the best five results. Give a brief summary of each. Why do you think these are the best?

7 How would you go about doing research into truancy? Draft a plan for a research proposal. Discuss it with your fellow students.

8 Text box 2.2 contains determinants for voluntary work. This is fundamental research. You can imagine that this may lead to applied research. In what way could this be applied research?

9 The research into art appreciation by teacher training students was fundamental by nature.

a Why would you call it fundamental?

b The research could also be applied, by referring to the tasks that teachers will be given later at primary school, among other things. Describe an appropriate research plan.

 In the section 'Chapter 2' (tab Assignment solutions) you will find the solutions to the assignments in Section 2.5. You will find information about the design cases under tab 'Design cases' in the section 'Chapter 2'.

Demarcating the Research Topic

In your research plan, you summarize all the research questions as well as your (provisional) answers. According to Verschuren, the approach that you use to draft your plan can be formulated as follows (see Text box 3.1).

First you present your research plan to the client (or your tutor). Once approved, it becomes the guide for your research: it gives your research structure. Bad research is often the consequence of bad preparation. If you don't set up your research properly, all kinds of things can go wrong during data collection and analysis. You can avoid these pitfalls by giving careful consideration to the subject and by writing an explicit and clear plan, one that everyone can stick to. Plan well and take your time to do this properly.

You start your research by defining the problem area, in other words: you formulate the problem and objective. We'll discuss this in Section 3.2. Apart from discussing question types, in this chapter we help you on your way with demarcating the concepts that you will be using in your research, drafting your plan and schedule, and choosing the method you will use to gather the data. You will also learn how to put your logbook to good use.

Learning objectives

After studying this chapter, you will be able to formulate a good problem and objective, and develop some sub-questions. You will be able to describe and demarcate the concepts contained in the problem and objectives formulation. You'll be familiar with the way in which the model will reflect the expected results. You will also know how to draft a research plan, what the different components of the plan are and what it should include. Finally, you will be able to set up a schedule and know what a research budget is composed of.

research path During the design phase of the research project, you reduce the overall subject to the core problem, preferably in one sentence. You know why you're doing the research: the client's (or tutor's) objective is clear. During your preliminary research, you gathered a lot of useful information. This enables you to start with the 'real' work. You are on the research track, as it were.

3.1 On with the Preparations: The Design Phase

What is designing research? By this we mean first and foremost all the activities that lead to the demarcation of the research subject (the *domain*): i.e., formulating the problem and objective, and perhaps sub-questions. Besides this, you address the issue of what information you need, where you will find this information and how you will gather it. The contours of your research will become clearer in the design phase. You will pass the first fork on your research path, and when you reach the fork, you have to make the right decisions. It is not only the domain that becomes clearer, but the questions and statements about the domain too. This is also known as the *claim*.

The design phase is made up of several sub-phases. The first and most important is formulating the problem and objective. You can then come up with a *provisional* answer to the question (i.e., the problem) based on the information you have found: this is the expected research result and it is the basis for your data collection. The core problem has to be relevant so that you know what information needs to be collected. After all, the answer to the question needs to contribute to solving a social or practical problem. The design phase can be subdivided into the following sub-phases (see Figure 3.1):

a orientation, from idea to design;

b describing the problem, defining the core question and objective;

c determining the data collection method, coming up with answers to the questions and a way of verifying the answers;

d drafting the research plan, writing down the answers, planning, budget and so on.

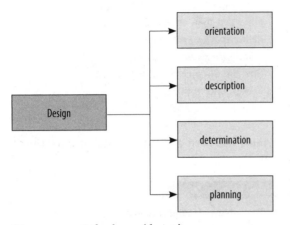

Figure 3.1   Sub-phases 'design'

The phases shown in Figure 3.1 are a guideline for designing your research. In actual research practice, they often take place at the same time. Some-times phases are skipped, and sometimes there is a pre-existing plan, in any event a budget and a schedule. If a client has commissioned the research, you'll have to take this into account. The various phases are just a guide to help you structure your research; their sequence is not carved in stone. What is important is that you demarcate the problem before you start col-lecting the data. Also, you can only start analyzing the data once it is com-plete. Reporting on the findings does not take place at the end of the research process but alongside it. There are even researchers that write down their results beforehand (or what they expect the results to be) so that they can see whether their assumptions were met at the end of it all.

Diagnosing or analyzing the problem takes place during the preliminary *problem* research, as we saw in Chapter 2. Migchelbrink uses six questions to do *analysis* this. He presents this problem analysis as the 5xW+H formula (five ques-tions begin with a W and one with an H; see Migchelbrink, 2002, p.62). For this book, this formula has been adapted to the 6W formula (Text box 3.3).

The 6W formula

1 *What is the problem?* How is it defined? Is it clear what it involves? Is anything missing? If so, what is missing?

2 *Whose problem is it?* Or who is responsible for the problem? You investigate who the players are, who is involved.

3 *When did the problem arise?* Fix the point in time that the problem first arose.

4 *Why is it a problem?* Try to establish the actual reason behind the problem. This means excluding ulterior motives and hidden agendas.

5 *Where is the problem located?* Are some aspects of the problem more important than others? Can you define specific problem areas?

6 *What is the cause of the problem?* How did the problem arise? Get the background to the issue.

Box 3.3

In Text box 3.4, the 6W formula has been applied to research into patient satisfaction in Mercy Hospital.

Patient satisfaction in Mercy Hospital (1)

A large hospital commissions research into how satisfied the patients are with the service in the outpatients clinic and whether there are any areas that could be improved upon. A number of complaints precipitated the research, complaints to do with the medical care in the outpatients clinic during the spring of 2010. Several patients sought care from hospitals outside their immediate area, which is why a survey, including interviews with patients, was conducted in the summer of 2010. The survey findings were used to draw up a plan for improvements. In terms of the 6Ws, the questions were:

1 To what extent are the outpatients in Mercy Hospital's outpatients clinic satisfied with the care they receive there and what suggestions for improvement do they have?

2 The subjects for this research are the patients. The medical staff (doctors, nurses and so on) are the other stakeholders.

3 In this case, the problem arose in the spring of 2010.

4 Complaints about service impact negatively on the quality of care that the hospital offers, resulting in patients seeking medical attention elsewhere. The hospital does not want to loose its customer base, which is why these complaints are seen as a problem.

5 The problem is in the outpatients clinic.

6 The cause of the problem is the complaints about the service in Mercy Hospital's outpatients clinic.

Box 3.4

3.2 Asking Questions

Formulating the problem is the most important aspect of a research project. Without a sound description of the problem, the research project will be an 'unguided missile': you have no idea which direction it should take. Without a well-formulated problem you will be unable to draw sound conclusions, let alone make the right recommendations. We mentioned this in the introduction: *good research is not so much about giving the correct answers, but rather about asking the correct questions.* This is why you must pay a great deal of attention to formulating the problem and objective for your research. Together they comprise the problem description. What is more, you don't always come up with the core question yourself: in applied research the client often presents you with it.

3.2.1 *Problem Description*

Before we deal with the various questions that arise when describing the *terminology* problem, we must first remove ambiguities in the terminology. When defining the core research question, some researchers talk about the problem definition, others about the problem description, research question or central/core question. Ambiguities can arise because of this. In this book, we use these concepts as follows:

The *problem description* consists of the research *objective* and the *problem formulation*, or central question. This is the main question being addressed by the research. It is not enough to speak of 'problem definition' because questions will be asked throughout the research project: about the content, set up, analysis, report etc. To distinguish all of these from the most important research question, we describe it as problem formulation or central question. Within this central question, there may well be several sub-questions that clarify the problem. They are a step in the direction of the research questions that will be answered during the analysis. These questions have more to do with coherence, tests, descriptions and so on.

Therefore: central question → sub-questions → research questions

Whether you are solving theoretical questions with fundamental research or *criteria for* addressing practical problems with applied research, the central question *good central* (also referred to as the problem formulation) always includes what you as *question* the researcher want to know and which question you want to be able to *formulation* answer when you get to the end of your research.

A sound central question has the following characteristics:

1 It is phrased in the form of a *clear question.*

2 It is *related* to the objective (see Section 3.2.3). In other words, the objective and the problem are inextricably bound together. Your problem may be: how satisfied are the customers of Supermarket BS with the range of products? Then your research objective will be to use your findings to make recommendations about extending or changing their range of products.

3 It is also clear *what knowledge* the researcher needs:

   a Which aspects are important: behavior, motives, facts, people's opinions?

   b Quantitative or qualitative?

4 It is also clear which section of the population the researcher needs to find out about and which period of time. It may be that no specific period is mentioned. This can be a disadvantage because it means that you won't know which period you'll be researching. The central question may therefore seem incomplete. But this is not so. The period is not mentioned because the research is being carried out in the present, which is also known as '*cross-sectional*' research.

5 Where possible or necessary, *sub-questions* about the subject may also be formulated (what do you need to know, about whom, where, when and in what context?).

6 *Specification* in research questions is also possible. This means that you can formulate *research questions* from the problem formulation (and also from the sub-questions), which can be answered through analysis.

7 There is a relationship between the central question and *expectations/ assumptions* regarding the research results. The central question is a question about a specific situation or, for example, an effect. The assumption is that you are only asking the question if you have an expectation of the research results. For instance: 'What is the extent of sick leave at "Swift" transport company and how can this sick leave be reduced?' Included in this question is the assumption that there is a problem and that something can be done about it.

8 A central question must be *complete.* A mistake that many researchers make is that their formulation is incomplete. For instance, the question may be: 'What are the reasons behind the high level of sick leave among staff at Ludlow College in Hartford?' You can't answer this question until you've investigated whether there is high absenteeism due to illness. Only then can you investigate why this is. The question is therefore incomplete. We'll come back to this issue when we discuss sub-questions.

9 Problem and objective formulations must be *unbiased*. This means that you draft your formulations as an independent and objective researcher, free from the client's motives and aims. For instance, you may be commissioned to carry out research into internal communications for a large bank, with the aim of improving communication. If the client's real intention is to fire people that are difficult to work with in the opinion of the organization, then there is a real danger that your research will be used for this objective. An unbiased central question can prevent this from happening.

Often the data collection method is quickly determined because it can be deduced from the central question. Obviously it also depends on other factors, such as the population, budget and time schedule. But it is the central question that plays a major role in this. It could be a descriptive question, an evaluative question or a question about a particular effect. Table 3.1 shows examples of these.

types of questions

Table 3.1   Types of questions

Question type	Example
Descriptive	What kinds of holiday jobs do young people aged between 16 and 25 have during the summer break on the East Coast?
Defining	What profile do visitors have to the Hermitage in St Petersburg?
Explanatory	Why is it that high school pupils are reading fewer books? (Or: why do high school pupils read fewer books?)
Predictive	What developments in social media can be expected in the next five years?
Comparative	What is the link between eating habits and health? Is there a difference in eating habits between the less well educated and the better educated?
Evaluative	How do patients rate the service at the outpatients clinic of the Lenox Hill Hospital in New York? What do they think of the proposed rise in retirement age in Greece?
Prescriptive	What suggestions for improvement can be put forward (which measures can be taken) to optimize the quality of the service in the 'Duck and Dog' pub?
Trend analysis	What trends can be detected in purchasing habits in web shops from 2000 onwards?

Text box 3.5 contains an example of a central question. It contains the research elements, the subject and the research objectives (see Section 3.2.3 as well).

Box 3.5

Youth orchestra (1)

The central question for research into the local youth orchestra that was carried out in 2002 was as follows: 'How can the organization of the Youth Orchestra as a whole be structured for the coming years?' (Verhoeven, 2002a). This is a 'how-question' that is not looking for an explanation; instead it is a question about a development perspective for the future. The research is based on the present and the past. The period about which statements will be made lies in the future. Further demarcation is given in a number of sub-questions. The objective is in the central question: the two are together in one as it were. In these kinds of *exploratory* questions, you will rarely find the researcher voicing assumptions about the findings of the research, which was also not the case here.

3.2.2 Sub-Questions

Often central questions are made up of more than one part: first there is a descriptive section followed by an explanatory section (for example, in a subordinate clause). Table 3.1 gives examples of one question type separately. For instance, you may first establish what the trends are in reading habits among high school pupils in recent years. You then go on to look for an explanation for this behavior. The central question would go something like this: 'What are the trends in reading habits among high school pupils in the last ten years, and what are the reasons for these trends?'

There are other ways of doing it, however. Many researchers choose to define a broad, general problem formulation followed by a number of sub-questions (also in the interrogative form) that go on to shed light on specific aspects (the target group, elements, subjects and schedule) of the central question. Verschuren and Doorewaard (2007, p.140) refer to this as 'unravel and regroup'. They discuss several methods to unravel the problem. You could, for instance, split your problem formulation into a number of simple core concepts. These core concepts are the subject of the sub-questions that you need to formulate. An instrument that you can use for this is a *tree diagram*. The concept that needs to be unraveled is the starting point, you then split it up, one step at a time, using questions. Figure 3.2 gives an example of this. Text boxes 3.6 and 3.7 contain examples of sub-questions.

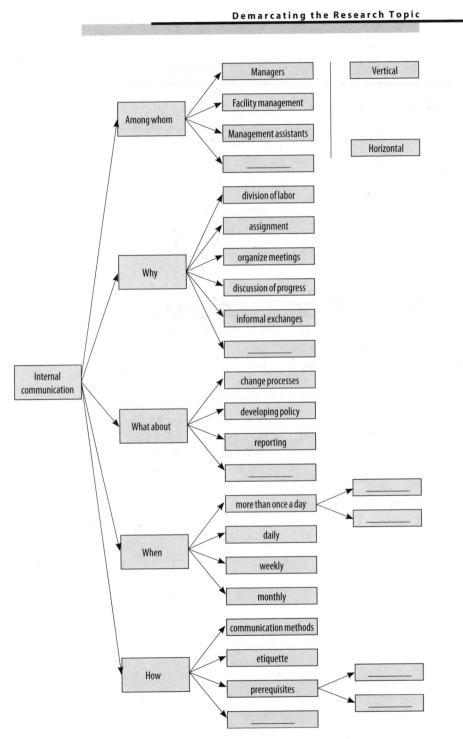

Figure 3.2   Possible demarcation for 'internal communication'

Box 3.6

Emeriti from Utrecht University

For research about emeriti from Utrecht university, Becker and Verhoeven formulated the following central question: 'What activities do retired professors get involved in, particularly those related to their field of expertise?' (Becker & Verhoeven, 2000). The sub-questions related to this include:

- How did they prepare for retirement?

- What is their situation in 2000? How has retirement been?
- What would they like to be able to do, work-wise, after they've retired?
- What are their aspirations and suggestions in terms of putting their knowledge and skills to use after they have retired?
- How will this research affect the policy-makers involved?

Box 3.6

Youth orchestra (2)

During the evaluation research into the youth orchestra organization, the following questions were asked (Verhoeven, 2002a):

- What would be the best legal form for the organization?
- How should the functions within the youth orchestra board and/or volun-

teer corps be demarcated, both in terms of their content and from a legal point of view (in terms of labor laws)?

- What is the best way to recruit sponsors and to raise funds?
- How does the orchestra want to profile itself in the future?

Box 3.7

You use the sub-questions to specify the problem by splitting it into specific questions. You write down the exact information you need to be able to answer the question. This information could be: a description of the situation, differences between groups, finding out about relevant factors, researching specific groups of people, in a specific period, with certain attributes. In Text box 3.8 you'll find an example about 'school leavers'.

High school drop-outs

Some pupils leave school before they graduate. It is a huge problem and the education board wants to do something about it. The board commissions research into the risk factors of dropping out of school. Two kinds of risk

factors are identified: classic and hidden. Classic factors include cognitive aspects, problems in the home and learning difficulties. Hidden factors are difficult to research because it's the pupil own decision to leave, often as a

<table>
<tr><td colspan="2" align="center">**Continued**</td></tr>
</table>

result of motivation problems or choosing the wrong course. Research can focus on the following central question: 'What is known about the hidden factors that influence dropping out of school?' The following sub-questions are relevant:

- Which classic and hidden risk factors are referred to in the literature about dropping out of school?
- How can the group susceptible to hidden factors be 'recognized': what is their profile?

- What do school drop-outs do?
- What measures have been taken to prevent dropping out and what are the main issues to do with these measures?

(This example is based on research carried out by Van Rooij, Pass & Van den Broek, 2010. The research was based on a study of the literature.)

Box 3.8

3.2.3 Research Objectives

Why do you do research? What is its purpose? Apart from underlying fundamental (i.e. elementary) considerations, research also has practical objectives. These are normally formulated with the client's point of view in mind. A well-defined objective includes the following aspects:

1 core definition (not too specific);
2 indication of the research type (practically orientated);
3 indication of the relevance (practically orientated);
4 mention of the objectives and requirements.

The research into the organization of the youth orchestra included the objective in the problem formulation. The issue was about the best form of organization. The objective was to arrive at an efficient organization of the tasks as far as legal structure, internal organization and attracting sponsors (funds) were concerned. The core question and the sub-questions made this very clear. The objective for the study among emeriti from Utrecht University was to use the research findings to give shape to policy regarding retired professors. Up until then, there was no such policy. Why is this policy important? When professors retire at the age of 65, they take all the knowledge and experience that they have built up over the years with them when they go. They generally get involved with all kinds of things in society, but the strict retirement age of 65 means that they cannot do much for the university any more, except on their own initiative. For the university and for the professors themselves, it is useful to consider how and where all their accumulated knowledge and experience can be used.

Finally, let's look at the objective of the school drop-out example. By looking at measures taken in the past (and their success rate), new measures may be put in place to combat dropping out. The objective is in the sub-questions.

3.3   Concept Demarcation

Once the subject and question areas of your research are clear, you can take the next step: you clarify the concepts used in your question formulation. After all, you can't jump from question to questionnaire! If you do, you may end up with inaccuracies when it comes to collecting the information. For instance, if you're conducting research into youth 'lifestyle', then you'll first have to define what you mean by lifestyle. That is why you establish the research domain (what am I making statements about?) and the claim (what statements am I making?)

Sick leave (1)
Imagine that you are doing research in a company into the issue: 'How can sick leave successfully be reduced?' Obviously the first thing you do is establish whether there is a problem: How serious is sick leave? Then you start interviewing people using a ques-	tionnaire. You approach all members of staff that have taken sick leave, at home with a cold, just out of hospital, suffering from burn-out, seriously ill and on their way to a disability pension. Is this the right approach?

Box 3.9

The example in Text box 3.9 is deceptive. What is the story? Often you can define the question areas in completely different ways. There are four ways to define 'sick leave' from the organization's perspective:

- the total number of sick days per organization per year;
- average duration of sick leave in an organization in one year;
- total working days for staff divided by all sick leave;
- the percentage of total working time absent due to sickness by members of staff.

From the staff's perspective, you can describe sick leave as
- illness due to health problems;
- illness due to psychosocial problems;
- illness due to emotional problems.

Another aspect is the subjectivity of the respondents because some people are more inclined to feel sick and stay home than others. If you don't define the concepts properly, you'll get nowhere. There's a good chance that you'll ask all the wrong questions, as you can see from the example. You wouldn't ask someone who is about to be declared unfit for further employment: 'When do you hope to return to work?' Note that you should be defining the concepts, not working out the questions for your questionnaire. You're not making sure the concepts are 'researchable' at this stage. That is known as *operationalization* and is done when you are structuring the data collection method that you intend to use. We will deal with this in Section 6.1.

The first thing you do is establish what you mean when you use a specific   *concept-as-* concept (concept-as-intended). The concept 'lifestyle' in the youth research   *intended* from the example above is described as 'the group that the youth consider themselves to be part of in terms of clothing and music'. There are several reasons why defining the concept is necessary. Here are three:
- The meaning of the concept is fixed and is clear throughout the research.
- You clearly delineate the boundaries of your research, what you intend to research and what you don't (Van Buuren & Hummel, 1997, p. 24-25).
- Demarcating the concept determines what information needs to be collected during data collection.
In short, you are demarcating the domain.

How do you arrive at the correct definition, i.e., the most workable defini-   *stipulative* tion for your research? For theoretical research, definitions are normally   *meaning* found in scientific literature. These definitions are generally unsuitable for applied research because they are too broad. Verschuren and Doorewaard (2007) generally recommend using so-called *stipulative* definitions, i.e., those that apply to a specific research project. The definition would then start with: 'In the context of this research, sick leave means ...'. It is important that the definitions are workable. The importance of this is emphasized if you consider the reasons given for defining the concept. Also, remember that definitions are given not only to indicate what falls within the concept, but also what does not. In other words: what is included and what falls beyond the boundaries of your research!

Suppose your central question is as follows: 'Why is it that sick leave at organization X is so high?' For this question, the staff will be the *domain* of your research, that part of the organization that you'll be making statements about. The situation to do with the high incidence of sick leave will be what you are making *claims* about (Verschuren & Doorewaard, 2007). This means that you will first have to prove that sick leave is high. You will also have to indicate what you mean by 'sick leave' and 'high sick leave'. Text box 3.10 gives an example of this.

Sick leave (2)

Sick leave is a concept that is open to interpretation: it is ambiguous. People decide for themselves whether they are sick or not. Sometimes they are not sick, in the strictest sense of the word (suffering physically from an illness). Emotional and psychological factors can play a role in sick leave. This is why distinction needs to be made between the physical and psychological reasons for calling in sick. In her research, Hopstaken (1994) divides sick leave into three types:

- *white*: there are demonstrable health problems;
- *gray*: it is not clear whether there are demonstrable health problems, but that is how they are felt to be;
- *black*: health issues are not the cause of the sick leave.

Box 3.10

3.4   Models and Expectations

After you have defined the concepts, you formulate the assumptions that you have regarding the results of your research. You can use a model to structure them, supported by the statements and findings of previous research. You can present your model in a simplified 'diagram' form, also known as a research model (Verschuren & Doorewaard, 2007). This is how you show how the various factors interrelate according to you, and what the expected relationship is between the factors. For example, you could present a model showing the factors that influence sick leave and the relation between these factors. As noted, you use existing theories from earlier research where you can.

A model is a simplified rendition of reality (or part of it); in it you show *conceptual* what you expect your research findings to reveal. There are many ways to *model* draw up a model, but it is important that it shows all the aspects that were included in your concept definitions. For this reason, it is often referred to as a conceptual model, comprising three parts:

1 the *elements* of the demarcated domain;
2 *building blocks*: all concepts and/or factors that play a role in the problem;
3 all possible *relationships* that you expect to find between these factors (or variables). In some cases the model will reflect causal relationships (possible effects), in other cases these relationships may be two-way (Swanborn, 2010; Verschuren & Doorewaard, 2007).

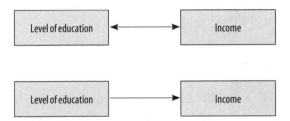

Figure 3.3   Two examples of models

Figure 3.3 illustrates two simple examples of models. The first model has an arrow with two arrowheads. This shows that the researcher expects to find a *two-way* relationship (or link) between level of education and income. The assumptions is 'There is a relationship between level of education and income.'

If the arrow only has one arrowhead, as in the case in the bottom (causal) model, then the expectation is that level of education has an *effect* on income level. The relationship therefore has a *direction*: we call this a *causal relationship*, or *cause-effect relationship*.

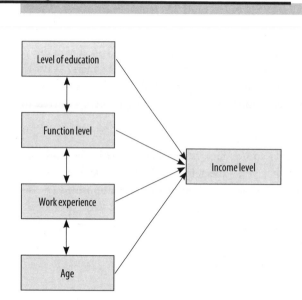

Figure 3.4   A conceptual model on level of income

Model building is mainly done in fundamental research. Applied research uses theoretical models much less frequently. Nevertheless, they are useful tools when it comes to visualizing the factors that play a role in your research and the relationships that you expect to find between these factors. So even if the model is not based on an existing theory, or you are research-ing a practical problem, it is still a good idea to structure your research in this way. The model in Figure 3.4 depicts a number of assumptions over the effects of income levels. This model is not comprehensive: it is just an exam-ple. You can see that the expectation is that age, level of education, job posi-tion and work experience all impact on income. This means that these attributes are not only *linked* to income, but also that this influence will be in a certain *direction*: i.e., there is an effect. You can describe these expecta-tions as follows:

- Education level has a positive effect on level of income. This means that you expect that those with a higher level of education will also earn more.
- Work experience affects income level. The assumption is that more work experience brings with it a higher income.
- Job position affects income.
- There are also arrows going between the various factors. This means that the assumption is that there are also relationships between these factors that are not purely random.

Research into sick leave (3)

To make a model of her research into sick leave, Hopstaken (see Text box 3.10) used the theory of planned behavior (Ajzen, 1987; Ajzen & Fishbein, 1980; Hopstaken, 1994, p. 34). This model shows how you can tell whether people will behave in a certain way (for example, taking sick leave) by asking them whether they *intend* to behave in a certain way. This 'intention' is in turn determined by *attitude* (What is your view? What is your attitude?) and *social norms* (What do those around you think?) regarding the behavior. Another influencing factor is *self-control*. Figure 3.5 illustrates this. It is a difficult scientific model that, despite this, is often used to explain behavior. This behavioral model is a 'causal conceptual model', because a model is used to indicate what causes behavior and what the consequences are.

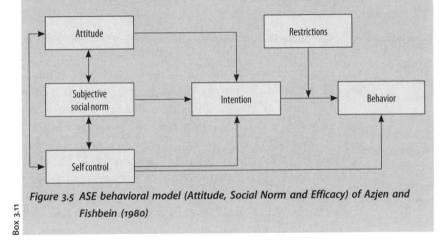

Figure 3.5 ASE behavioral model (Attitude, Social Norm and Efficacy) of Azjen and Fishbein (1980)

The relationships in your model will indicate what your *expectations/ assumptions* are regarding the findings. In the example given in Text box 3.11 you can see that the assumption is that sick leave is high. Obviously your assumption is not a shot in the dark, you have to be able to back it up with sound arguments. For this you use literature, research that has already been carried out and has produced certain findings, theories about the subject, and so on. When you start your analysis, you will define your assumptions more precisely. You make them testable, by defining them as a *hypothesis*. Hypotheses (predictions) are testable statements about the research group (population) that you expect will be confirmed by your research. You test these predictions normally through analyzing your data quantitatively. The hypothesis is derived logically from the general assumption (or expectation) of your theory (or model). Testability of theory is discussed at length in Chapter 8.

3.5   Design Choice

In this section we'll be getting a preview of what is to come in the chapters that follow. We'll discuss the criteria that you use when deciding which data collection method to go with. Apart from the decision-making process itself, we'll discuss the various pros and cons that come with each method and we'll show you which methods go with which questions types. A detailed discussion of a number of data collection methods follows in Chapters 4 and 5.

terminology Although there is more to research design than choosing the way you intend to go about gathering information (data collection methods), in this section we'll restrict ourselves to this part of the research plan. While some researchers call this research strategy, others refer to research method, type, angle (point of view) or design. Choosing a strategy is often seen more broadly than choosing a data collection method. You may opt for qualitative or quantitative research as a strategy, or you may agree with the point of view on which a specific type of research strategy is based. The choice of data collection methods is restricted within each research strategy. Methods such as surveys, experiments, analyzing existing data and so on fall under quantitative research. Within qualitative research, you can choose to do open interviews, observations, focus groups, and so on. The empirical-analytical movement has its own 'dominant' data collection methods. In this book, by 'design choice' we mean choosing the data collection method. The terms 'data collection method' and 'research type' will both be used.

question   You choose the data collection method that can best address your research
areas as   problem depending on the question areas, objective, research group, budget
starting   and time aspects of your research. Take note: The most important reason
point   for choosing a method is that it will help to find an answer to your problem. Text box 3.12 shows you a method that you can use to decide which method to choose. Sometimes you need to tackle the question areas using more than one method, i.e., from a triangulated approach. Read about it Text box 3.13.

Other important aspects are what we call 'possibilities and limitations'. These *possibilities* include things such as available budget, the number of people that can and *and limita-* are willing to participate, the amount of time that you are given, and the cir- *tions* cumstances surrounding the research, at the client's organization for instance. The factors that influence all these aspects can be both theoretical and practical:

a Knowledge about the skills required for particular methods.

b Views on how you should tackle the research (it could be that you lean towards a particular research principle). In this respect, a number of strategies were discussed in Chapter 1 (*empirical-analytical, critical-emancipatory* and *interpretative*).

c Is the research going to take place at a certain point in time (also known as *cross-sectional* research) or is it going to be repeated at various points (i.e., Is the research going to be *longitudinal*)? You could be asking someone their opinion on a certain subject, but you could also be researching a person's life by assessing that person at various points during their lives.

d How much time do you have?

e How big is your budget?

f What research elements are available (normally people, sometimes organizations, administration, databases, books etc.)?

g What other possibilities (not forgetting limitations) do you as the researcher have?

Box 3.12

Election time

A question often asked at election time is: 'How will the seats be divided after the coming elections based on current voting trends?' To answer this question, the obvious choice would be a survey: use a questionnaire (by phone) at one point in time (*cross-sectional*). Within a short space of time, a large amount of numerical information can be gathered and processed concerning a randomly selected sample (also known as *non-probability* sampling).

Working atmosphere

The method may be somewhat less obvious when it comes to the research question: 'What do the staff at Advise consultancy firm think of the working atmosphere?' To answer this question, you could circulate a questionnaire among staff members. You may, however, fail to answer the question if you use this method. This is because of the definition of 'working atmosphere'. The one member of staff may like the atmosphere because he has lots of

Continued

colleagues that he likes; another may like the atmosphere because they get free coffee in the coffee break. You can also come up with all kinds of negative things about the atmosphere. Also, some people may give answers that they think the department would like to hear (this is called 'social desirability'). There is more to assessing working atmosphere than ticking the boxes: the meaning that lies behind the perceptions and the explanation that the respondents themselves give are both crucial. First a literature search needs to be done to demarcate properly the concept that the research is exploring. Then open interviews or focus groups with those involved could be organized. By doing this, you will discover what lies behind the answers to your questions, what it is that they mean by positive or negative atmosphere. You can opt for a qualitative or quantitative approach, or even a combination of the two.

Box 3.13

Text box 3.14 contains an example about mental healthcare that gives the practical arguments for choosing a particular data collection method. In Text box 3.15, you'll see an example about voluntary work policies that highlights the strategic and methodological considerations for choosing methods.

Mental healthcare (1)

In 1998, the Organization for Health Research and Development commissioned research to assess the effect of preventative measures for psychiatric and behavioral problems within the mental healthcare sector. This kind of research may well have entailed setting up long-term and expensive experiments involving assessing groups of patients while exposing them to the various measures. But the researchers were restricted both in terms of time and money. They were expected to come up with the answers within a couple of months. This was one of the reasons they decided to carry out a *literature study* that involved looking at what has been written about the effects of certain measures.

Box 3.14

Box 3.15

Organizational structure

In another research project, a consultancy firm carried out research into the organizational structure of a voluntary organization – a hiking club – with the aim of coming up with recommendations for their future policies. A number of different groups were involved in this research. Beside those of the volunteers, the opinions of the board and sponsors as well as those of the hikers themselves were important. However, because of the high turnover among the members (the hikers) and the reluctance of the sponsor to get involved in the research, they decided to limit the research to the board and voluntary staff. The methods they chose were *open interviews* and *focus groups*. The limitations of the sample did not allow for a large-scale survey. However, their chosen method gave the researchers the opportunity to explore the background behind the views of the volunteers. It allowed them to put themselves into the world of the volunteers and to get a very good idea of their views about the organization's structure.

The central question gives an indication of the way the study is to be carried out. It can be at a certain point in time (cross-sectional) or intermittent, or at various points in time (longitudinal). The latter involves collecting data about trends or developments on a certain subject or area.

In anticipation of the information given in the chapters that follow, Table 3.2 gives an overview of the methods that *can* be used for certain types of questions.

decision process

Sometimes it is obvious from the description of the problem which method should be used; sometimes it is not. An example of the latter can be found in Table 3.2 under the title 'recommend'. Whether or not the research design is obvious depends on the subject that the question relates to. In policy research, written questionnaires can be used to get opinions about policies from a large group of people. Focus groups and interviews would be appropriate if the research is about internal communication within a specific group of people. This would give them the opportunity to make suggestions for specific measures to improve communications. Document analysis – for example, minutes of meetings – can also be carried out to see what measures were taken in the past, and what their impact was. You can describe the behavior of toddlers by asking their playgroup teachers how the children behave in groups. But remember: you'll be getting the teachers' opinions if you do this. A better approach would be to carry out research in the classroom, and get your own observations of a group of children. You'll get first hand assessments and notes that you can analyze. In short, various selection criteria play a role in your research design, the problem formulation being the most important one.

Table 3.2   *Question types and appropriate model*

Question type	Question	Method
describe	What?	Analyze existing material a.k.a. secondary analysis
		Survey
		Content analysis
		Case study
define	Which attributes?	Observation
		Secondary analysis
		Content analysis
		Survey
		Literature research
explain	Why is it that …?	Survey
		Observation
		Experiment
predict	What developments, expectations?	Secondary analysis
		Experiment
		Content analysis
		Survey
compare	What is the link, the difference?	Survey
		Experiment
		Observation
		Secondary analysis
evaluate	How is … assessed?	Open interviews
		Survey
		Focus groups
recommend	Which measures?	
develop	Which developments?	Monitor

While you are designing your research, you take the time to stop and take *iteration* stock of your work so far. Are you still on the right track? If so, then proceed. If not, go back a step, to the previous phase, go over your options once more, and make your choice again. This process of repetition is known as *iteration*.

3.6   Research Plan

Once you have completed your preliminary research, you've formulated your objective and question, your models are ready and you've defined your assumptions, then you take the next step: you put your research plan together. We have deliberately chosen not to use the word 'write' here. This is because when it comes to developing your plan, there's a lot of work to be done. You have to propose which data collection method you intend to use, you have to work out your schedule, and, if it hasn't been done already, you have to work out your budget and the way you intend to report on your findings.

3.6.1   *How Do You Compose a Research Plan?*

When composing a research plan, the following aspects are dealt with: the choices you have made, how you intend to apply the chosen method, how to put your plan together (structure it) and your research schedule. A sound research plan comprises the following parts:

a *The reason* for your research, the background. You describe how you have demarcated the research using the findings of your preliminary research.
b *Problem formulation.* The formulation of the central question.
c *Objective.* The aim of the research: what is the client going to do with the findings? But also: what is the researcher's goal?
d It may have a provisional (theoretical) answer to the question, a *model*, an overview of existing findings on the subject. Theoretical models are crucial in scientific research. In applied research, where researchers are inclined to make do with an introduction to the subject, they tend to get overlooked.
e *Research design* and arguments to support it. Which method have you chosen to address the core question and why? How will the study be carried out?
f *Schedule.* By when must your research be completed? What are the important milestones along the way?

g *Communication plan.* In this part of your plan you discuss aspects such as: how often and how will communications take place between the researcher and the client? How will the findings be presented and discussed? Who will assess the results and how will discussions about this assessment take place? How will the PR aspects of the report be handled?

If you have referred to literature during the preliminary research, then it goes without saying that a reference list will be attached to your research plan.

3.6.2   Timeline

Your research plan will make clear which activities will be part of your research. You draw up a 'to do' list. The time has arrived to draw up a plan of how to spend the time that is available. If you are very experienced at doing research, you will know that you have to set aside enough time for each part of the research project, including extra time as a contingency. You will not always have a lot of room to maneuver. Often the client will indicate when they expect you to make your findings known. You'll have to cut your cloth accordingly.

making decisions The example given in Text box 3.16 shows that deadlines restrict the options that you have in terms of how you carry out your research. In this case, not all the various aspects of the subject were researched. Priorities had to be made. Decision time!

When you draw up your timeline, you have to bear the following in mind:
- what your *objectives* are;
- the various *parts* of your research (the 'to do' list);
- the *sequence* of events;
- the *priority* given to each of the parts;
- the *deadlines* (or milestones); which milestones have to be reached regardless, and which are relatively flexible; deadlines that you can influence and those you can't;
- which parts of your research need to be carried out *concurrently.*

Mental healthcare (2)

The researchers in Text box 3.14 were only given three months to carry out their literature study. This deadline forced them to restrict their research as follows:

- They only studied prevention of illness from a social and psychological point of view (biological aspects and previous studies into these were not researched).
- They did not study publications dealing with the consequences of taking recreational drugs.
- They only looked at publications that discussed reducing psychologi-

cal problems (known as primary and secondary prevention).
- Only reports on particular research topics were studied.

In their research report, the researchers discussed the number of publications on the various subjects that had been determined by the client, and the various research designs that had been used for each. They also described the nature of the interventions and they mentioned the restrictions that the time limit imposed on them (Van Gageldonk & Rigter, 1998).

Box 3.16

The next thing you do is mark off the research period in your diary and specify within that period how you intend to divide your time. You do this for each phase of the research. Always make sure you leave enough spare time for overruns and other unexpected events. Figure 3.6 shows an outline of a timeline. Make sure you discuss your timeline at length with all the parties involved, it is important because will be steering your research. Those who help you with your research also need to plan their time, so be sure to discuss it with them. It's no good planning a milestone that none of your co-researchers can reach.

Figure 3.6 has rows and columns. The columns show the weeks, the rows show the tasks, from A to D and so on. The figure also has dark yellow blocks, each covering a period that ends in a certain week: your milestone. At the end of each block, you can read in the column the week number of your milestone. Task A will be done in weeks 1 and Task B in week 2 and 3 and so on.

It is also useful to be able to see which tasks are undertaken concurrently. For example Tasks B and C run at the same time. Task D starts before Task C is finished. If you look at your own preliminary research, you will be designing the research at the same time as developing your strategy. Demarcating the population and the sample could also be done at the same time as the last changes to the questionnaire. And it is possible to be working on the conclusion while new research material becomes available.

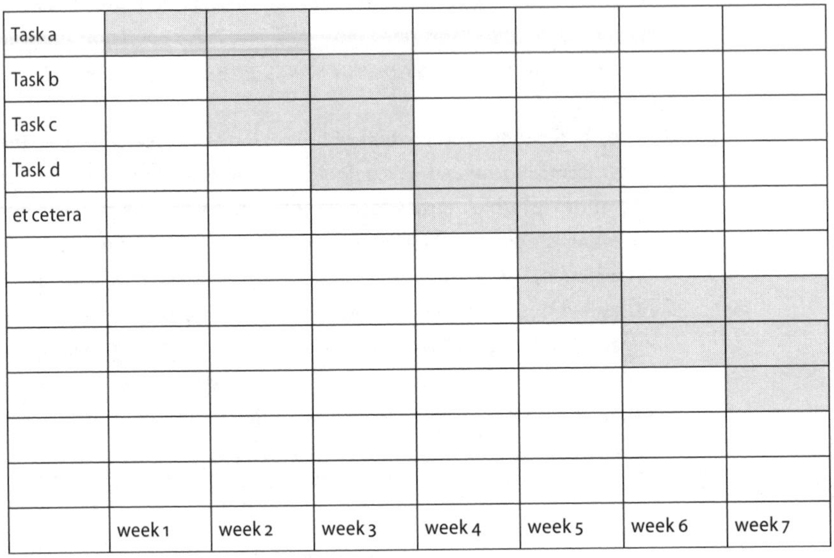

	week 1	week 2	week 3	week 4	week 5	week 6	week 7
Task a							
Task b							
Task c							
Task d							
et cetera							

Figure 3.6   Timeline

overlap Sometimes it is really easy to see where certain tasks will overlap and where they will run consecutively. Sometimes it is not that obvious. Phases in surveys often run consecutively, while in *case studies* (i.e., the study of one aspect of research, for example an organization) phases can run concurrently. Researching an organizational structure is often done using a recurring process (i.e., iterative), during which a number of phases (design, data collection, analysis and report writing) can all be done at the same time.

Your research logbook will be a useful tool in all this. In it, you will have noted the tasks that need to be done, their relative priority, what you have agreed with the clients in this regard, as well as the possibilities and the limitations in your research. You can note some of these aspects on the timeline. From this overview, it will become clear which aspects need to be dealt with concurrently.

Sometimes timelines can be quite general, as shown in Text box 3.17.

Tools for Timelines

Creating a timeline is important for every study, but especially longitudinal research needs a thorough timeline. The British organization ESDS Longitudinal developed a tool to organize international longitudinal studies in a timeframe, such as studies on 'birth cohort':

'This timeline plots the majority of UK/British birth cohort studies alongside their major international equivalents.

This resource builds on the Centre for Longitudinal Studies (CLS) – International Zone – and the UK Longitudinal Studies Centre's (ULSC) – Keeping Track.'

According to its developers this tool will enable researchers to put their study in an international context.

Source: www.esds.ac.uk/longitudinal/resources/international.asp

There are software programs that can help you set up a timeline. Ms Project and Excel come to mind (see Figure 3.6). MS Project charts plans: the tasks are noted in the time axis. Although MS Project is a very good instrument for planning research projects, you can also make your own time chart with all the relevant deadlines yourself, using Excel for example. *planning software*

After you have plotted your timeline, two things are important:
1 You must check whether you will be well ahead of the deadline according to your planning. You do this by adding up the periods between each milestone. If you don't make the deadline, then you must adjust your timeline.
2 You must structure your research by making the contents page of your research report.

It is difficult to say anything specific about setting up a *suitable* budget. It is dependent on so many factors. The main thing is to find out whether the maximum amount needed will be available for your research, then you can take it into account. It is also important to gather financial information. Find out the following: how much each part of research will cost; how long it will take; what it will cost you personally; cost of printing, postage, hiring venues, equipment, laboratories and so on. Try to be as realistic as possible about the costs. If you overestimate the costs, you won't get the project. If you underestimate them, you may have to scrimp and scrape during the research, and you don't want that either. *budget*

3.6.3   Preparing for the Report

You work on the report throughout the course of the research. It starts when you demarcate the problem during the preliminary research. The last thing you do is leave report writing to the end. Researchers who make this mistake often underestimate completely how long it takes to write a report. Start early and write as you go along. This makes it easier to write a clear, well-delineated report. Documents that you can use to prepare your report are as follows:

a your research proposal and design;
b your logbook, in which you'll have notes that you make during the study;
c the outline of your research report that you draft before your start.

Many researchers make an outline of their final report when they start the research project. They do this by deciding on the chapters that it will include: what will the report contain, in the broadest brushstrokes? It goes without saying that you can always change it, but the main outline of the report should always be fixed (see Text box 3.18).

Patient satisfaction at Mercy Hospital (2)

A large hospital commissions research into the quality of service in its outpatients clinic. When they were preparing the questionnaire, the researchers made an outline of the report. They did this by making a list of contents which included all the aspects that would probably be addressed. They also came up with a working title 'Listening to the patients. Opinions about the service in the emergency rooms.' The list of contents looked like this:

1 Introduction
  a reason for the research (Why is the researcher doing this project?)
  b question areas (problem description: central question and research objective)
  c theory (possibly theoretical solutions; model; expectations regarding the findings)

2 Research design (i.e., method)
  a defining the strategy (How can we best address the client's question? Which solutions does the research offer? What will we be assessing?)
  b sample (Which people will be involved in the research and how will we select these people?)
  c data collection (Which research methods will be used and why? How will we tackle data collection?)

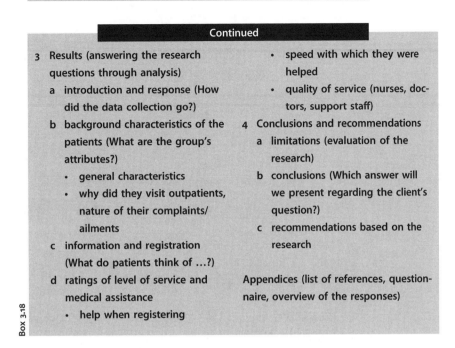

Continued

3 Results (answering the research questions through analysis)

  a introduction and response (How did the data collection go?)

  b background characteristics of the patients (What are the group's attributes?)
- general characteristics
- why did they visit outpatients, nature of their complaints/ ailments

  c information and registration (What do patients think of ...?)

  d ratings of level of service and medical assistance
- help when registering
- speed with which they were helped
- quality of service (nurses, doctors, support staff)

4 Conclusions and recommendations

  a limitations (evaluation of the research)

  b conclusions (Which answer will we present regarding the client's question?)

  c recommendations based on the research

Appendices (list of references, questionnaire, overview of the responses)

Box 3.18

3.7 Assessing Research Proposals

Once you've completed your research proposal, it gets assessed. Your tutor or the client can do this. It is a good idea to ask a colleague (or fellow student) to assess it, to see if you have forgotten anything, whether there are any mistakes, or perhaps there is a better way of approaching the questions. This kind of assessment is known as *peer assessment* or *peer examination*.

Sometimes for your study or work you will have to assess research that was designed and carried out by others. It is good to know what to look for when you do this. Here are a few pointers regarding aspects to look for when you assess research proposals: *points of interest*

1 Is the reason for the research clear?
2 Does it have a problem description?
  a Is there an objective?
  b Is there a central question formulation that meets all the requirements? Is the question a logical consequence of the reason? Is there a link with the objective?
- Has a question been asked?
- Is the question clear and unambiguous?

- Is it clear what knowledge the researcher needs, who it must come from and to which period it relates? It could be one question, or it could be a number of sub-questions.
- Is the relationship with the objective clear?

3 Is it clear which concepts are important to the research?
a Have these concepts been well-defined and demarcated?
b Have assumptions about the research findings been noted?
- Are these assumptions a logical consequence of the question formulation?
- Can these assumptions be outlined in a model?

4 Is the research design a logical consequence of the problem description and sub-questions?
a Has the research design been sufficiently justified?
b Is there a timeline and a budget? Are the figures and data realistic?
c Has the population been well described?

Depending on the nature of the research (qualitative or quantitative, theoretical or applied), you will focus on different aspects when assessing research proposals. The most important thing in all assessments is that the emphasis should be on the quality of the formulation when it comes to problem description, and on motivating the choice when it comes to the design.

3.8   Glossary of Most Important Terms and Their Meaning

Domain	The whole 'area' related to your research, or what you will be making statements about.
Claim	What statements are you making?
Problem description	Your research objective and central question.
Objective	The purpose of the research, both for the researcher (for applied research) and the organization or client.
Sub-questions	A number of sub-questions that together form the problem formulation.
Iteration	Repeat of research process or parts of it in order to get a reliable answer to the problem.
Research questions	Specific questions that you answer during your analysis.
Tree diagram	A model designed to help you delineate abstract concepts.

Concept demarcation	Establish what you mean by certain concepts (concept-as-intended).
Stipulative meaning	Definition of a concept for a specific research project.
Triangulation	Addressing the problem areas using more than one data collection method.
Hypotheses	Testable expectation about the findings of your research.
Relationship	Relationship between variables $(X \leftrightarrow Y)$.
(Conceptual) model	Simplified reflection of reality in which (within the domain) the most important concepts of the research and the expected relationships between these concepts are shown.
Causal relationship	The effect of one variable on another $(X \rightarrow Y)$.
Research plan	A proposal showing the procedure you intend to follow in your research that includes the results of your preliminary research.
Design choice	The data collection method that you have chosen which is included in the research plan.
Timeline	Outline showing the milestones of your research, included in your research plan.
Milestones	Important points in time during your research that mark deadlines or moments in which decisions must be made.
Operationalization	From concept to question: see Chapter 6.
Case study	Study that has one research element $(N = 1)$.
Peer examination	Assessment from other researchers or fellow students.
Cross-sectional	Research at a particular point in time.
Longitudinal	Research over a longer period of time, with more than one assessment moment.

3.9   Assignments for Chapter 3

1 Read through the example about patient satisfaction (Text box 3.4) in Mercy Hospital carefully. Answer the following questions:
 a What is the domain?
 b What are the problems and objectives?
 c Give a stipulative definition of the concept 'patient satisfaction'.

2 Describe the following concepts:
   a concept demarcation;
   b hypothesis;
   c iteration;
   d conceptual model.
3 In Figure 3.7 you will find part of a list of contents for a research report.
   a Which sections refer to the design and how is this done?
   b Based on the list of contents, what can you say about the research set up?

1	Introduction	4
1.1	Background and reason	5
1.1.1	Structure of the report	7
1.2	Demarcation	8
1.2.1	Introduction	8
1.2.2	Volunteer work and possibilities for professionalization	9
1.3	Central question and subquestions	11
1.3.1	Constructs	11
2	Research design and method	12
2.1	Data collection methods used	12
2.1.1	Population and demarcation	13
2.1.2	Looking for information	13
2.1.3	Open interviews	14
2.1.4	Group interviews	14
2.2	Operationalizations	15
3	____________	___
Appendix I Topic list open interviews		54
Appendix II Brown paper session (1)		55

(1) A brown paper session is a brainstorm session involving a small group in which you think about the research process and the possible outcomes

Figure 3.7 First part of the list of contents for a research report

4 Look at the example of the reason for the research into dropping out of school (Text box 3.8) and answer Migchelbrink's six questions (Section 3.2).
5 Read through the research into dropping out in Text box 3.8 once more. Several factors play a role in the decision to drop out. Design a model that shows the effects of these factors.
6 How would you 'unravel and regroup' the example in Text box 3.9?

7 You are asked to research internal communications in a department of an IT company. Detail three central questions, one of which is descriptive, one is explanatory and one is evaluative. Compare your questions with those of your fellow students.

8 What questions *types* belong to the following problem formulations?

  a What do parents and children in the highest class of Blakiston Primary School think of the learning environment?

  b What do publishers expect the growth to be of e-books in the next five years?

  c What is the effect of reducing the speed limit on carbon emission from cars in the UK?

  d What is the prevailing situation regarding criminality at Pennsylvania Station, NYC?

  e What are the developments in terms of reading habits of young people between the ages of 12 and 18 years, and are there any differences between girls and boys in this respect?

  f How long do patients have to wait for specialist healthcare and how can this problem be addressed?

9 A client asks you to draft a proposal for research into burn-out. Burn-out is a common cause of long-term illness, and one of its causes is stress in the workplace. The aim of the study is to develop a treatment plan for doctors in corporate healthcare to use to treat patients suffering from these symptoms. There is an address database available from which you can draw your sample. It contains a cross-section of the population. Over the course of the last fifteen years, a lot of information about people suffering from chronic exhaustion has been gathered. Various problem formulations are produced during a brainstorming session. Give the pros and cons of the following central questions and choose the most relevant one for the research:

  a Why is it that so many people suffer from burn-out these days?

  b What causes burn-out?

  c What is the current state of affairs regarding symptoms of burn-out compared to fifteen years ago, and what can be done about it?

  d What is the current state of affairs regarding symptoms of burn-out compared to fifteen years ago, and what is causing this?

  e What symptoms do people suffering from burn-out have at the moment, how do these compare to those of fifteen years ago, and what causes of burn-out play a role?

Use the information in Section 3.2.1 to support your answer.

10 Read the following research conclusion carefully.

Nordic Walking

Compared to 'normal walking', Nordic Walking barely relieves strain on the joints, which has been the assumption up until now. 'It is a great way to get fit or to lose weight. It is also very suitable for people with certain physical limita- tions.' This is the conclusion of exercise physiologist and movement scientist Wil van Bakel, who carried out his own research into the effects of Nordic Walking on the body' (*Tweevoeter, 2005*).

Box 3.19

a What central question was most probably used for this research?
b Design a model that you can test.
c What were the expectations? Were they confirmed, according to the researcher, or not?

WEBSITE In the section 'Chapter 3' (tab Assignment solutions) you will find the solu- tions to the assignments in Section 3.9. You will find information about the design cases under tab 'Design cases' in the section 'Chapter 3'.

Part II
Fieldwork

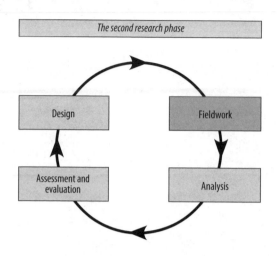

Part II of this book is all about fieldwork. The time has come to go into the field. We'll be answering questions like:

- How (in what way) will you be conducting your research?
- Who will be the subjects of your research?
- When will you be conducting your research?

Chapters 4 and 5 will be dealing with the data collection methods that are appropriate to certain methods. This is because core questions can be answered using specific methods, so we will be discussing the criteria for those methods. Chapter 4 discusses quantitative data collection methods and Chapter 5 deals with qualitative methods.

Chapter 6 discusses how to convert concepts into measurable 'instruments'; questions in a questionnaire; parts of observation sessions and interview guidelines. We also talk about how you define your sample and how your select research participants. Finally we talk about assessing the quality of your research.

In Chapter 7 you go back to your research plan. What was the objective? If you intend to carry out a survey, then you make decisions about its structure. Is it going to be a written questionnaire, a telephone survey or online? You will learn how the method you choose influences the way to approach the respondents. If you are going to do face-to-face interviews, then you will have personal contact with the respondents. You learn how to go about this in Chapter 7.

Quantitative Data Collection Methods

4

When you formulate the problem area of your research, it soon becomes clear which data collection method you will use. Although these methods are discussed in Part 2 (Phase 2: data collection), you must bear in mind that choosing the method took place in the first phase: this decision was discussed at length in Chapter 3.

When doing applied research, and scientific research for that matter, you have to give serious consideration to the circumstances in which your research is to take place. For instance, you are unlikely to want to carry out interviews on a noisy factory floor. Also, if there is conflict in the workplace, you can't just approach people willy-nilly clutching a clipboard with questionnaire attached. Conflicts are sensitive issues and you're unlikely to get to the bottom of it with a few straightforward questions.

The choice of data collection method depends on the question areas and various other circumstances – not least of which being the client's requirements. Obviously the client will make their wishes known. Remember that you are the expert. It is your job to advise your client about the best way to address the questions. A good relationship with your client is crucial here.

Quantitative research entails collecting numerical information. This information is entered into a database, after which it is analyzed using statistical techniques, so-called quantitative analysis. This analysis method is often used for surveys, secondary analysis, in experiments and as part of monitoring. This chapter will discuss the data collection methods involved, what they entail and the criteria that you must use for each. Structuring surveys, questionnaire design and conducting the fieldwork will be discussed at length in Chapter 6. Alongside data collection we will also be talking about monitors, a research type in which you can use *various* methods to collect the data.

content and objectives

circum-   Besides talking about the prerequisites (criteria) for each of the methods, we
stances   will also discuss the circumstances that can impact on the various types of
research. It is your job to advise the client about the best way to go about
collecting the information; you're the expert after all! But negotiating with
the client is essential because they are the ones fixing the budget and the
deadline. There may also be other special circumstances to contend with, as
we saw in Chapter 3. Maybe you won't be given permission to conduct
experiments with patients, maybe it's not a good idea to carry out interviews
because of factory shutdowns or because too many people in that department are on sick leave, and so on.

Learning objectives

By the end of this chapter you will be
able to select a suitable quantitative
data collection method, supported by
the correct arguments for doing so. You
will also be familiar with the parts of a
survey and an experiment, and you will
know what secondary analysis comprises and how a monitor works.

Box 4.1

4.1   Surveys

The most frequently used method for measuring the opinions, views, attitudes and knowledge of a large group of people is the survey, also known as
opinion poll. Originally this method was mainly used by sociologists, but
these days it is widely used for market research, policy research, communication research and opinion research of a more general nature. Text box 4.2
describes an example that uses scales to measure perceptions.

Surveys use structured data collection methods, i.e., the questions are fixed
in the sense that the number of possible answers is fixed and limited. The
respondents' answers form the basis of the dataset that the researcher then
uses for (mainly) quantitative analysis. Open questions (those for which the
respondent is free to provide their own version of the answer) are kept to a
minimum because these are difficult to include in *quantitative* analysis. They
require a certain amount of *qualitative* analysis.

Box 4.2

Response scales

If you want to elicit people's opinions about 'complicated' subjects, for example 'customer satisfaction' in a supermarket, then one way to do it is to use so-called *scales* (see Babbie (2005); Swanborn, 2010). You can measure customer satisfaction in various ways, for instance by assessing satisfaction with the helpdesk, product pricing, range of goods, opening times, and friendliness and helpfulness of staff. You can do this by presenting respondents with statements or by asking them sub-questions. In this method, respondents are given a limited choice of answers that are presented in an obvious order. Respondents can then choose from four, five, six or seven answers that are ranked from 'completely disagree' to 'completely agree'. The number of options in the scale may vary, but rarely beyond seven. We discuss these scales at length in Section 6.2.3.

Box 4.3

Election polls

A research bureau asks a respondent which party he would vote for three times in the run-up to the election: once in January, once in February and once at the beginning of April. The first time he says the Republicans, the second time the Democrats and the third time, the Republicans once again. No information was elicited about the background and reasons for this change. Had the bureau conducted an in-depth interview, they may have found out it was because of the oil spill in the Gulf of Mexico. The respondent was very unhappy to hear that Republican cronies in the House of Representatives tried hard to cover up government involvement in failed safety regulations at the time that the well was dug, and that his state representative was one of them. Given that his business is now under threat, this has serious implications for his livelihood. But then after a time, his true colors show and he reverts to the party he has voted for since he was 18, 20 years ago.

4.1.1   Taking Part in a Survey

How do you get people to take part in a survey? It's not easy, particularly when you bear in mind that there's a lot of 'background noise' these days. By that we mean that people are hassled a lot by people selling stuff under the guise of 'doing research'.

population   The first thing you need is a domain, all the elements of your research that you will be making statements about. This is known as the research population. Your population may consist of all the students in the next door city's college, all people eligible to vote, people suffering from a certain disease, people shopping on 5th Avenue NYC, people visiting the Getty Museum, the staff of a large bank, and on and on.

sample   Depending on its size, it is virtually impossible to interview all the people in the relevant population. They may be difficult to access and a comprehensive list of all these people probably does not exist (a list of this kind is called a *sample frame*); or you don't know which people belong to the population (for example: shoppers). This is when you approach a section of the population. This section is known as a *sample*: a portion, which may or may not be selected randomly, of the population that is available for the research. It is advisable to select your sample randomly if possible. By random we mean that everyone in the population has a calculated chance of being selected (also know as 'equal chance', even though that is not true strictly speaking). All of this is discussed in Chapter 6.

respondents   People who take part in research involving questionnaires (mainly surveys) are known as *respondents*. Participants that take part in other types of research, such as experiments, are not respondents, but subjects. Respondents take part in your research, they have agreed to do this, they are participants in the research.

4.1.2   *Types of Surveys*

There are several types of surveys. All of them use questionnaires as their main research instrument, but the way they do this differs. Here are a few possibilities:

- *Self-completion (postal) surveys.* Questionnaires are disseminated by post.
- *Telephone surveys.* Respondents that fall within the sample are contacted by phone and asked if they are prepared to take part. The survey is conducted by phone and entered straight into the database by the interviewers. This is often done by call centers that have trained and experienced interviewers.
- *Face-to-face (personal) surveys.* Interviewers go round to the respondents to conduct the interviews and to note the answers. Appointments are made for these interviews. They have to give their permission to be interviewed.

- *Online surveys.* This is a very popular type of survey these days. People are approached at work, by e-mail or sometimes when they're surfing on the web. The electronically collected data is sent straight to a database. Online surveys often suffer from 'self-selection' on the part of the respondents, for instance when they are surfing on the web. You can draw a sample (via e-mail), but the respondents do need to have an e-mail connection. In Text box 4.4 we give an example about breast cancer patients. This survey was carried out on the web.
- *Panel surveys.* In this kind of survey, a large group of people are approached regularly to discuss a certain subject. This is normally done using Internet questionnaires. You just put yourself forward to participate in the panel, your name is noted on a list from which a sample is drawn.

Waiting times for breast cancer patients

In many European countries, breast cancer is the most common form of cancer among women. On average, one in nine women will suffer from breast cancer in the course of her life. Some forecasts suggest that breast cancer will be found in 13 out of 100 women. Despite being the First World, breast cancer associations in Northern European countries report appalling examples of unacceptable waiting times that some breast cancer sufferers have to endure. In 2004, extensive research was conducted into hospital waiting times among breast cancer patients. Using the quantitative information that was gathered, the breast cancer association was given an objective picture of the situation and was able to use this information to take action to address the issue of long waiting times.

Survey

Between February 19 and July 19, 2005, 1,527 respondents took part in an online survey. These respondents had either suffered or were still suffering from breast cancer. They supplied data about the most important landmarks in the course of their illness, from diagnosis to the end of treatment, including: visits to the GP, mammograms, diagnosis, operation, and the course of their therapy. These women also reported on their experience (using data from their diaries and medical histories) from 2000 to 2005.

The invitation to take part in the survey was sent out through various media: from direct invitations to the members of the Breast Cancer Association, invitations in the main newspapers and women's magazines, websites from affiliated associations and journals as well as through questionnaires and flyers distributed at relevant conferences.

Source: Breast Cancer Association, 2005

Box 4.4

New BBC School Report Survey

In a nationwide survey, more than 24,000 pupils (ages between 11 – 16) in more than 300 schools participating in the BBC's School Report program filled in a questionnaire. According to the BBC, this gives a unique insight into the daily lives, fears and aspirations of a generation of young people in the UK. One-third of the respondents said their families have cut back on spending amid the economic downturn. Crime topped the list of personal fears of the young people surveyed, while terrorism and climate change were their biggest global concerns. Most respondents had Internet access at home; 67% had it on a mobile phone. The survey was carried out by the Royal Statistical Society Centre for Statistical Education (RSSCSE) at the University of Plymouth. It is said to be one of the biggest in its kind.

Source: London, March 24, 2011. BBC News

Box 4.5

Often when the media report on research, it's about a survey that has been carried out. Text box 4.5 is about a large survey among school children, the results of which were used in the media (the BBC commissioned the study). The survey was cross-sectional, i.e. administered at one moment in time.

representativeness   If you have drawn your sample randomly, and this group's most important attributes resemble those of the population that you are studying, then your sample is what is known as *representative*. If this is the case, then we can extrapolate the findings to a larger population: in other words, they become valid for that population. The larger your sample, the better the chance is that it is a good reflection of the population as a whole. So if you have a *generalization* large representative sample, your findings will be more valid. This is called generalizing the research results. The article 'Sex education helps!' (Text box 4.6) discusses the findings of a survey with a sample size of 2,019, which is a large group. If you take into consideration the size of the total population, however, it's only a small fraction. In the conclusion, the results are extrapolated to the general population of school children. From the article it is not clear whether this is justifiable or not. You would first have to establish whether the sample is representative of the general population before you can judge. In this case, however, external validity is high because the data used was from the National US Survey of Family Growth in 2002 and this data is representative of the nation. Often it is not clear from newspaper articles how sound the sample is in terms of representativeness.

Box 4.6

Sex Education helps!

Teenagers who have had formal sex education are far more likely to put off having sex, contradicting earlier studies on the effectiveness of such programs. Researchers found teenage boys who had sex education in school were 71% less likely to have intercourse before age 15, and teenage girls who had sex education were 59% less likely to have sex before age 15.

In order to obtain these results, a re-analysis of a national (US) 2002 survey was conducted that among 2,019 teens aged 15 to 19.

They found teenage boys who had sex education in school were nearly three times more likely to use birth control the first time they had intercourse. But sex education appeared to have no effect on whether teenage girls used birth control, the researchers found. 'Unlike many previous studies, our results suggest that sex education before first sex protects youth from engaging in sexual intercourse at an early age,' they wrote (Mueller, Gavin & Kolkarni, 2008).

Text box 4.7 gives the main features of surveys.

Box 4.7

Features of surveys

1 They research a large group of people.
2 They are done at one point in time.
3 They research Knowledge, Attitudes and Perceptions (and are known as KAP surveys).
4 They ask descriptive and/or evaluative questions.

5 The questionnaires are structured or semi-structured.
6 They involve a large number of questions.
7 The samples are drawn randomly.
8 The data is analyzed quantitatively.

4.2 Secondary Analysis

If your research involves using existing datasets with quantitative information that has been collected by other researchers, then what you are doing is carrying out secondary analysis. You are using the dataset again, but this time you are addressing a new question. Statistical overviews are often 'reused' in this fashion (see Text box 4.8). This is what is known as quantitative desk research. There is also qualitative desk research and it will be discussed in Chapter 5 (Section 5.4). You use data from existing databases: data from other researchers.

Box 4.8

Geographic distribution of the population

Many archives offer researchers the opportunity to perform a secondary analysis on their data. For instance, census data, electoral data and data on social and cultural topics are widely available, provided they are used conscientiously. The Dutch Interdisciplinary Demographic Institute (NIDI) collects longitudinal demographic data. One of the research programs is the Netherlands Kinship Panel Study that collects data on family relations. This data was used by students in their senior year to perform a secondary analysis and answer the question to what extent early childhood experiences influence depression among older adults.

Source: www.nkps.nl

Reasons for doing secondary analysis could include:

1 *Saving time.* Going into the field to carry out a survey is time consuming.
2 *Financial advantages.* Collecting data yourself is a costly business.
3 *Availability of the data.* There are so many datasets available that have been put together for other research. This data is ideal for new analysis. Research institutes make it available through special databanks.
4 *Usability.* This is not only a reason to use it, but also a precondition. It is not easy to find a dataset that is exactly what you are looking for, but there are sets that will meet a few of your requirements or that take you a step in the right direction. There is a huge amount of data that lends itself to analysis.

Databanks based on censuses are often used to track developments in the population. For example, they may be used to see if there are any changes in the number of women admitted to hospital due to complications during pregnancy; or whether there is an increase in the number of couples seeking IVF treatment. This information can be gleaned by processing the information that is supplied to the census bureau from hospitals. By comparing data from different points in time it is possible to carry out tracking studies.

disadvan- Secondary analysis does have disadvantages, one of them being that you
tages don't have any control over the data. The structure, coding and questionnaire have all be decided and used. You also have to find solutions for any

errors that may have occurred during original data collection. It may be that you have to adjust the central question in your secondary analysis in order to be able to use a particular dataset.

Example of secondary analysis (1): social networks

For research into the social networks of men and women in the labor market, secondary analysis was carried out between 1995 and 1996 on six existing databases that contain information about networks (Verhoeven, Jansen & Tazelaar, 2000). It was fundamental research (i.e., theoretical), based on the question: 'Why is it that wide social networks affect behavior in the labor market and work mobility for men, but have little or no affect on these aspects for women?' A comprehensive answer to such a research question is only possible if you have an extensive database to work from. That is a time consuming and costly business. That is why the researchers decided to analyze existing and available datasets from the '80s and '90s. These databases contained information about the networks of both men and women, as well as data on the careers and backgrounds of these people. The databases formed the basis of the analysis. None of the databases contained all the information that was needed, but each one had part of it. The researchers also had to process many of the attributes to make comparison between the sets possible.

Box 4.9

Example of secondary analysis (2): volunteers

The Social and Cultural Planning Office conducted research into voluntary work (Dekker, 1999). They looked at voluntary work from an *international perspective*. This means they compared how voluntary work is done in various countries. For the research, they used the information gathered from two international surveys that studied partaking in and being motivated to do voluntary work. The availability of this data saved a lot of time and, in turn, work and money. The data was not always usable from every respect. For example, the study could not answer questions about voluntary work as part of being 'an active member of society' (involvement in society). Although the research was fundamental in its approach, the usability of the data for practical research was good, especially for policy makers.

Box 4.10

Often data has to be thoroughly processed before it can be used for further analysis, as you can see from the examples in Text boxes 4.9 and 4.10. This was definitely the case in the first example where six different databases were compared to each other. Despite this, using existing databases still has its advantages because why would you collect information that is already available? There are so many available archives, ready to be used by others. For what often amounts to a small fee you can access data and use it to supplement your own or to carry out renewed analysis. National archives and census bureaus have this information, and it can often be accessed over the Internet. Sometimes you need to get permission first, or to register, and sometimes you need to pay for it. In brief, the fact that it is available and that it is cheap in comparison to fieldwork is more than enough reason to take advantage of it.

meta-anal-ysis If you want to *re-analyze* several databases, on one and the same topic, so that you can come to a conclusion that summarize them, then you are conducting a *meta-analysis*. What is the difference between this and secondary analysis? When you do secondary analysis, you collect and analyze the data gathered by other researchers, based on one existing dataset. When you do meta-analysis, you collect whole databases before going on to compare them: meta-analysis is therefore based on a different unit of analysis. Meta-analysis is extremely in-depth and extensive, and not always used for practical applications. Using the Internet, the whole world is scoured for research on a given subject. If research is found that could be usable, it is first tested to see if it is indeed usable. Only once a thorough comparison of all the databases has been carried out does the analysis begin. In retrospect, it may turn out that it is still an expensive and time consuming undertaking, but one that offers way more options than was previously possible thanks to the arrival of the Internet. Medical research is a prime example of meta-analysis in practice. It involves looking at the results of treatment across a broad spectrum of research, cancer research is one such example.

4.3   Experimental Research

In experimental research, data is collected about people in a controlled situation (as shown in Text box 4.11 for example), in order to test a hypothesis. In other words, by way of an experiment you test the effect of a specific situation, stimulus and/or factor, based on an (assumed) result. You may carry out your experiment in a laboratory so that you can restrict outside influences as far as possible. But this is not necessarily always the case, although the situation will have consequences for the conclusions you draw from your findings. In this section we will describe both kinds of experiments.

The impact of alcohol on driving

Suppose you want to research the effects of alcohol on driving fitness. The obvious choice would be to collect your data by way of an experiment (not using your own car, mind you!) You suspect (your hypothesis or assumption) is that people that have downed a few glasses of alcohol will be less able to drive well than those who have not had anything alcoholic to drink. You divide a group of people into two subgroups: the people in the one group each drink four glasses of beer, those in the other group get nothing. The two groups carry out a few driving exercises, in a parking lot. You assess their driving and compare the results.

4.3.1   Aspects of Experimental Research

An inherent characteristic of experiments is the so-called 'effect measurement' or 'cause-effect relationship'. You measure the effect that X has on Y. This is what is known as the *causal relationship*. In such a relationship, X always precedes Y in time, and the cause (logically) always comes before the effect. The effect of attending classes on your exam results comes to mind. In the social sciences, experimental research is generally carried out by psychologists. It is also a frequently used method for collecting data in medical and scientific research. Some see it as the basis of all research methods.

causality

Experiments are not only used to find causal relationships; in many cases the experimental setting is also created especially for the experiment. If this is the case, outside influences are removed as far as possible, as we mentioned in the introduction. This is called 'unbiased'. The experiment is not carried out in a 'real' situation, but in a created one: an experimental situation. During the experiment a number of subjects are exposed to a cause variable, i.e., an experimental variable. This is often done in a laboratory. The variables are characteristic of your research elements. It could be a test that the subjects have to undergo, or medicine that they have to take. Whatever the case may be, the aim is to measure the effects of the situation on the subjects.

unbiased experiments

internal   In your research into the effects of alcohol, you don't sit in a bar and watch
validity   what happens if someone drinks more than three beers. You create your
own setting so that you can control it. The aim is that all your guinea pigs
should drink exactly 4 glasses of beer, no more and no less, and not gin or
wine either. The test, the experimental variable, is the consumption of four
glasses of beer containing a specific amount of alcohol. The circumstances
of the experiment must be the same for each subject. Why is this? The
purer the experiment is in terms of set up, the greater the chance is that the
effect is the result of the experimental variable: X → Y (X has an effect on
Y). If this is the case, we say that the *internal validity* of the experiment set
up is high. The effect is not caused by some external factor, the conclusions
that you draw will be correct in this respect at least. In 'pure' experiments
there has to be at least one experimental group and one control group. In
Chapter 6, we'll discuss at length the concept of 'internal validity'.

randomiza-   In an experiment, the composition of your group of *subjects* (we don't call
tion   them respondents in experiments) is crucial. The subjects have to have
shared characteristics (they are 'interchangeable', that is on average they
don't differ much). When the groups are split into subgroups, a number of
attributes play a role, but the division into the experimental and control
groups is done randomly. This is known as *randomization*. Randomization
is the second criteria used to judge whether the experiment is biased or not.
You will find an example of this in Text box 4.12.

Medication
In order to test the effect of a medicine to combat high blood pressure, a group of people are assembled that all share the same condition: they have high blood pressure. One of the subgroups is given pills containing an ingredient that lowers blood pressure; the others are given a placebo (a tablet that does not contain the active ingredient). The division of the group into subgroups is done randomly. The selection of the whole sample is done on the basis of blood pressure measurements.

Box 4.12

Does it   If you want to test the effects of medicine, then it will never do to test one
actually   group and then see if the medicine has worked. The researcher will never
work?   know whether the effects are the results of the medicine or some other factor
that was brought about by the experiment itself. The internal validity is at
stake here. The best solution to this problem is to use a control group. This

is a group of subjects that do not take the medicine so that their results can be compared with the ones from the group that do, to see whether they differ.

To some people, just the thought of taking medicine makes them feel better, even if it doesn't contain any active ingredients. This is called a *placebo* effect. The medicine might 'help' you, but does it actually 'work'. *placebo effect*

In order to exclude the placebo effect, subjects are assigned to the groups randomly. This means that they have no idea which group they're in. The doctor in question may also be suffering from the placebo effect by subconsciously projecting their assumptions onto the subjects. In cases like these, *double-blind* experiments are used: neither the subjects nor the doctor in questions knows which of the pills are real and which are placebos. *double blind testing*

In brief, if you want to carry out an experiment that is free from outside influences, then opt for an unbiased laboratory experiment. For this you'll use a lab, with a control and an experimental group, consisting of people that share an attribute and that have been randomly assigned to either group. If this is not possible, then the alternative is to carry out a quasi-experiment. The following section will discuss how to do this.

4.3.2   Types of Experimental Research

There are several ways to carry out experiments. The basis for all is an unbiased laboratory experiment, as discussed in the last section. For the rest you decide how you will measure the results, what the subgroups will be and what the setting will be.

Before you start your experiment you may want to carry out a 'baseline' or 'pretest'. The measurement that takes place after the experiment is known as the 'posttest'. You may also decide to just do a posttest, by assigning two groups of people to the experiment, exposing the experimental group to the experimental variable and then measuring the effects by comparing the two groups. Text box 4.13 gives an example of an experiment using two measurements: one directly after the experiment and one a couple of weeks later. *pre- and post-measurements*

Box 4.13

Green electricity

To investigate the effects of informing people about green electricity, subjects are divided into an experimental group and a control group. The experimental group is shown a film about green electricity that discusses the environmental consequences if we carry on using fossil fuels. The control group is shown a film that doesn't contain any information about green electricity. After watching the films the subjects fill in a questionnaire about the environment. After a while, the subjects are approached to see if they have switched to green electricity.

opting for a
control
group
It is not always necessary to use both types of groups, nor is it always possible. Imagine that you want to test the effects of anti-depressants on two groups, one that gets the medicine, one that gets the placebo. Your subjects must meet the condition that they suffer from depression. But how can you divide this group into people that will get the medicine and those that won't? In this kind of experiment, it is not ethical to use a control group. It would be irresponsible to withhold medicine from this particular group of people. For this reason, experiments sometimes only use one group of people.

The study into arachnophobia in Text box 4.14 is an example of a laboratory experiment with only a posttest. The experiment is not pure because the assigning of the subjects was not done randomly.

Box 4.14

Arachnophobia

Let's have another look at the study into arachnophobia carried out by Birgit Mayer (2000). In order to assess reactions to arachnophobia, she conducted several experiments. One of them was as follows. Subjects that signed up for the study were divided up according to whether they were scared of spiders or not. Mayer put two groups of people together: one group of 47 people who claimed to be scared of spiders (and snakes) and another group of 47 people who were not scared of these creatures. She felt that it would be unethical to divide the people randomly in case those who were scared of spiders ended up in the experimental group. In an experimental facility (a laboratory), the two groups were shown slides of spiders and snakes, as well as flowers and toadstools. Mayer measured their reactions using electrodes on the skin. She then compared the results between the two groups.

Laboratory experiments, be they unbiased or not, can be exposed to all kinds *Solomon* of interfering influences. When we discuss validity in Chapter 6, we will talk *four group* about a number of these elements. Here we'll talk about one of them. Some- *design* times subjects react differently because they are aware that they are part of an experiment. This is known as a *test-effect*, or *Hawthorne effect*. This magnifying effect also takes place if the researcher carries out pretests as well as posttests. Because pretesting draws the subjects attention to certain factors that are relevant to the research, the experimental variable may have a different effect to what it may have had if there had been no pretesting. To avoid this, a special type of experiment was designed: the 'Solomon four group design'. It is an expensive experiment, but extremely effective when it comes to filtering out this type of test effects. Alongside the experimental group, the researcher puts together three control groups, as shown in Table 4.1.

Table 4.1   Solomon four group design

Group	Subjects are exposed to experimental variable	Pretest	Posttest
Experimental	yes	yes	yes
Control group 1	yes	no	yes
Control group 2	no	yes	yes
Control group 3	no	no	yes

Text box 4.15 lists the characteristics of experimental research.

Characteristics of experimental research

1 Causal relationships are investigated: $X \rightarrow Y$.

2 X is the independent or cause variable, Y is the dependent variable or effect variable.

3 The cause variable precedes the effect variable in time.

4 Hypotheses are formulated about the results.

5 Groups are exposed to the experimental variable (cause) under circumstances that are as unbiased as possible (controlled, free from outside influence)

6 Subjects within an experimental group have attributes that are similar.

7 Subjects are assigned randomly to the experimental and control groups (randomization).

Box 4.15

unbiased or quasi-experiments If you can't or won't use laboratory experiments then you can opt to conduct a field or quasi-experiment. You use an existing situation within which you carry out your experiment. You could send males and females out to sell magazine subscriptions and see who are the most successful. Gender would then be the experimental variable. This kind of experimental set up is often used in applied research. Another example would be if an area of grassland were not mown during the bird-breeding season. During this period the number of breeding pairs would be counted and compared to the number in the fields that were mown.

Using computers in math lessons

What if you want to assess the effect of using computer during high school math lessons. It would be difficult to measure this effect in a laboratory setting. You would have to replicate a math lesson and assign the pupils randomly. That wouldn't really work. It would be better to look for a setting that is as normal as possible. You could use classes that have already been assigned, for example at school. Trying to replicate a lesson would seem contrived and it begs the question whether the pupils would react in the same way to the variables anyway.

Box 4.16

In quasi-experiments you can't control disruptive external influences, which means that the internal validity is affected, as discussed in Text box 4.16. This is often not the researcher's intention. Making use of existing situations as far as possible is easier (and often cheaper), but it is also more 'real'. Read about this in Text box 4.17.

Are stats fun? The effects of humor on pupils' attitudes

A researcher wants to find out whether pupils' attitudes are 'statistically' more positive when humorous examples are used during classes. He carries out two field experiments among two groups of freshmen students who are studying to be teachers at university. Throughout the term, at specified times, humorous examples are used in the one group, while the other group gets the standard (unfunny) examples. He also carries out pre- and posttests: one at the beginning of term and one at the end. In this way he hopes to measure pupils' attitudes towards statistics. His analysis shows that using humor in examples results in a positive change in attitude, while those in the group that had the standard examples did not show any significant change in their attitude towards stats.

Box 4.17

4.4   Monitor

A fairly recent development in research is 'monitoring'. These come in various shapes and sizes and in many European countries include education monitors, poverty monitors, city policy monitors, security monitors and so on. Monitoring is a popular method for communication research, policy research and evaluation research. Policy makers, in particular, like using this method. In Text box 2.11 you read about an example of a monitor. How do monitors work? In monitors, data is collected so that developments in certain areas can be tracked. This kind of data collection resembles 'ordinary' research, but monitors are a specific kind of research. To qualify as a monitor, two important conditions must be met:

1   *Time* plays a crucial role in the analysis. Data collected at different points in time is compared (*longitudinal research*). In this way developments can be established and tracked.
2   *The same instrument* is used to measure the same phenomena in the same way. The research is repeated as it were. This enhances the reliability of the results. By reliability we mean the extent to which the research is free of *random errors*.

Monitoring research is not a form of data collection: it is type of research design. Triangulation is normally involved because various data collection methods are used to collect the information: focus groups and in-depth interviews, questionnaires, observations and so on. At a certain point, all the data about the same phenomenon is collected and processed. The processing is done both quantitatively (for the surveys and analysis of key figures) and qualitatively (for focus groups and in-depth interviews).

A lot of the data is collected using existing databases. This data is mostly analyzed using quantitative methods. For example, if you are doing an education monitor, you can check with educational institutes that collect key information (indicators) about student and pupil enrollment and graduation. For a monitor to do with unemployment allowances, you would need to check with the relevant section of the Social Welfare Department. For a monitor to do with housing, the department of housing at the relevant municipality would do. A monitor to do with healthcare could draw on various databases held at hospitals and other healthcare institutions. Government departments that organize their own monitors obligate the participating institutes to provide data periodically. An example of this is the Security Monitor, which is carried out in several European countries.

Text box 4.18 gives an example of an IT education monitor organized by a government department. Text box 4.19 shows the set up of the Security Monitor.

IT Education Monitor

Since the '90s IT education monitors have become the norm. Schools are free to take part in these monitors on a voluntary basis, and they can do so by submitting information about IT implementation at their school. They can use feedback to adjust their policies. In turn, ministries at national level get information about what is happening in the nation's schools.

'The IT education monitor links information to your school or college so that you can assess how advanced your institution is in terms of IT implementation, compared to other schools and colleges. You can use this information to approach things differently where necessary. The IT monitor also serves as a source of information for the education department at government level. By studying the IT monitor they can see where the problem areas are. This can only take place thanks to the participation of schools, educational institutions, educational boards, IT coordinators, teachers and pupils.'

Many IT monitors are funded and commissioned by central governments.

Box 4.18

Security Monitor

The Security Monitor is a large-scale investigation into feelings regarding security among the population. It is carried out in several European countries, including Belgium and the Netherlands. All aspects of security are measured: the general living conditions in the neighborhood, neighborhood problems, crime reporting patterns, anti-social behavior indicators, victim rates and police presence and how well they function. Most security monitors were started shortly after the turn of the century. They gather data by way of large-scale surveys that are held annually (in some places every two years), among people aged 15 years and over. These monitors are generally conducted at the same time of the year, for example from mid September to the end of December. Normally they are held at both national and provincial level.

Box 4.19

Section 4.2 tells you about how using existing databases (secondary analysis) has a disadvantage, namely they may not contain the exact information that you require. The information in these databases is often very general in character: it gives a global view of things. Because these monitors also use existing databases, they too are very general, which means that the information from their results is not detailed. No individual, detailed data is given. If it's in-depth information you need, there are other methods that lend themselves far better.

Starting a monitor will make demands on all your research negotiation skills. It is often a difficult job to get the client and the institutes involved to agree to give the correct information in the correct format to you at the right time. It'll take a lot of talking, planning and stress to get it off the ground. In summary: you carry out a monitor if you want to track developments over time, evaluate a situation or you want to develop new policies (measures, instruments). For this you use the same kind of data, collected at specific points in time. Methods for collecting the data can vary from secondary analysis to focus groups and in-depth interview or surveys.

4.5   Glossary of Most Important Terms and Their Meaning

Data collection method	The way in which you collect data.
Survey	Research that uses polling methods (questionnaires) to assess knowledge, attitudes and perceptions (KAP studies) among large groups of people.
Population	All the elements that your research will make statements about (domain).
Sample	A segment of the population that you may or may not have selected randomly, and that may be asked to participate in your research.
Likert scale	Lists of questions about the same subject (concept) that have a limited number of possible answers.
Respondents	People that take part in surveys involving questionnaires
Generalizing	Extrapolating conclusions to the population.
Secondary analysis	Research based on existing data.
Meta-analysis	Re-analysis of a large number of databases or texts.

Laboratory experiment	Assessing the effects of experiment variables on subjects, in a situation that can be controlled as far as possible.
Causal relationship	The presence of a 'cause-effect' relationship.
Internal validity	The extent to which the correct conclusions can be drawn.
Subjects	Participants in an experimental research project.
Randomization	Random assignment of subjects to conditions.
Pretest	Measuring of characteristics at the start of the experiment.
Posttest	Measuring of characteristics at the end of the experiment.
Pure experiment	An experiment that is free from outside interference.
Experimental and control groups	An experimental setting in which two groups are used, one that is exposed to the experimental variable and one that is not.
Placebo effect	Subjects who are not given the active ingredient, but are of the opinion that they can notice a difference suffer from the placebo effect.
Test effect or Hawthorn effect	Skewing of results because the presence of the researchers has a positive effect on the results.
Solomon four group design	Special experimental setting consisting of four groups.
Quasi-experiment or field experiment	Experiments that use 'existing' groups; not a pure experiment (not done in laboratory).
Monitor	Data collection done about the development of a particular phenomenon using questionnaires more than once, and generally on a regular basis.
Variables	The characteristics of the unit that you are assessing in your research.

4.6   Assignments for Chapter 4

1   Complaints come in at a company about the quality of the air in the offices that staff are expected to work in. The windows can't be opened, an air conditioner is used to circulate and refresh the air. People complain about dry throats and itchy eyes, saying that it is interfering with their work. Management are desperately keen to improve working conditions and the atmosphere at their offices, so an experiment is set up.

Two groups of people are chosen. In the one office, the windows can be opened, in the other they can't. The researchers spend a couple of days at the offices; staff productivity and working atmosphere are observed. What do they find out? Both groups are more productive and the atmosphere improves. There is no connection with the windows. Describe what the researchers are confronted with.

2   Read about the effects of Nordic Walking in Text box 4.20. What method of data collection did the researcher use? Describe the research set up.

Research: Nordic Walking hardly eases strain on joints

Box 4.20

Compared to 'normal walking', Nordic Walking barely relieves strain on the joints, which has been the assumption up until now. 'It is a great way to get fit or to lose weight. It is also eminently suitable for people with certain physical limitations. This is the conclusion of research into the effects of Nordic Walking on the body.' An exercise physiologist and movement scientist got experienced Nordic Walkers to walk with and without sticks and then mea- sured their pulse rates and the pressure on their joints. The pressure on the feet and joints was the same when walking normally and doing Nordic Walking. Nordic Walking exercises the shoulders, back, chest and arm muscles much more than normal walking does. The heart rate is also higher, which means more fat is being burnt.

Source: *Tweevoeter*, December 14, 2005

3   Read the article in Text box 2.5. It outlines the reasons given for conducting the research into the effects of Ritalin usage on driving ability. How would you approach the research? Which data collection method would you use?

4 Text box 4.4 describes the set up for research into waiting times for treatment of breast cancer. Several different methods were used to collect the data.

   a Which methods were used? Describes the characteristics of these methods. Why do you think the researchers chose these methods?

   b The method used has one huge downside, especially if you take the subject into account. What is this disadvantage? Describe an alternative method. Describe an alternative method for collecting information about waiting times.

5 Suppose you were asked to conduct research into the effects of an information campaign about the dangers of smoking on the smoking habits of young high school pupils. The client wants to know whether, and if so, to what extent, smoking behavior changes as a result of this campaign. Design a Solomon four group design for this experiment. Remember to assign an experimental and a control group, and also to carry our pre- and posttests. Use the outline in Table 4.1 as an example.

6 Read the text box about the study into social networks carefully (Text box 4.9). A lot of research has been carried out into how social networks operate, but this research used existing material: it was secondary analysis.

   a Describe the pros and cons of this data collection method.

   b This information had already been collected. How do you think this was done?

7 A research bureau designs a questionnaire to assess customer satisfaction with the new chip tickets for the train and subway system. The population is all users of the ticket. Their physical addresses, e-mail addresses and telephone numbers are known. These people also travel often by train and subway. How would you administer the questionnaire? There are several ways to do this. Motivate your choice.

8 Revisit the study in Question 5. Think of arguments to support doing a field experiment for this project.

9 Read about the experiment in Text box 4.21. How was this data collected? What are the pros and cons of this data collection method?

The National Search Engine Monitor (NSEM)

In the most recent National Search Engine Monitor, research was done into usage and perceptions of toolbars. Of all Dutch users, 66% had heard of toolbars. Of these 70% know about the Google toolbar, 50% the MSN toolbar and 25% the Yahoo toolbar. So Google is ahead of its rivals in this respect too. Awareness of toolbars is higher than usage: 15% use the Google toolbar, while the MSN and Yahoo toolbars are used by 3% and 1% of Internet users respectively. Blocking pop-ups (48%) and searching (76%) are the most popular toolbar functions for Google and this toolbar scores an average rating of 7.6 among its users.

A new item in the NSEM is that it investigated the use of desktop search programs. With this function, one that is offered by several search engines, you can quickly search the content of your own computer. A surprising research finding was that no less than 72% of Internet users had never heard of desktop search programs, while 91% have never used this function.

This is the seventh time that the NSEM has been presented. Since 2002, Search engine Media Bureau, Checkit, and research bureau RM Interactive have researched the use of search engines in the Netherlands using web questionnaires. The research is representative of Dutch Internet users.

Source: Checkit, 2010

Box 4.21

10 Read the following problem formulation carefully. Which data collection methods would you use?
   a Who are people going to vote for at the next general elections?
   b What is the effect of taking multi-vitamins on immunity?
   c What do people think of waiting times at the cable car in Gstaad?

In the section 'Chapter 4' (tab Assignment solutions) you will find the solutions to the assignments in Section 4.6. You will find information about the design cases under tab 'Design cases' in the section 'Chapter 4'.

WEBSITE

Qualitative Data Collection Methods

Chapter 5 discusses qualitative methods of data collection. These are methods that use virtually no numerical information. Instead, they use texts, interviews, observations, and videos etc., which are all analyzed.

Qualitative research has nothing to do with gathering numerical information, the search is not for causal relationships based on numbers. The researcher can change the research as they go along, making this approach open and flexible. The main thrust of this research is to explore the background of the information that is gathered. In qualitative data collection methods, such as observations and open interviews, it's about how people *perceive* things. This makes qualitative research interpretative by its nature. The crux of the matter is the significance that people give to situations, in other words their subjective perceptions. *perceptions*

Qualitative is much more than an alternative to quantitative research. Qualitative research may not be based on figures, but it is the method that takes researchers into the 'field' ('in reality' as researchers sometimes put it). In qualitative research the research elements are studied on their own turf, in their normal surroundings. This is also known as *holistic research*. *holistic research*

If the central question calls for finding out how people perceive a situation, what their underlying arguments and motives may be for behaving in a certain way then qualitative research is the way to find out. Literature research and content analysis do not gather numerical information either, but they collect information using texts. It is the meaning of the texts that is important in this case, not how many there are.

In this chapter we'll discuss a number of well-known qualitative methods, such as observation research, literature research, and content and secondary analysis of qualitative material. One of these methods, in-depth interviews, will be discussed at length in Chapter 6, but it will be introduced in this *contents of this chapter*

chapter. In Section 5.6 we'll discuss a special method: case studies. We will once again talk about the best way of choosing a method in this chapter. In some cases it is better to opt for a combination of different data collection methods (*triangulation*). How to do this is also dealt with in this chapter.

5.1   Observation

We all observe things from time to time. Sitting having a beer on a sidewalk café somewhere, we may observe the passers by. At the office, we try to assess the mood by observing the faces of our colleagues. In the queue at the supermarket, we observe the behavior of others waiting ahead of us.

systematic observation Scientific researchers also use observation as a method. By observation we mean: the *systematic observation* of certain behavior. Of interest are only those aspects of behavior that are relevant to the research. In observation research, small groups or individuals are observed in their normal surroundings.

5.1.1   Types of Observation Research

in the field or not Observation research comes in various types. You can observe in the 'field', i.e., in everyday situations. The people you observe are then not selected for the research, and it often involves existing groups, for example observation of the San people in the Kalahari Desert.

You can also observe behavior in areas that have been specially designed for this (see Text box 5.2). This kind of observation research strongly resembles an experiment. The difference with an experiment is that in this case only the behavior is observed, and no experimental variables are used. You don't research the effect of a certain variable that has been introduced by the researcher, instead you study the behavior that is of interest to the experiment.

The Assessment Center Method

Box 5.2

The Assessment Center Method (Vander Meeren & Gerrichhauzen, 1993) is an instrument used to judge candidates for a given function in an organization. The applicants are observed in certain situations by trained observers. Afterwards it is decided who would be the best candidate based on the results of the observation.

Another distinguishing factor in observations has to do with the *structure*. If you compile a list of this behavior that you will be observing, then your observation will be structured. You could also opt to simply observe what happens during your observation, in which case your method would be unstructured. *— structure*

You can also *directly* observe the subjects, so that they are aware that you are there, or you could observe them *indirectly*. In indirect observations, you make use of one-way mirrors, as the police do, or you could video tape the subjects. You can also decide to let those being observed know that you are observing them (*unconcealed*) or not (*concealed*).

The final distinction that we will discuss is that between more or less 'normal' observation and so-called *participant* observation. In this type, the researcher takes part in all the activities of the persons being observed, while at the same time observing them. As we saw in Section 1.3, this kind of research is often used by anthropologists to describe the lifestyles of certain population groups and/or cultures. Over the years, many cultural anthropologists have visited the Bushmen of the Kalahari. This would have been participatory research. Text box 5.3 contains a fitting example of current observation research. Figure 5.1 summarizes the various types of observation research. *— participant observation*

Participant observation in neighborhood shops

Everyone does shopping, that goes without saying. But small neighborhood shops are fast disappearing and being replaced by large supermarket chains in a society that is becoming more and more individualistic. How do small neighborhood shops survive? To find out more about it, it is important not to

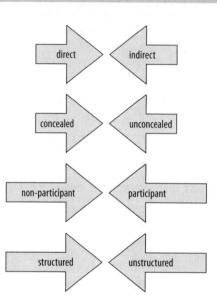

Figure 5.1   Applications of observation research

observation When do we consider observing behavior to be a type of scientific research?
as a scien- When does watching people from a sidewalk café become research? For this,
tific activity observation must meet various requirements:

1 The central question must lend itself for this kind of research: it must be
   an issue that can be resolved through observation. Take the following
   question: 'What happens at the intersection 5th Ave and Main Street?'
   Some of the sub-questions could be: 'How do pedestrians behave at this
   intersection?' and 'Do motorists stop at the zebra crossing?' These two
   sub-questions can easily be answered by using observation research. You
   go to the intersection in question with a list of possible answers which
   you tick whenever you observe the behavior, for example pedestrians jay-
   walking and motorists who ignore pedestrians waiting at the zebra crossing.

2 Behavior must be studied. This could also be so-called negative behavior
   (someone who ignores traffic regulations) or intimate behavior; behavior

of one individual or behavior of a group of people. You can observe solitary behavior, or interaction between people.

3 *Subjectivity* must be avoided. Because you are observing behavior not only as a researcher, but also as the observer, your own opinion will soon come into play. If you see someone walking past with a glum look on their face and with their shoulders drooping, you may quickly conclude that this person is unhappy. That is your interpretation of the behavior, your explanation for it. Those who conduct scientific research using observation try to keep their subjectivity to a minimum. It is not possible to do so completely, but there are ways to keep your own opinions at bay. By being systematic in your research you can avoid giving your own, subjective interpretation to things and events.

One way to avoid subjectivity is to develop an *assessment procedure*, to be systematic. The concepts from the central question and demarcation are converted into measurable observation categories: elements of behavior that you can observe (see Text box 5.4).

An example of behavioral categories	
The notion 'unhappy' can be characterized using the following measurable behavior categories:	• drags feet;
	• mouth down at corners;
	• staring into the middle distance;
• doesn't smile;	• frowning;
• drooped shoulders;	• crying.

Box 5.4

4 Reliable conclusions should be drawn from your observations, in other words: they are good quality. There are various ways to draw reliable conclusions from observation research:

- It can be *replicated*. Often it is said of observation research that it is a one-off opportunity to collect the data. The same situation is unlikely to repeat itself. To avoid this limitation, you can use video recording equipment to tape what you are observing. You can replay the tapes and, as the researcher, focus on a different aspect of the behavior each time.
- *Intersubjectivity*. The more inclined researchers are to agree in their coding of the behavior, the more usable the system is because *intersubjectivity* exists. This is a difficult concept. There is agreement about how the behavior should be interpreted, but that doesn't remove the subjectivity altogether. The agreement is only to do with how to inter-

pret an 'unhappy' demeanor. How did you reach this agreement? By making the coding known, among other things, so that it could be looked at critically, or by conferring with your colleagues (*peer consultation*).

- *Systematic observation.* A third way to avoid subjectivity is to be *selective.* By this we mean that you don't observe everything someone does, rather you concentrate on certain elements of their behavior. You boil it down to a *category system*, a system of usable behavioral elements, one that the researchers agree on and one that you can use for your observations. A popular category system is Vrolijk's (Vrolijk, Dijkema & Timmerman, 1972), which was designed for observing dialogues. Understandably this system is more useful for structured observations than for participant observations, for example, when circumstances dictate the course of the research.

5.1.2   Scoring Observed Behavior

How do you score observed behavior? This is a difficult question and each researcher will tend to answer it differently. Often notes are made of observations but there are more systematic ways to go about it. We'll mention two here. Both methods use a score sheet (Van den Sande, 1999):

1 *Time sampling.* In this method observations are made for a short period of time, say ten minutes. Every fifteen or thirty seconds, there's a signal and at that point you note down what the person is doing.

2 *Event sampling.* In this method, you also observe the person for a certain time but instead you simply note how often they display a certain kind of behavior. The score that you arrive at is called the *frequency* of that particular behavior.

triangula- Observation can be done in combination with other research techniques (tri-
tion angulation). For research at a crèche, the question may be: 'How do toddlers behave when their parents leave?' or 'What is the difference between new toddlers and toddlers that have been at the crèche for six months?' These questions can be answered by observation but you can use other methods as well, for example, through discussions with the day care people and the parents or a combination of the two. Text box 5.5 gives an example. We'll come back to this later in the chapter.

Observation research into telephone booths in Malaysia

The President of Malaysia wanted to improve the state of telephone booths in his country. He engaged an ergonomic institute to carry out the assignment. Using observation research, the problem was pinpointed. From the observations it became clear that people often leant against the booths, damaging them over time. This is called diagnostic research. The researchers also conducted interviews among users. From these interviews it became clear that people also had trouble hearing above the noise of the traffic and the weather when it was stormy. The ergonomic institute came up with an improved design for new telephone booths.

The researcher (on the right) observes.

Source: www.ergonomie.nl

Box 5.5

5.2   Interviews

An interview is a conversation in which the interviewee's perceptions are paramount. The aim is to gather information about a particular subject. Interviews normally take the form of a dialogue, i.e., between the interviewer and the interviewee. It can, however, also take the form of a focus group. In Chapter 7 we'll go into the details of organizing and conducting interviews. In this section we'll briefly discuss types of interviews, starting with the conditions required for holding open interviews. These are interviews that mainly consist of open or unrestricted questions (Swanborn, 2002, p. 163).

Whether conducting open interviews is the right kind of research for you depends on your central question, among other things. If you are investigating the underlying motives that respondents may have, if the subject matter is sensitive, or if the *perceptions* of the respondent are important, then open (in-depth) interviews are what you need. Suppose the question is: 'How do teachers of Groups 1 and 2 at Brixton Primary School perceive their interac-

respondent's perception

tions with children of new immigrants?' This is a sensitive and *complex* subject: it is all about how refugees integrate with the local community. It also involves how the teachers themselves perceive their dealings with these children. In each interview you are looking for new information from the teachers: an interpretative research design! You don't have a fixed questionnaire; at most you have a discussion guide. In brief, using open interviews is the ideal way to tackle this subject.

There is another good reason for using open interviews in the previous example: the *size of the population*. Because it is only one primary school in a particular neighborhood, and because only the teachers from the first two classes will be interviewed, we are talking about a *limited group* or population. If the group is *small*, then the decision to use interviews is made easier. This is because preparing, conducting, processing and analyzing interviews is an intensive and time-consuming business. Interviewing large groups of people is not always feasible.

In the First World, it is easy to assume that 'everything under the sun' has been researched. Yet it is still possible to come across a topic for which no research literature is available. In this case, open interviews are a good method to use because you can use the interview to *orientate* yourself in the subject (see Text box 5.6). Open interviews are often used in the preliminary research so that the subject and the concepts involved can be well-defined.

Emeriti from Utrecht University

Open interviews were held with ten professors during the preliminary research into the activity patterns of retired professors (see Text box 3.6). The aim of these interviews was not only to get a very good idea of how these professors spent their time, it was also to use the results of the interviews to design a questionnaire. This questionnaire was later sent to 381 emeriti who were eligible to participate in the research (Becker & Verhoeven, 2000).

Box 5.6

---

subjectivity   As is the case with observation research, you are close to the participants of your research. You are closely involved with the subject; you empathize where necessary. You draw conclusions from your discussions, and so once again you must be careful to avoid subjectivity. Similar to methods used in observation research, there are techniques that you can use to do this. You can tape the discussions, stick to a discussion guide, or use a loosely structured list of open questions. You can also learn discussion skills that help you to keep the right distance from the respondents and the subject. You collect the information 'from the sideline' as it were, thus maintaining your objectivity. We will discuss these special interviewing techniques in Chapter 7. Finally, the same preconditions that you have to deal with regardless of the research technique apply to open interviews: you have to have available manpower, time and money. Conducting and processing interviews is an intensive and time-consuming job. For every hour you spend interviewing expect to spend at least six processing the results. *Practical considerations* will determine whether you can conduct interviews and how you go about it. Text box 5.7 lists the criteria for using open interviews.

Criteria for using open interviews

- Small groups of people.
- Perception, motives, experience, meaning.
- Complex subjects, taboo subjects.

- Gathering new information, defining concepts.
- Practical considerations.

Box 5.7

Interviews can be completely open, but also very structured. There are three basic types of face-to-face interviews: *interview types*

1 *Unstructured interviews* (also known as *in-depth* or *open interviews*). As the researcher, you normally use one main question and/or topic. So each interview will take its own course, depending on the respondent. The guiding thread will however stay the same. Respondents are completely free to offer their own contribution.
2 *Semi-structured interviews*. In these kinds of interviews, the interviewer has a list of questions or subjects (*topic list*). Respondents still have a great deal of freedom to contribute what they feel is relevant. The researcher is flexible and goes with the flow of the discussion.
3 *Structured interviews*. This is similar to conducting a face-to-face interview using a structured questionnaire. It is more quantitative in nature.

Often discussion guides are used in open interviews; at the same time, structured interviews can also be very open. In other words, this division is not very strict. If you decide to use open interviews, it is a good idea to use a topic list to fall back on.

In *focus groups*, groups of people are interviewed at the same time. The *focus groups* researcher is in charge, they ask the questions and function as the *moderator*

– this means that the researcher structures the discussion as well as the information.

Focus groups can comprise of anything between 5 and 25 people (although 25 is extreme). Focus groups take on many different forms, depending on the objective and the selection criteria. They can be *work conferences* or *workshops* (in which the group leaders are known to each other), but they can also be *focus groups* (during which only one subject is discussed; Swanborn, 2010).

Group participants are sometimes selected because they have a certain skills or knowledge (experts), and sometimes not at all. The objective of the discussion may be to reach consensus, to arrive at the same conclusion. Other discussions are held to gauge a range of opinions on the subject. There is a lot to setting up focus groups, and many of these aspects will not be covered in this book. It is important to bear in mind that moderators have a lot on their plate when controlling and steering focus groups: there's an extra dimension to it all that is beyond the scope of this book.

5.3   Literature Research

Generally speaking, literature research is part and parcel of all research. Prior to the 'main research', but also when you are defining the problem demarcation, it is a good idea to check whether research has been done into the subject. It could be that literature research is the main course of your research meal. This is why we'll treat it as a separate data collection method.

Literature research takes place at all levels. It can be seen as a type of desk research because technically you don't have to go 'onto the street' to do it. You can search for documents at macro level, for example policy documents, but also on an individual level (micro level), for example biographies. Literature research is used a lot for historical research. There may be several reasons for wanting to carry out literature research, for instance:

- To address descriptive and/or comparative questions (such as: 'What characteristics are prominent in the literature on the subject of …?, 'What is known in the literature about …?', 'What do previous research results say on the subject of …?');
- for orientation into a problem area;
- as theoretical support for your research project.

In brief, literature research is almost always part of your project. A lot of applied research is carried out without it, for example to save money, or simply because the research is addressing a specific, practical issue. But if you want to plan your project properly and you want your research to be sound, don't start without carrying out literature research.

In Chapter 2 we discussed how you can best go about searching for literature (or information) and which methods you can use for this. You will generally visit the following sources during your search: libraries, existing archives and the Internet (see Text box 5.8). Obviously you'd inspect your own book-shelves first to see if you can find relevant books there. In your search for literature, you'll come across various grades (i.e., levels). The ones referred to the most are: *grades of literature*

- *Primary sources*
  The subject is being addressed for the first time. It is new.
- *Secondary sources*
  The subject is not new, instead it is literature in which authors refer to and report on topics that have already been researched, for example because of new research or insights.
- *Gray literature*
  Books, reports and documents that are not held in the usual book collec-tions, for example unpublished dissertations that stay within the research institute for which they were written, policy documents at ministries and so on. A lot of this literature is available on the web or in institutional libraries. A well-known Internet library for gray literature is GLIN.

In applied research the differences between the various literature types is not that important, which is not true for scientific research: there it is important. Often if you work as a researcher for a scientific institute, you are judged by the number of publications you have produced. The extent to which you refer to primary and secondary literature counts. If you have taken too much 'gray' literature into account then your publication will not be regarded very highly. Publications that make it into journals with a high *impact factor* are also taken more seriously. Incidentally, gray literature may well be primary, if it is the first time the subject is being written about. Scientific journals are an important source of information when preparing research. There are special journals that describe the latest developments and research in certain fields. These would be secondary literature.
Special indices have been developed for scientific articles, such as the *Social Science Citation Index* (can be found nowadays under *ISI Web of Knowledge*) *impact factor*

or *Scopus*. These show you which articles refer to other articles and how often it occurs. The more an article is referred to, the wider its reach, i.e., the more important it becomes. This is known as the *'impact factor'*. It can be a handy tool when it comes to doing literature research, especially if you are looking for leading articles on a particular subject.

There has, however, been a lot of criticism about the way things are valued scientifically. The reasons are because some journals are given preference, journals about research into education are not included in these indices, and nor is there a rating of the quality of the article itself in the indices. This *impact factor* may be important if you want to write articles. When you cite articles, you don't have to pay too much attention to it.

Articles are registered using key words so that they are easy to find, especially on the web. Scientific articles also have short synopses, known as *abstracts*. You can also find articles by their abstracts. There are even special journals that only contain the abstracts. You can also find articles through *reviews*, which are critical accounts given by peers and colleagues. There are also special journals for this.

tertiary sources   There are also so-called *current content* journals which contain a summary of all the published editions of a given journal (by subject or in alphabetical order) and a short summary of their contents. This search key or instrument is also known as *tertiary sources*. They are not sources in the real sense of the word, but rather references to the sources. This is why this type of literature was not mentioned on the list of 'grades of literature'.

WEBSITE   Some large databases can be accessed by students and staff using a login name and a password, others are freely accessible to all. On our website you will find more information about libraries that you can access via the Internet in the section 'Chapter 5' (tab Extra material).

Literary research into mental healthcare

For their research into mental health-care (see Text box 3.14), Van Gageldonk and Rigter (1988) conducted literature research into the effects of preventative measures on psychological and behavioral problems in mental healthcare. They did not research anything themselves, but instead searched the literature to see what research had been done into the impact of prevention. The research results that Van Gageldonk and Rigter found were mostly quantitative and they included, among others, results of experiments into the effects

Continued

of special preventative measures. The literature research itself is, however, qualitative. The categories used by the researchers are the same as the research subjects in the literature they found. For the research, the researchers mainly looked in electronic sources and libraries, and via reference lists of the articles they found. In their report, the researchers indicated how much literature was available in the various categories and what research designs were used. A closer look at this research reveals that the categories were chosen in close collaboration with the client.

5.4   Content Analysis and Other Kinds of Desk Research

Content analysis involves more than just studying the literature, or reading through documents that you have found. It is a kind of qualitative desk research in which the documents or, as Swanborn puts it, 'the account of verbal behavior' (Swanborn, 1987, p. 220; 't Hart, Van Dijk, De Goede, Jansen & Teunissen, 1998, p. 297) is studied closely for the meaning of and the relationship between the words that have been used. These analyses can be as deep and wide as you want. They are conducted at all levels, i.e., from government and organizational to individual, and from macro to micro level. An example of the last would be an autobiographical investigation, a document analysis of the life of one person. Bear in mind that content analysis is not restricted to the study of written texts. Videotapes, sound recordings and so on can also be part of a study. *Language* is what the analysis is based on (see Text box 5.9).

The quality of hypotheses

In 1999, research was conducted into the quality of hypotheses in PhD dissertations, i.e., the reports that doctoral students present at the end of their studies. The researcher gathered a large number of dissertations produced between 1994 and 1995, by students from six scientific fields. He subjected these dissertations to intensive analysis, looking at the most important question that the PhD research projects were intended to address. He analyzed them in terms of a number of characteristics, such as the link between the subject and its connection with the research design. He also assessed how precise the questions were, their relevance, and so on. This is a typical example of qualitative desk research (Oost, 1999).

To analyze documents properly, it's a good idea to use qualitative variables. Before you start, you decide which characteristics you'll be researching (i.e., 'variables') and which categories (i.e., aspects) you will use. We call these variables qualitative because it is not numerical information you'll be gathering. You'll be studying the text according to these variables. You group the information, look at relationships and study meanings. On the basis of all of this you try to draw conclusions about what the texts purport to say. In Chapter 9 we'll be discussing how to analyze documents. You'll be shown a short text analysis, done on the basis of specific theoretical principles.

Apart from qualitative analysis, there is also a more quantitative variant that entails counting how often an attribute is mentioned in the source (document, text, tape etc.). Text box 5.10 gives an example of this. Swanborn mentions a problem that arises with content analysis: the sample. You have to select a number of documents (newspapers, magazines and so on), but the question is: which ones? And how many? (Swanborn, 2010). When is enough, enough? Also, there is no fixed method of analysis, no set of rules.

How can you uphold the quality of your research? By repeating the analysis (iteration), by discussing the issues with co-researchers, by giving your work to your peers for reviewing, and so on. In brief, content analysis is a complex and intensive method, and as data collection option, by no means the easiest.

Preventative measures in mental healthcare

In Section 5.3 we discussed the example of the literature research done by Van Gageldonk and Rigter (1998) into the effects of preventative measures on psychological and behavioral problems. The researchers not only studied literature, they also analyzed it using content analysis. They investigated the general methodological quality of each research undertaken using a scale. They used Randomized Control Trials (Jadad, 1998) to assess experimental projects. For the rest they either based their study on the attributes mentioned by the research or they used a set of criteria that had been fixed beforehand (Van Gageldonk & Rigter, 1998). The content analysis was to a certain extent quantitative because of the coding exercise that they undertook.

Box 5.10

Reduction in bonus levels as focus on costs increases

Content analysis showed that 2009 proved to be one of the most challenging in US employment markets of the last 30 years. The majority of organizations, from the largest corporates to small businesses, were impacted by the global economic downturn and national unemployment rates rose beyond 10%. At the beginning of the year, widespread cost-cutting exercises meant that redundancies and recruitment freezes were commonplace across a number of sectors, including legal, banking and finance. The influx of candidates onto the market caused competition for roles to rise and resulted in a decrease in salary levels. A greater focus on costs also reduced bonus levels compared to 2008.

Source: www.robertwalters.com

Text sociology is a method used for autobiographical research whereby the researcher analyzes the meaning of words and their relationships in autobiographical texts. The meanings behind the words are not studied from a historical point of view, but rather from a current perspective, and they are interpreted within the current language system. Research into life stories is a good example of this. By analyzing life stories, an image of the era is sketched, or a particular social development is followed (Nijhof, 2000).

text sociology

As we saw in Chapter 4, analyzing existing data can offer a cheap and efficient solution to the problem of how to collect data. This is also true for qualitative data. Existing quantitative data can be reused to test hypotheses. This is more difficult with qualitative research because the analysis is inductive (theory forming) and not deductive (theory testing). What is less problematic is re-analyzing information qualitatively, using an open approach for example. This well-grounded theoretical approach then becomes the guideline for summarizing, coding and structuring the information so that sound conclusions can be drawn (Glaser & Strauss, 1967; Boeije, 2005). In other words: a theory is formulated. This approach is discussed at length in Chapter 9. Text box 5.12 gives an example of this method.

secondary analysis of existing qualitative data

The Veteran Tapes

Proof of good qualitative analysis based on existing documents can be found in the analysis done by researchers at the Veterans Institute. Entitled 'Veteran Tapes', the research was put together by a group of researchers from different fields and comprised a collection of interviews with war veterans. They

Continued

re-analyzed the interviews, and this time from different perspectives. The findings give an idea of how veterans perceive their tours of duty, from the Second World War to the conflict in Afghanistan. The researchers described these perceptions from several points of view, such as morality and religion, but also how they experienced appalling incidents, their perceptions of what it's like to come home and so on (Van den Berg, Stagliola & Wester, 2010).

Box 5.12

Text box 5.13 shows you once more what the main characteristics are of content analysis.

Main features of content analysis

- Impression of behavior as reflected by texts, images and/or sound and video recordings.
- Uses existing data.
- Investigates the semantics of language.
- Explorative by nature.
- Uses qualitative analysis techniques.
- Not dependent on level.
- The sample size can range from one (case study) to dozens of documents.

Box 5.13

5.5   Case Studies

Research that involves one organization or one group is referred to as a case study. This so-called 'N = 1' research only investigates one case, such as a hospital, a school or a department. The study takes place in the 'natural environment', in other words: within the hospital or school. Text box 5.14 gives an example of such a study.

Youth orchestra

The research project for the youth orchestra (see Text boxes 3.5 and 3.7) is a good example of a case study. Changes needed to be made to the organization, but in order to do this the researchers needed to study the existing structure first. During this evaluation research, a perspective for the future was developed after the organization had been studied from several points of view: a document analysis (a.k.a. content analysis), in-depth inter-

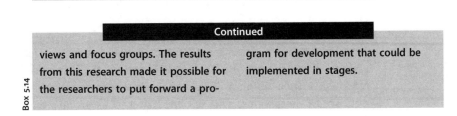

Continued

views and focus groups. The results
from this research made it possible for
the researchers to put forward a pro-

gram for development that could be
implemented in stages.

Box 5.14

Case studies are qualitative research that uses a range of data collection methods, such as open interviews, observation, document studies and focus groups. Researchers from the *interpretative* movement often use case studies for exploring the perceptions and experiences of people within an organization (Boeije, 2005, p.21).

Case studies are used for a wide range of applications, as you can see from Text box 5.14, and they are used in organization and policy research in particular (Boeije, 2005, p.21). After analyzing the problem within the organizations, the findings are used to put forward recommendations for changes and new policies.

Researchers are sometimes called in to monitor and evaluate proposed *action* changes. In such cases, the client (the organization) and the researcher are *research* equally involved in the process. While the measures are being implemented, the researcher observes to see if they have the desired effect. This method (often implemented within one organization) is an interactive, emancipatory learning process for both the organization and the researcher. It is also an iterative process, as illustrated by Figure 5.2. This approach is also known as action research (Ponte, 2007).

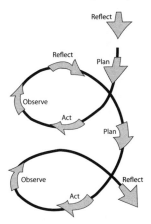

Figure 5.2   *Action research as an iterative process (source: www.qualiteit.nl)*

Delphi It is sometimes the organization's objective to reach consensus about a certain plan, change or measure. If this is the case, then the Delphi method lends itself for the process. In Delphi research, those involved and other experts give their opinion of the new policy, measure or change during a sequence of discussions. This is done using focus groups, dialogue, workshops and communication audits (which involves collecting information about the issue from the organizations internal communication sources), and as such is a triangulated approach. The objective is to investigate what all the various layers of the organization think and to reach a consensus on the issue.

biographical research Biographical research is another example of a case study in which the life of one person is investigated. For this, historical sources are researched using document (or content) analysis. Interviews are also conducted with those acquainted with the person concerned, where possible that is. Text box 5.15 gives an example of a biographical case study.

Biography Roosevelt's Geographer

In 2002, Prof. Neil Smith won the LA Times Book Prize for Biography on a study of the life and works of Roosevelt's Geographer, Isaiah Bowman. By researching and describing his life and works, Smith also uncovered the history of geography or, as he says, 'the geo-graphy of history' (Smith, 2002, xvi). In his book, Smith also links late 19th and early 20th century American history to contemporary developments such as acting as the world's police force, and the 'war on terrorism'.

Box 5.15

---

other types of case studies In the psychology, education and medical sciences, you'll come across a lot of case studies. Examples of these would be research into individual medical case histories. Anthropological case studies would be those investigating individual villages or population groups, such as the research into the Yanomamö (a South American tribe) or, a little closer to home, research into the causes of RSI among students of the faculty of Industrial Design carried out by students of the Technical University of Delft (De Bruin & Molenbroek, 2001).

intensive research Case studies are a type of *intensive* research. This research investigates the relationships *within* the case using participatory observation (by spending time working among the staff in a department) and or in-depth interviews.

Opposed to this is the *extensive* approach, in which the organization is approached 'from the outside', by way of a survey for instance (Swanborn, 2000, p.14-15; Sayer, 2000).

5.6   The Right Way?

In the past two chapters, we've discussed a number of data collection methods. We also indicated which criteria apply to each method. With every research question you have to ask yourself which is the correct method to collect data. You can make the decision based on the criteria we have listed. You will also be dependent on the client, the possibilities and limitations of the research locations, the size of the population and the sample, what's possible in terms of time and money, and so forth.

The title of this section is actually a bit misleading. There is no 'right' way. There is a 'best' way if you take into account the circumstances that we've mentioned. Obviously, it's possible to go into the fundamental aspects of it all and discuss the pros and cons of qualitative versus quantitative research, or the principles of research that you consider to be important when conducting research, or the various movements within the science of research. The most important criterion when it comes to choosing a method is that you can get an objective and unbiased answer to the problem. It is also important to provide your client with a solution that will be implemented within the organization or institution instead of disappearing into a drawer somewhere.

We've reviewed many different kinds of data collection methods. In some cases, one of these methods will suffice; in others it is not possible to get a straightforward answer using one method alone. And sometimes you have to use a multi-faceted approach to delineate the subject first and then use a range of different methods when researching it. The result of this will be a research design. Here we have in mind evaluation research, policy research, market research, and communications research. These concepts are not data collection methods per se, instead they indicate in broad terms what the subject of the research is. *research design*

On our website www.doingresearch.nl, under the Extra material tab, in the section 'Chapter 5', you will find information about communication research as a research design, and where you'll find the answers to questions about internal and external communications within and between organizations.

using trian- As noted above, triangulation is used when the problem needs more than
gulation one kind of data collection method to find a solution. You can cast your
net wide and do quantitative research, and combine this with in-depth interviews or focus groups to get to the nitty gritty of the matter. Triangulation
enhances the quality of the research findings, but bear in mind that triangulated research is time-consuming and therefore expensive too!

collabora- Once you have completed your research design, you go back to the client.
tion Conferring with client is a regular, recurring aspect of research. Normally
you will have a contact person within the organization who reads your progress reports, advises you of the client's perspective, and puts you in touch
with other relevant people within the organization. Always bear in mind
that research, especially if it's within the organization, often has consequences for the staff. First and foremost it may mean more work for them.
They have to organize things for you, and make sure that you have everything you need in terms of people, material and facilities. But above all it
will require the active participation of some members of staff.

5.7   Glossary of Most Important Terms and Their Meaning

Holistic research	Research elements are studied within their environment as a whole.
Observation research	Research which uses observation of people or groups to collect information.
Participant observation	The researcher takes part in the daily lives of the people being researched, gathering infor-mation at the same time.
Triangulation	A combination of various research techniques.
Intersubjectivity	The researchers are in agreement among themselves about the findings of the research.
Peer consultation	Researchers review each other's work critically in order to increase the quality of the results.
Time sampling	Over a short period of time, at a given signal, the behavior of the subject under observation is noted at that time.
Event sampling	Over a short period of time, the incidence of a given type of behavior is noted.

Unstructured interviews	Information is gathered during conversations (in-depth interviews) using a limited number of general discussion topics.
Semi-structured interviews	Information is gathered during an interview using a discussion guide covering specified topics.
Structured interviews	Interviews conducted by interviewers using structured questionnaires containing closed questions.
Focus groups	Interviewing of people in groups (focus groups).
Primary literature	Literature dealing with a new subject or a new perspective on a subject.
Secondary literature	Literature that reports on the research findings of other scientists.
Gray literature	Unpublished literature that is not generally available from the usual sources, such as reports, papers presented at conferences and so on.
Tertiary literature	Literature containing synopses of primary and secondary literature.
Impact factor	A measure of the relative importance of scientific publications.
Content analysis	Analyzing texts from literature/interviews transcriptions.
Case studies	Research with a sample size of 1, i.e., N = 1.
Delphi research	A combination of methods aimed at gaining consensus on a given issue within an organization by going through several cycles.
Intensive research	Addressing a research question 'from within' as opposed to extensive research, which addresses the issue from the outside.
Action research	Research that assesses the impact of change at the same time that it is implemented.
Communication audit	Collecting information about the organization's internal communications.

5.8   Assignments for Chapter 5

1 Come up with an observation method for research into the learning behavior of students during a lecture. Use the outline given in Figure 5.1 and
 discuss the differences in the various approaches possible.

2 The Eastleigh Municipality has commissioned research into care for the
 elderly. The research is expected to last several years. The municipality
 wants to know what the state of affairs is regarding care for the elderly at
 the start of the research and how the users themselves experience this
 care. The municipality also wants the suggestions and requirements of
 the elderly so that they can use this information to draft a new policy.
 This policy will be designed to ensure that the elderly stay in charge of
 their own lives as far as possible. Finally, the municipality wants to assess
 the impact of their new policy some time after its implementation. What
 research approach and data collection method would you advise? Why?

3 Read the example in Text box 5.15. Formulate the problem correctly.
 Which data collection methods do you think the researcher probably
 used?

4 How can you avoid subjectivity when conducting interviews and observation research?

5 What is the difference between time sampling and event sampling? Give
 an example.

6 A secondary school wants to improve the way they teach math. The
 pupils are not motivated during lessons, they don't like the subject and
 they find it difficult. Not only that, the achievement levels are low, i.e.,
 the number of pupils who pass is not high, and this is reflected in their
 poor grades. The school wants to introduce a new teaching method that
 involves using a software package. They want to research the effect of
 this method on pupils' grades.
 a How would you formulate the problem?
 b Which data collection method would you advise? How would you
  approach the project?
 c Suppose that you as the researcher were involved in the whole process
  of implementation and evaluation. What is this kind of research called?
  Outline an overall design.

7 What would you say are the pros and cons of triangulation in research?

8 Read Text box 5.3 on participant observation in the neighborhood shop.
 a Formulate the problem and research objective.
 b Come up with an alternative way of conducting the research.

9 The municipality of Brookville wants to build a new apartment complex, preferably with the support of the local community. They want to carry out research to gauge local support. The problem has been formulated as follows: 'How much support is there for the new apartment complex among those who live in the suburb of Newlands?'
The municipality uses the meeting of the local community club to discuss the subject and to gauge opinions. The researcher acts as the mediator. What data collection method is the researcher using? Motivate your answer and design the research.

In the section 'Chapter 5' (tab Assignment solutions) you will find the solutions to the assignments in Section 5.8. You will find information about the design cases under tab 'Design cases' in the section 'Chapter 5'.

Applying the Method: Operationalization and Sample

You have now arrived that the stage where you apply your method of data collection. You've decided which one you are going to use, your research plan has been approved. Now is when you take the following steps:

1 You develop the concepts in your design until they are so-called 'measurable instruments', which is called *operationalization*. This means that if your research is using a questionnaire, you will use the concepts to phrase the questions properly. If you are using open questions, you will design an interview schedule. After this, you will go over the techniques you intend to use during the interviews (see Chapter 7).

2 Together with the client, you have delineated the domain, so you know which group of people/units you will be making statements about. In short, the *population* has been established. Now you are going to select a part of this group: you will draw the *sample*.

3 You carry on preparing the report. To what extent will the results be *usable*? How objective and reliable will it be? You can already comment on this based on the operationalization and sample selection.

The topics discussed above will be applied to two data collection methods: surveys and in-depth interviews. These are the two kinds of data collection that you are most likely to come across in practice. In this chapter, we will start elaborating these two methods and will continue the discussion in Chapter 7 when we talk about data collection.

content and objectives

Learning objectives

Box 6.1

When you get to the end of this chapter you will be familiar with the way in which you translate the theoretical design of your research into research in practice. You will be able to turn concepts into measurable instruments for both surveys and interviews. You will also be able to draw the sample correctly. Finally, you will also be able to discuss the usability, validity and reliability of your research design.

6.1   From Theory to Practice

When setting up your research, you work from the abstract to concrete, from theory to practice. You start by describing the problem areas, you then go on to define them by formulating a researchable problem and objective. You then search the literature for relevant theories, models and research findings. The aim here is to find clues as to how to structure your research and where to look to formulate your assumptions about the results. You apply any results that you find concretely to the subject of your research ('Previous research shows …'). The next step is to investigate whether or not your assumptions can be confirmed. You do this by collecting data. You decide which is the right method to use and then you take a step further and operationalize the method. You take the concepts that you used in your model and you design tools to collect the data, the so-called instruments.

operationa-lization Often it seems that when it comes to operationalizing your concepts, you go over the same ground that we've just described all over again. And in fact you do. You take another long hard look at your research model and the concepts that you have formulated, but this time you go one step further: you decide which questions you are going to ask to actually measure these concepts. This step – from research questions to so-called observational questions ('t Hart et al., 1998, p. 80) – is what is known as operationalization.

measure-ment instruments When you operationalize your research, you take the concepts from your research design and turn them into measurement instruments. *Measurement instruments* are tools that you use to collect the information. Included in this would be the questions in your questionnaire, the subjects for your in-depth interviews, observation categories for your observation research, the experimental variables for your experiment and so on.

WEBSITE On our website you can find more information about the concept 'measurement instrument' in the section 'Chapter 6' (tab Extra material).

Figure 6.1   From theory to practice in surveys

In Chapter 3 we talked about how you define the concepts you will use in *from* your research. You demarcate the concepts theoretically by indicating the *concept* boundaries of their meaning that is relevant to your research. Take for *demarcation* example the concept 'work climate' that you have defined for your research *to measure-* into perceptions of the work climate at a supermarket (see Text box 6.2). *ment* For this you would define: *instrument*

- what you mean by work climate;
- the definition that you yourself have used for the research (i.e., the *stipu-lative* meaning);
- whatever sub-aspects there may be of this concept;
- which 'perception of work climate' model you will be using to answer the research question.

When you define the concept you mention what you would include, but in particular what you would not include.

Operationalization work climate at Supermarket 'NS' (1)

Imagine you've been asked to find out about how the staff at Supermarket 'NS' (short for Neighborhood Supermarket) in Borrowdale feel about the work climate. When you operationalize, you expand the concept 'work climate' into a number of questions. Why is operationalization necessary? Because you can't ask people about abstract concepts. If you ask twenty people 'What do you think about the work climate?' you'll get twenty different answers. That's not only because people have a different view of the work climate, it's also because they attach their own meaning to the concept 'work climate'. In order to get reliable results, you formulate questions that have the same meaning for everyone: lucid, clear and completely unambiguous. So you go from an abstract concept to a measurable question.

How do you operationalize 'perceptions of work climate' at a supermarket? First you look at your theoretical model. Suppose you describe perceptions of the work climate in your model as 'job satisfaction'. By that we understand the extent to which a member of staff enjoys their work. Applied to the work climate in a supermarket, we could look at aspects such as relations with colleagues, working conditions (working in the cold rooms is not the same as at the tills), work pressure or relations with management and supervisors.

Box 6.2

The next step is to develop some so-called 'observational questions' so that *observa-* each aspect of the concept is addressed. We start operationalizing, i.e., we *tional questions* go from the concept 'as intended' to the concept 'as determined' (see Figure 6.2). We determine how we are going to measure the concept.

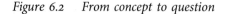

Figure 6.2   From concept to question

6.2   Developing Survey Questions

Designing a good questionnaire is a long process of deliberating, evaluating, scrapping and changing, all in consultation with your co-researchers and the client. Don't take this step too lightly, you only have one chance to interview your respondents. You can't say 'Sorry, my mistake, can we start again?' It is crucial that the questionnaire:

- is usable;
- is easy to understand and clear, so specific and unambiguous;
- is comprehensive;
- contains questions that 'measure what you want to measure';
- is neutral so that respondents are not steered in one or other direction;
- is not too long: it should be as concise as possible;
- is not a catch all for everything you ever wanted to know but never got a chance to ask.

6.2.1   *Asking Questions*

There are several ways to ask questions. You can link your questions so that they follow a route through your questionnaire. You can ask stand alone questions or questions that consist of several sub-questions and open or closed questions. The way you structure the response options is also important. How will you tackle this?

standard Bear in mind when it comes to designing questionnaires that using standard
question- questionnaires may enhance the credibility and reliability of the results. This
naires will only be the case if you ensure that:

- the questionnaire structure is the same for all respondents;
- the question formulation is the same for all respondents;
- the formulation of the possible answers is the same for all respondents;
- there aren't too many open questions;

- the questions are logical (don't ask those under the age of 18 how they intend to vote, for instance);
- questions about the same subject are in the same section;
- each section of questions is preceded by an introduction outlining its intention.

It is important that you ask the questions in the correct order. The way you *question* order the questions can affect the way they are answered. Boeije et al. (2009) *sequence* see this as a sequence effect. For example, you may have put a lot of questions with the same answer categories together. On the face of it, this is not a bad thing, but it may mean that the respondents will stop thinking about their answers and just mention the first thing that comes to mind.

The following tips will help you to make sure that there is logic to the sequencing of questions:

1 Start with simple, general and engaging questions (for example, facts and background characteristics).
2 Be straightforward about your intentions, i.e., your main subject: don't skirt around it.
3 Don't put difficult questions right at the end of your questionnaire. There's a good chance that the respondents won't take their time to answer them properly. The best place for difficult or sensitive questions is at the beginning of the second part of your questionnaire. Put easy questions at the end.
4 Group questions with the same answer categories but make sure that there is some variety so that you can avoid uniformity in the answers.

Linked to this is the *routing* of a questionnaire (Boeije et al., 2009). There *routing* should be logic to the sequence of questions. If there is no rational route, it can be very irritating for the respondents. Make sure there is one!

Another thing to remember is this: you can only ask someone questions *filter* about their spouse if you know they are married. In the same way, you can *questions* only ask someone what they think of a product if you know they use it. If they are not familiar with the product, then there is no point in asking them questions about it: skip the questions, they are not applicable. For instance, you first find out if someone has a driver's license before asking them questions about driving ability. These selection questions are known as *filter questions*.

6.2.2 Giving Answers

It is well-known that, apart from the sequencing of questions, the way the response options are structured also influences the way respondents answer the questions. For instance, if you first structure the response options from positive to negative and then from negative to positive, the respondents may not be aware of this. As a result, the question maybe incorrectly marked, and you'll no longer be 'measuring what you intend to measure'.

Below we first give a list of the various *types of response options*, followed by a few examples:

- *Single item answer*. For example: 'How old are you?' Or: 'How many hours a week do you take part in sport?' The number of years or hours is the answer.
- *Scale (Likert)*. You can ask people's opinions of related things by presenting them with a scale. The answers then range between, for example, 'completely agree' to 'completely disagree'. In Section 6.2.3 we'll discuss this further.
- *List*. The respondents can choose a word from a list.
- *Open answer*. The respondents are free to formulate their own answer.
- *Semi-open answers*. In this type of answer category, you have closed and open questions. For example, if the response options on offer don't match the respondent's answer, then they can fill in their own answer. This category is then know as *other* (see Text box 6.3).
- *Multiple answers*. More than one answer may be possible; the respondent can choose as many options as they consider applicable (see Text box 6.4).
- *Dichotomous answers*. There are only two options to choose from (see Text box 6.5).

 WEBSITE Would you like to know more about analyzing multiple answers? Visit our website where you will find an example in the section entitled 'Introduction to SPSS'.

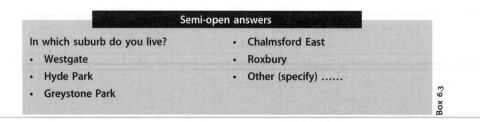

Semi-open answers	
In which suburb do you live?	• Chalmsford East
• Westgate	• Roxbury
• Hyde Park	• Other (specify) ......
• Greystone Park	

Box 6.3

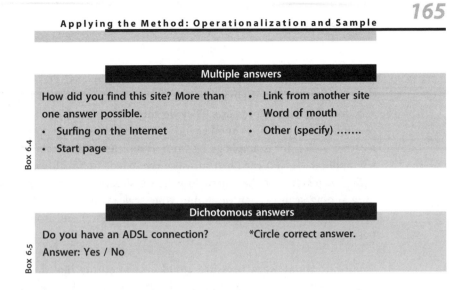

Multiple answers

How did you find this site? More than one answer possible.
- Surfing on the Internet
- Start page

- Link from another site
- Word of mouth
- Other (specify) ....

Box 6.4

Dichotomous answers

Do you have an ADSL connection?   *Circle correct answer.
Answer: Yes / No

Box 6.5

6.2.3 Likert Scales

A Likert scale is a so-called 'composite instrument' comprising a list of related (i.e., about the same subject) questions, statements or items that the respondent is asked to answer by choosing from an increasing scale of responses (Swanborn, 2010). For instance, you can gauge people's opinions on a subject by asking them a series of related questions. The respondents then choose from the same range of answer categories, normally in ascending order.

Operationalization work climate at Supermarket 'NS' (2)

For the research project among staff members at Supermarket 'NS', you designed research that entails conducting open interviews and organizing a survey. The open interviews are part of your preliminary study into finding out more about the background to perceptions of the work climate. You then develop the concept 'work climate' into detailed questions that you will use in your survey. For this you are going to use the results of the open interviews. One of the aspects of perceptions of the work climate is 'work pressure'. For this you devise a scale. The questions will relate to things like working hours, starting and knocking-off times, shift work, irregular hours, sick leave, sick leave of colleagues, public holidays and other special occasions, the number of staff on the shift and so on.

Box 6.6

In Text box 6.6 there are a number of observational questions about 'work pressure'; they are also known as *items*. Together they gauge the perceptions

multiple

item scales

that staff from the supermarket have about work-related pressure. You put these items in a list. Using this list, the staff from 'NS' can tell you how they feel about work pressure. They do this using a *multiple item scale*. The respondent has a limited number (odd or even) of response options given in a certain order, for example going from 'completely inapplicable' to 'completely applicable'. You can then measure the extent to which someone agrees with a statement, or the extent to which a situation is applicable to them, on a sliding scale. When designing your scale, you can decide how many options you want, from three to seven (or even more) and from negative to positive (or vice versa).

Questions about work pressure could go something like the example in Table 6.1. In the same way you can design questions about working conditions, staff relations, communications, customer service and so on.

Table 6.1   Operationalization of 'work pressure'

QUESTION 3 WORK PRESSURE Below you will find a number of factors that have to do with perceptions about work pressure. You can indicate how you experience work related pressure by ticking the appropriate box.					
	I experience:				
	No work pressure at all	Hardly any work pressure	Neutral	A little bit of work pressure	A lot of work pressure
Number of working hours a day					
Starting and knocking off times					
Number of colleagues on duty					
Own sick leave					
Colleagues' sick leave					
Job content					
Special days, e.g., Christmas, New Year					
Irregular working hours					
Uncertainty about shifts					

Multiple item scales usually have an *odd* number of response options of which *odd or even* the middle one is *neutral*. You will find an example of a seven point scale in Table 6.2. Between 2005 and 2009, research was carried out in the Netherlands and Flanders among social science students at universities and colleges to find out what they thought about courses on statistics. The questions in Table 6.2 were part of this research into 'attitudes towards statistics' (Verhoeven, 2009). One of the risks of using odd numbers of response options is that an error occurs because respondents interpret 'neutral' as 'I don't know' or 'no comment'. An alternative is to force respondents to abandon the neutral terrain by giving them an even number of response options (see Table 6.3).

Table 6.2   *Attitudes towards statistics*

	Strongly disagree			Neither agree nor disagree			Strongly agree
Statistical formulas are easy to understand.	1	2	3	4	5	6	7
Statistics are useless.	1	2	3	4	5	6	7
Statistics is a difficult subject.	1	2	3	4	5	6	7
Statistics should be a compulsory subject in my study.	1	2	3	4	5	6	7

Table 6.3   *Motivation for doing voluntary work for Highlands Sports Club*

	Completely inapplicable	Not applicable	Applicable	Completely applicable
When you work for Highlands, you meet a lot of other volunteers.				
It's fun to work with other volunteers.				
It feels good doing voluntary work for Highlands.				
I have enough spare time to do voluntary work for Highlands.				
Helping to organize sports events is fun.				
It's good to help others.				

Researchers often use Likert scales when investigating 'motivation', as did Lindeman (1996) when she researched what it is that motivates people to do voluntary work. In her theoretical model, she uses four different objectives that people aim for when they do voluntary work:

- *investment* (in human capital): gaining experience that you can put to good use elsewhere;
- *caring*: doing something for others;
- *stimulating*: voluntary work is good for your own mental and physical well being;
- *social relationships*.

These concepts were used in applied research into the motivations for volunteering to help organize a sports event. Lindeman developed a number of Likert scales because in research like this you can't just go 'onto the streets' with these concepts.

Likert scales were also used in the research into voluntary work that was done at Highlands Sports Club (see Table 6.3). The questions have a high level of uniformity (also known as *homogeneity*, *internal consistency* or *reliability*). In other words, *together* they measure 'motivation to do voluntary work', 'attitude towards statistics' or 'work pressure' (Lindeman, 1996; Verhoeven, 2002c) and the relation between the items is strong.

WEBSITE On our website you will find more information about how you can analyze the reliability of Likert scales in the section 'Chapter 8' (tab Extra material).

6.2.4 Good Questions – Good Answers

It is amazing how often you come across very extensive (and especially long!) questionnaires because the client thinks that, now that they have the chance, they'll ask all those other questions that really have nothing to do with the research. That is not the way to go. Of course there's nothing wrong with assessing a concept from several different angles, but wandering off the point is not good. It is irritating for the respondents and they quickly get 'survey fatigue'. The end result is that you get incomplete questionnaires back, or that people refuse to take part at all. Don't make your questionnaire unnecessarily long and restrict your questions to the subject you are researching or you'll risk annoying or losing your respondents. In the summary that follows we mention a few pointers that you can use to devise good questions and formulate good response options.

Good questions

When is a question a good question? There are a few rules for this:

Good questions:

- *are clear and simple.* They are written in straightforward language that is easy for all in the target group to understand;
- *are unambiguous.* They are not leading and the respondents understand the intention of the question without being steered;
  - Wrong: 'Do you also hate it when people breed animals for their fur?'
  - Right: 'What do you think of breeding animals for their fur?'
- *are never double-barreled.* You only ever ask one question at a time;
  - Wrong: 'Did you vote during the last elections, and if so, for which party?'
  - Right: 'Did you vote during the last elections? If so, carry on to 2b. If not, skip to question 3. 2b: Which party did you vote for?'
  - Wrong: 'What do you think of the waiting times and customer friendliness of Sure Insurance's call centre?'
    This is an example of a double-barreled question.
  - Right: 'What do you think of the waiting times of Sure Insurance's call centre?' And: 'What do you think of the customer friendliness of Sure Insurance's call centre?'
- *do not contain double negatives;*
  - Wrong: 'Do you disagree with the fact that the US is not taking part in the winter Olympics?'
  - Right: 'What do you think of the fact that the US is not taking part in the winter Olympics?'
- *are objective;*
  - Wrong: 'Are you also annoyed that train tickets have gone up in price?'
  - Right: 'What is your opinion of the increase in the price of train tickets?'
- *are unbiased;*
  - Wrong: 'Will you vote for the Republicans or Democrats at the next election?'
  - Right: 'Which party will you vote for at the next elections?'

Good (quantitative) answers

Similarly, there are a few rules for 'good response options'. Good response options are:

- stated in *recognizable categories.* Response categories should be recognizable. Don't use abbreviations, jargon and other terms that your respondents may not be familiar with;

- given in a *logical sequence*, for example in ascending order. Level of education would go from 'primary school' to 'university degree' and opinions go from 'completely agree' to 'completely disagree' or vice versa;
- *exhaustive.* All possible response options must be given, or there must be an 'others' option;
- *mutually exclusive.* There should be no overlap in the response options so that respondents can only choose one option;
- *measurable.* The categories should be numerical (or can be converted to digits) so that calculations can be made. If the response option is open, so that text can be inserted, then the answers have to be analyzed qualitatively.

When you design your questionnaire, you use appropriate language. By this we mean: you use the kind of language that your target group is most familiar with, for example you would use a different register for young people than you would for the elderly (see Text box 6.7).

Lifestyles of the young

In 2005, research was conducted among the youth focusing on their choice of clothing and music. The question asked of respondents was 'Which group would you say you belong to in terms of clothing and taste in music?' The respondents could choose from Gothic, Skater, Hiphopper, Rich kids, Alto, Trendy/Fashionista, Gabber/Hardcore, Normalo, and so on (*de Volkskrant*, November 24, 2005).

Box 6.7

---

pilot survey Once your questionnaire is ready, the best thing to do is test it. This is known as a pilot. You test your questionnaire to see if there are any mistakes, if the sequence is correct, if the questions 'flow' properly and to check whether you've overlooked anything. Often these pilots give you a lot of useful pointers to improve your questionnaire.

6.2.5 *Preparations for Quantitative Processing: Variables*

Once you've completed the operationalization process, then you'll know what the characteristics of your questionnaire are and how long it is. You will also know what kind of analysis you intend to use so you can start preparing for this. The preparation for this consists mainly of compiling your codebook. A *codebook* is the list that shows how the attributes that you intend to measure will be converted into the *variables* that you will be using for your analysis. This codebook will be the basis for the data entry of the quantitative information into Excel or SPSS.

In your codebook you include:

- the attributes that measured in all the questions (variable *label*);
- what they are called (*variable name*);
- the *categories* that they belong to. These are all the possible values that a variable can have;
- what you will do when answers are missing, so-called *missing values*.

The next step is to process these categories numerically. You do this by assigning a number to each category so that the variables also become 'numeric' and as such can be processed by the software program. How this is done will be discussed in Chapter 8 when all of these terms will be explained at length. Here we will restrict ourselves to an example of part of a codebook (Table 6.4).

Unanswered questions (missing cases) can also be coded so that they can be easily identified later. You can also set up the program to ignore these codes. They are known as *missing values*. In Table 6.4 they have been given the code '99' or '999'.   *missing cases*

Table 6.4   Part of a codebook

Variable name	Label	Categories	Missing values
AGE	Age in years		999[1]
SEX	Gender	0 = male	99
		1 = female	
STATUS	Marital status	1 = married/living together	99
		2 = single	
		3 = widow/widower	
		4 = divorced	
LEVEL	Highest level of education	1 = primary school	99[2]
		2 = high school	
		3 = college	
		4 = university: bachelor	
		5 = university: masters	
		6 = university: post grad	

[1] The code '999' is used to indicate that the age is missing given that 99 could also be an age.

categories Assigning numbers to the categories is not difficult. For example, 'age in years': any age possible is a category. Numbers and measures are generally easy to code, but it's not that simple when the categories are less logically ordered. Categories in questions about opinions are normally given numbers in ascending order, say from 1 to 5. The category 'gender' is two, and you're free to choose whichever number you like because they will not be used for calculations. So for gender you can choose 1 for male and 2 for female, or 0 for female and 1 for male.

multiple If the question has several possible answers (multiple answers) then the
answers respondent could choose any number of options, from 1 to 5. In this case, you give the category 'ticked' 1 and 'not ticked' 0. These variables are also known as *dummies*. Each response option becomes a separate attribute. In Text box 6.8 there is an example of dummy variables from research in which people are asked about their hobbies.

Dummy variables

Respondents are asked the following question: 'Please indicate which hobbies you have. Multiple answers possible.' When assigning the codes, the researcher does as follows:

- reading   1 = ticked, 0 = not ticked;
- walking   1 = ticked, 0 = not ticked;
- gardening   1 = ticked, 0 = not ticked;
- sports   1 = ticked, 0 = not ticked;
- travel   1 = ticked, 0 = not ticked.

Box 6.8

6.3   Interview Topics

Although you don't generally use structured questionnaires for in-depth interviews, you do have to operationalize the questions. After all, you have to deliberate long and hard about the topics you want to discuss and the information you intend to gather. Sometimes semi-structured questionnaires are the answer. These are questionnaires that include both closed and open questions. In this way, in-depth interviews resemble face-to-face interviews conducted during surveys. Alternatively, the topics may not be that fixed because there is only one, general subject. The interview then is extremely open and free.

In most cases, a topic list is compiled based on the concepts used in the   *topic list*
research design (see Text box 6.9). This is then used to steer the discussion,
but the starting point for everything is still the central question. Think carefully about what you want to talk about, you won't get another shot at it.
Often concepts on topic lists are much closer to the demarcated concepts
than the ones on questionnaires. This is because the discussion will be
about the meaning that the concept has for respondent. You don't have to
turn it into a question or explain it: the respondents will indicate themselves
how they perceive the subject and what they think about it.

Always bear in mind that in in-depth interviews it's the respondent's point   *steering*
of view that is the focus point. If the interview starts to head towards something other than your topic, go along with it. Naturally you try to steer the
respondent back to the issue using the appropriate interviewer techniques
(we'll talk about this in the next chapter), but you must be flexible and
allow the respondent enough space to have their say.

The extent to which you steer the interview also depends on the subject. If
you are exploring opinions, then you can give the respondent a free rein. If
you need to get specific information about certain aspects of the subject,
then you can steer the discussion more. In Chapter 7 we discuss tools that
are used in open interviews (interviewing techniques). In Text boxes 6.9
and 6.10 you'll find examples of topic lists.

From the perspective of kidney patients

Two universities carried out in-depth interviews with kidney patients. The focus during these interviews was on living with kidney disease. Two subjects were covered: the history of the illness and perceptions of everyday life. The objective of the project was to establish a research agenda for the years to come. The topic list that was used to assess perceptions of daily life as a patient contained the following sub-jects:

Continued

Daily life

1   Own feelings

2   Education

3   Work

4   Social life and leisure time activities, vacations, relaxation

5   Social relationships: family/partner, having children, care

6   Hates

7   Perceptions of their own body: puberty, marriage, sexuality

8   Diet (pre-dialysis and dialysis)

9   Medicine

10   Treatment, communication and contact: the environment

11   Formal measures

From the results it emerged that information about how to live with their disease is what helps kidney patients the most, as opposed to information and insights about the disease itself.

Source: Abma, Nierse, Van de Griendt, Schipper & Van Zadelhoff, 2007

Box 6.9

question sequence   As is the case with surveys, the way the questions are ordered can also affect the way they are answered. The most important thing to take into account in an interview is the respondent's perceptions. In order to get as much useful information as possible, it is important that the conversation goes well, and the sequence of the questions impacts on this. Generally you should start with a few easy questions (facts). After that you go on to talk about opinions and the reasons for them, and then later you can introduce more sensitive subjects. Towards the end, you wind down again with some less demanding questions.

pilot interview   In in-depth interviews, like in surveys, it is advisable to try out your topic list in a trial interview so that you can see whether there is anything missing or superfluous. If so, you can adjust it accordingly. You can also check the sequencing of the topics and sub-topics if there are any.

Image of a department store

What is the difference between the identity and the image of a department store? Armed with this question you go off to conduct a number of open interviews with store managers. The central question is the same as the main question for the interviews. What you are researching is the image that the managers themselves have of their store, and the one they think customers have of it. The topic list may contain the following subjects:

- *service*: product knowledge, customer orientation, efficiency;
- *human resources policy*: staff component;
- *merchandising and house style*;
- *communication*: advertising message;
- *image*: staff perceptions of customer perceptions, desired image, suggestions.

6.4 Population and Sample

Once your questionnaire and topic list are ready, you can start conducting interviews. For this you need to know who it is you are going collect information from. Normally the client will have an idea of who it is they want to interview and how many of them there are (the domain). Also, it is generally not possible to interview the whole target population so you have to make a selection by drawing a sample. It is important to take into account rules that enhance the reliability and validity of your results and therefore the credibility of your findings. In this section, we'll talk about these rules but not before we've discussed how you determine the population, what this entails and what a sample is.

6.4.1 *What Is a Population?*

In Chapters 2 and 3 we introduced the concept 'population'; now we'll discuss it at greater length. By population we mean all the 'elements' (people, companies, organizations etc.) that you will be making statements about in your research. These are the *domains* that your research will be investigating. Take note: this means *all* the people or businesses that you *would like* to make statements about. This does not mean that you actually interview all these people. Suppose you want to collect information from high school pupils. If you were to interview every single high school pupil it would be a costly and long-drawn-out business given that the population comprises

population = domain

hundreds of thousands, if not millions of people. There is another very practical reason for not interviewing all of them: there is no way you could reach all of them! For this reason you draw a sample (see Section 6.4.2), i.e., you select a section of the population using a specific method.

operational   Sometimes it is possible to define the population more specifically because
population   the original, intended population is very large. Taking the example of the high school pupils. Suppose you research the experiences of final year pupils. The population is all high school pupils, but the *operational population* (i.e., a section of the population, a specific segment as it were) is all high school pupils who are in their final year. That is the operational population that your research will focus on, and that is the group from which you will draw your sample.

6.4.2   Conditions for Drawing Samples

As we have already noted, it is not always possible to interview all of the elements in the population. Not only is respondent availability a problem, it would also be an extremely costly and protracted business. Drawing a sample is the best solution. A sample is a small part of the population that you want to gather information from. But you don't just pick people, there are rules for drawing samples.

reach   These rules have consequences for how you handle the processing and the results, and what the reach is of your results. Ideally the sample should lead to reliable results. There are three important conditions that must be met when drawing the sample. The extent to which you meet these conditions will determine the scope of your research. We will now explore these aspects.

Random samples

The sample should be *random*. This means that each element (person, business, organization) should have an equal chance of being part of the sample (Boeije et al., 2009; Swanborn, 1987, p. 271). If your sample has been selected randomly, then you can verify quantitatively whether the correlations between characteristics (variable) that you have found are valid for the whole population. You can also make estimations about the whole population based on the results of your sample's responses (for example, the mean) or indicate the ranges within the population that a given characteristic occurs (with a certainly of say 95%). This is also known as the *confidence interval* (see Boeije et al., 2009).

Generalizability

A second important condition is *generalizability*.

The generalizability of the results is determined by the extent to which your sample is *representative*. In other words, the elements in the sample have similar characteristics (that are of interest to the research) to the rest of the population. This is what is known as the *external validity* of your sample: we'll come back to this in 6.5.2. Figure 6.3 shows what the sample for our research into high school pupils would look like. The outer circle is the intended population, the next circle is the operational population and that's where we draw the sample from. For example, the ratio boys to girls should be about the same as that of the overall population.

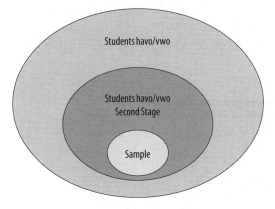

Figure 6.3   Sample of pupils

Sample size

The sample has to be *big enough* to be able to carry out statistical analysis on it. This rule of thumb is difficult, what is 'big enough'? It's an issue that researchers have debated for a long time. There is no easy answer.

In quantitative research, it's important to be able to make accurate state-ments based on the results. The larger the sample, the more accurate it will be. Generally speaking, larger sample sizes yield more reliable results because the replicability of the instrument is possible (see Section 6.5.1). Assessing reliability is best done with random samples. How high should reliability be? In most cases researchers look for 95% reliability (Swanborn, 2010, p. 158-160; Boeije et al., 2009). Broadly speaking, quantitative analysis can be done on samples sizes of 100 or more, but a lot of research has been done using sample sizes. And once you've divided the total sample into smaller

accurate statements

sub-samples, for example males and females, the groups being compare are much smaller (i.e., 50 males, 50 females). Statistical analysis then becomes problematic. This means that you must take into account the groups within your sample that you intend to compare.

expected response Another aspect to consider when deciding on the size of the sample is the expected response rate. If you are doing quantitative research, you use a random, representative sample. You demarcate the operational population and determine how many people have to be included in the sample. Bear in mind that some will not participate! If you ask 100 people to take part in your research, you won't get all your questionnaires back and completed. If you get 60 back, then we say the *response rate* is 60%. If you need at least one hundred completed questionnaires to be able to extrapolate the results to the whole population, then you'll need to estimate the response rate and base the number of questionnaires you send out on that estimate (see Text box 6.11).

Taking into account the expected response rate

Suppose you send out a questionnaire for your research and you expect that about 60% of the sample will respond. How many questionnaires do you have to distribute in order to get 100 completed and returned questionnaires? To calculate this you can use the following formula: divide the number of questionnaires that you need (100) by the expected response rate (60) and multiply by 100:

$$100/60 \times 100 = 167$$

In order to get 100 completed questionnaires back if your response rate is 60%, you will need to distribute 167.

Box 6.11

In this example the expected response rate was 60%. Sometimes the response is higher than expected. In telephone surveys the response rate can be between 70 and 80%. But normally the response rate is much lower, for example, for postal surveys that rarely score higher than 30%. Internet surveys also generally don't get a high response rate.

population size The size of the sample also depends on the size of the population. A sample size of 100 for the state of Texas is very small, but if the whole group comprises 200 people, then it would be 50% of that population.

Qualitative research uses intensive methods of data collection, for instance in-depth interviews. For this you use small sample sizes, perhaps 10 to 15 interviews. Generalizability is not the objective of qualitative research, so the research objective also determines the sample size. *research objective*

No matter how much information you'd like to collect, if you don't have the time or the money, it will impact on the sample size. These are the practical considerations that you have to take into account. *practical considerations*

On our website you will find more information about sample sizes in the section 'Chapter 6' (tab Extra material).

First and foremost you need to decide whether the sample will be random or not, then you decide to what extent it needs to be generalizable and how large it should be. If the sample is not random, then you don't need to meet the same conditions. Using structured, non-random samples is often useful and it makes sense. In the next sections we will discuss a number of random (or probability) and non-random (or non-probability) sampling methods.

6.4.3 *Probability Sampling*

There are several ways to draw random samples. The first thing you do is find out whether there is an existing database that contains the population that is relevant to your research: staff lists, municipality registers, members of organizations or institutes etc. These databases are often protected by privacy laws, but it is possible to draw *blind samples* (a sample in which the names remain anonymous) from them so that you don't contravene these laws. If databases like this are available, make sure you use them! They will be your *sampling frame*. *sampling frame*

Simple random sample
The sample is selected randomly from the database, for example using a computer. Every data *entry* has a calculable (equal) chance of being selected.

If your database (sample frame) is numbered, then there is a useful tool that you can use to select random numbers (entries): the *random number generator*. You can find this on the Internet. It is a method of selecting numbers randomly from a series of numbers, i.e., a random selection method. This method uses a mathematical model (an algorithm), in other words a series *random number generator* of commands. You enter some information, such as the total number of entries in your database, the first and last numbers and the sample size (i.e., the amount of numbers you need). The result is a string of numbers that you then apply to your sample frame. The people who correspond to the entries are the ones you approach for your data collection. Figure 6.4 gives an example.

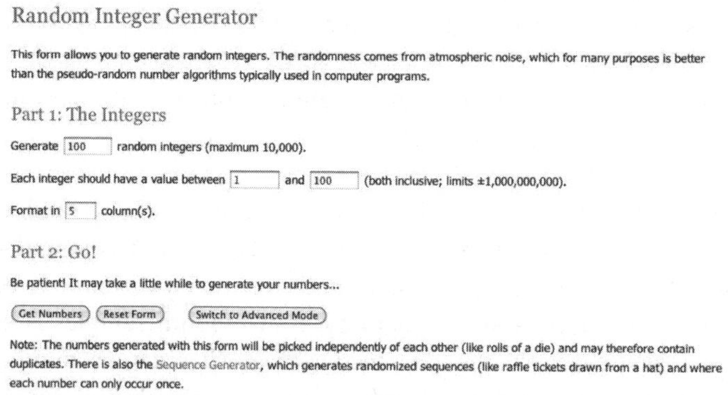

Random Integer Generator

This form allows you to generate random integers. The randomness comes from atmospheric noise, which for many purposes is better than the pseudo-random number algorithms typically used in computer programs.

Part 1: The Integers

Generate [100] random integers (maximum 10,000).

Each integer should have a value between [1] and [100] (both inclusive; limits ±1,000,000,000).

Format in [5] column(s).

Part 2: Go!

Be patient! It may take a little while to generate your numbers...

(Get Numbers) (Reset Form)   (Switch to Advanced Mode)

Note: The numbers generated with this form will be picked independently of each other (like rolls of a die) and may therefore contain duplicates. There is also the Sequence Generator, which generates randomized sequences (like raffle tickets drawn from a hat) and where each number can only occur once.

Figure 6.4   Random number generator

Systematic sample (with a random starting point)
This method entails drawing a sample by selecting every tenth or fifteenth 'person' from the database. Your starting point (the first person in the sample) is decided randomly. You can use this method on address databases by randomly selecting a street and then choosing every tenth address for example.

Cluster sampling
Sometimes it is easier to research a whole group instead of drawing a random sample. This would involve 'existing' groups that are similar to each other in a number of respects. An often-used example of this is research at schools ('t Hart et al., 1998, p. 237). Schools consist of classes that comprise an existing group. If you want to investigate the perceptions of high school pupils, then it makes more sense to interview the whole class. First you randomly select the class from a list of all the schools in the state, or city, and then you use the whole class for your sample. This method of cluster selection is also used for example in residential areas: a suburb is first selected and then blocks of streets within that suburb. Costs could also play a role in deciding to use this method.

Stratified samples

If you are carrying out research in a large city, say Chicago for example, you can draw your sample systematically based on an initial random selection. There's a good chance, though, that not all parts of the city will get proportional representation. A way to deal with this is to divide the population into sub-populations, for example into suburbs. These sub-populations are what are known as *strata*. You then select the sample randomly from the strata, the residents that is. Within each stratum you can make sub-samples. In this way you can ensure that all the various areas of the city, or that particular part of the city that you are interested in, get proportional representation in your sample.

Multi-stage samples

Multi-stage sampling is a combination of several sampling methods. For instance, it takes Cluster sampling cluster sampling a step further by drawing a sample randomly from the clusters you've selected. You draw the house addresses randomly from the street blocks you've just selected.

6.4.4   *Non-Probability Sampling*

It is not always possible, or necessary, to select your sample randomly, particularly for qualitative research. Sometimes the interviews are held with experts or stakeholders: these groups are never selected randomly. The objective is not to extrapolate the findings to the general public, but to use the results within an organization, for example. Sometimes it is simply not possible to draw the sample randomly, perhaps because there is no existing database from which to draw the sample, or because it is not practical to do so. One such practical consideration would be availability of interviewers, another the size of the budget (see Text box 6.12). In short, the conditions of generalizability and reliability will not be met if non-probability sampling is used, but then nor is the objective of the research to extrapolate the results.

Non-probability sampling among senior citizens in Soest	
In 1988 research was conducted into the requirements of people aged 55 and above in terms of the facilities in the service centre at Soest and Soesterberg.	For this a questionnaire was distributed among residents of these areas who were above the stipulated age. The municipal register was used as the

Continued

sample frame; the municipality was divided into sub-populations (strata) and all those above the age of 55 were selected. Four suburbs were *chosen*, so it was not a random sample. The criteria used for selecting the suburbs were: the presence of a service center and the status of the suburb in terms of the ratio of homeowners to tenants. This restriction of the sample selection was necessary because there was not enough manpower and money available to carry out a survey in all the suburbs of that municipality. But for the rest the sample was drawn by using a systematic technique (every tenth house with a resident older than 55 years) and using a random starting point (Verhoeven, 1998).

Quota sampling

Quota sampling is when each interviewer is given the task to complete a specific number of interviews, within a certain suburb and according to a given quota: i.e., 20 men and 20 women, 20 under the age of 35 and 20 above the age of 35, 20 home owners, 20 tenants and so on. The sample is in no way random given that the interviewers do the selecting and it is not always representative (in reality there may be more younger people living in that neighborhood than older, for example). And while it may be easy to distinguish between men and women, it may not be so easy if the other attributes are harder to recognize or find.

Self-selection

Sometimes the sample needs people that meet certain criteria. These people are invited to participate in the research through advertisements asking for participants who are eligible. An example of this is given in Text box 6.13. If you meet the requirements and you feel like taking part in the research then you sign up. Medical and psychological research often uses self-selection to recruit participants.

An example of self-selection

For research into the effects of cortisol (a stress hormone), we, psychology students from the University of Leiden, are urgently seeking people to take part in a research project. We are looking for: Men above the age of 30 years who are in good mental and physical health, are right handed, have normal eyesight and a good command of the Dutch language.

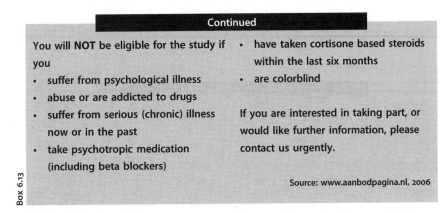

Source: www.aanbodpagina.nl, 2006

Purposive sampling

Purposive sampling is used to select samples on the basis of given character-istics. Your research would then be into specific issues, critical or typical cases or unique cases. The aim is to find the information at the source. An example of this is the research into the activities of retired professors by Becker and Verhoeven. There the researchers used purposive sampling to draw the sample from the group that represented the population, namely emeriti that have continued to work or carry out various and many activities in their field after their retirement (Becker & Verhoeven, 2000). For research into the implementation of environmental legislation in organizations, a number of interviews were held with people specialized in the field, for example because they were tasked with implementing the legislation, i.e., they are *experts.*

Convenience sampling

In this kind of sampling, people are approached ad hoc and asked whether they would be willing to take part in research. Street research is an example of this. Interviewers choose a venue where there are plenty of passers by (for example in a shopping mall) and then approach people and ask them for their co-operation.

Snowball sampling

Sometimes when the research starts, there is no existing database, no sample frame available. The people you need to interview are not registered any-where as such and it's difficult to find them. You have to come up with another way of approaching them. One way of doing it is to use the snow-ball method in which you use networks of people. If you find one person who uses the product, say, or has experience in the area you are interested in, you then ask them if they know anyone else who does and so on (see Text box 6.14).

Changes within relationships

For research into changes within relationships, the interviewer first looked within his own circle of friends and acquaintances. After the first interview with a couple from his own circle, he asked the pair if they knew of another couple who may be interested in taking part in the research. A number of criteria were used for the selection. In this example, it could be the length of the relationship (for example the couple would have to have been together for a period of at least five years), marital status (they have to at least live together) and be resident within a certain area. Slowly but surely the researcher would find couples who were eligible and willing to take part in the research. The only thing is the sample is neither representative, random nor large for that matter: in total 30 couples were interviewed. But this is a sizable sample for qualitative research.

Box 6.14

This snowball method has another application: for literature research. The results of the first search for literature is studied carefully: the list of references in the back of the books are used to continue the search, as are articles in journals and so on.

6.5   The Quality of Research

Nobody's perfect. Everyone makes mistakes, and researchers are no exception. But at the end of the day you need to be able to draw well-founded conclusions from your research. How do you assess the quality of your research? The main criterion has to be *usability*: can the client use the results? But apart from this, there are the more formal criteria of *validity* and *reliability*. We use these two criteria to track two kinds of error that can occur in research (Boeije et al., 2009). By validity we mean the extent to which *systematic errors* occur: we check the soundness or accuracy of the research. When we check for reliability, we assess the incidence of *random errors*. One of the conditions needed for assessing reliability is that the research is feasible, if it is not then you can't assess its reliability. In this section we'll look at reliability and validity and how they impact on drawing conclusions from your findings (how sound your research actually is).

Predicting election results (1)

Differences in research designs for research into voter behavior for the elections, so-called polls, resulted in different predictions of the outcome in 2004. The same thing happened again in 2008 and 2010. Reliability was in question because different data collection methods were used, the samples were structured differently and were different sizes. Methods used to analyze the data also played a role in this.

Often you'll find clients, policy-makers and the media trotting out research results to bolster their arguments without paying attention to how the results came about (see Text box 6.15). To find support for their ideas they point to research results (preferably 'significant' findings) as though they are automatically of sound quality. Before you can be convinced of the quality of your research, as the researcher you have to look at it systematically. How was it conducted? How was the information collected and analyzed? How was the sample structured?

The quality of the research comes into play at various stages: during the design and operationalization, when deciding on the sample size and structuring the sample, during the fieldwork (response rate) and when you analyze the results. Often what you'll find is that a critical study of the various research phases will bring to light shortcomings that may undermine the value of your findings. Be careful with this though. Even if the methodological value of your research is not particular high, to the client the results may be extremely *valuable* and *useful* even though the research has some shortcomings.

6.5.1 Reliability

Random errors occur during research. The reliability of the results is an indication of how free your research is from these random errors. In order to adequately test the reliability, the research must be replicable. If it leads to *similar* results (which is not the same as the *identical* results!) then your research is *reliable*. This condition of replicability means that it must be possible to replicate the research at another time, by another researcher, using other subjects and under different circumstances. Not an easy thing to do.

What are random errors? Take time keeping as an example. Reading time accurately is quite difficult. If you repeat the reading a number of times, you'll get small variations, both negative and positive. This is the result of 'human intervention'. Other examples of random errors are:

- Someone doesn't know the answer to the question.
- When you are completing the questionnaire you are distracted by very loud music; another respondent is not distracted by music at all.
- You tick the wrong box by accident.
- When entering the data, the data capturer makes a mistake.
- The tape you're using to measure something is slightly elastic. Unwittingly you pull it too hard every now and again and so your measurements are all slightly different.

Researchers come up with all kinds of ways to enhance the reliability of their research. They can be applied to both quantitative and qualitative research. Below are a few examples:

1 *Sample size*: the larger your sample, the more accurate your statements will be. On the basis of the sample size, you can estimate the possible outcome of your research. NB: It's an estimate! You have to take into account the *margin of error*: the extent of the error that you will allow. If you want to get the average height of high school pupils, and you use a sample size of 100, your estimate will be much more accurate than if you use a sample of say 15. Using a large sample size is not always possible or necessary; we saw that in the previous section. Sometimes a large sample is not available, or your research is within one organization. Then you'll have to safeguard the reliability in another way.

2 *Intersubjectivity*. This measure is often used in observational research. Various researchers observe the situation. The extent to which there is agreement in the results determines the intersubjectivity. Obviously you can only claim that your research is reliable if the level of intersubjectivity is high.

3 *Using a triangulated design*. Reliability is enhanced because you check whether the findings are correct by comparing them with the findings of research done using a different method.

4 *Standardization of the method* is another way to increase reliability, by designing a standardized questionnaire, for example, or Likert scale (Swanborn, 2009, p. 237).

5 *Test-retest in quantitative research*. By repeating the method you can check whether your research is reliable. For instance, you can use a scale twice in a questionnaire and if the results correspond, then the scale is reliable.

6 *Pilots*. In qualitative research, you can enhance the reliability of your topic list by carrying out test interviews with it. In quantitative research, this can also be done with surveys.

7 *Peer examination.* You can ask your colleagues to check your results or read through your findings.

8 *Reporting and justification.* It is important to be able to justify all aspects of your research. Keep an accurate log of everything in your logbook! You don't only make a note of all your decisions and the progress that you make, but also points along the way when you learned things, changes that you made and why, circumstances that brought about problems, things that went wrong. If you repeat the research, you can avoid these things, which will improve the reliability of the results next time.

If your research is quantitative, then it is always possible to check the reliability by carrying out statistical tests. You can check the homogeneity of a set of questions by running a reliability analysis (see Text box 6.16). This is what is known as *internal consistency.*

Opinions about government measures

In a survey, respondents are asked about their opinions of government measures related to education. They are shown a series of statements and are asked to indicate to what extent they agree with them, on a scale of 'completely disagree' to 'completely agree' (i.e., it's a Likert scale). A test is then carried out to see if the items reflect a reliable measure of the term 'government measures in education'. A statistical procedure has been developed for this. For example, they check to see if all the items have similar averages. They then go on to see whether, and if so, how strongly, the items are corre-

lated. If each item hardly correlates with other items in the scale then this can impact negatively on the reliability (and therefore the quality) of the scale. The reliability (also known as internal consistency) is expressed in one common measure: coefficient alpha. If the test gives a high coefficient alpha score, then it means that the scale is highly reliable. Each item correlates strongly with all the other items in the scale. The conclusion would be that together the items form a reliable measure of the concept 'government measures in education'.

Box 6.16

On our website you will an example of a coefficient alpha calculation in the section 'Chapter 8' (tab Extra material).

6.5.2 *Validity*

When assessing the validity of research we go one step further. Validity determines the extent to which the research is free of *systematic errors*. You do this once you have checked to see to what extent your research is free of random errors. Reliability is a prerequisite for determining the validity of your research. What you're looking at here is how credible the research is, whether it is a true reflection of reality. A well-known example of a systematic mistake is when someone deliberately gives the wrong answer. If the subject is sensitive, then respondents may be inclined to give answers that they think you want to hear: socially desirable answers, that is. This will systematically skew your results. There are several ways to check how valid your results are. The two most important indicators for validity are the *measurement instrument* and the *research group*. The fewer mistakes, the more your results are likely to be a reflection of reality. There are various kinds of validity, we'll discuss the three most important here.

Internal validity

When we say that results are *internally valid*, we mean that we can draw the correct conclusions from them. But what are 'the correct conclusions'? They are conclusions that can be upheld and withstand the criticism of other researchers. This kind of validity often plays a role in so-called 'cause and effect relationships' that are researched in experiments. If, for example, your central question includes measuring environmental factors on behavior, and you intend to test a theory, then the extent to which the results are internally valid will determine whether you are will be able to give, find and test the correct explanation.

There are several situations that can jeopardize the internal validity of results. We'll mention a few here:
- *Selection* of the participants. If this is not done correctly, the opinions of this select group will not count beyond the group itself.
- *Maturation*. If the research goes on for too long, changes will automatically take place. Look at methods used to teach children words. In the end, no matter how they are taught, they learn them anyway.
- *History*. Election forecasts, for instance, may suddenly go awry after an external event such as an assassination or death.
- *Instrumentation*. Suppose you adjust the questionnaire during the research. This means you won't have used exactly the same instrument all the way through: this will skew your results.

- *Mortality (drop outs)*. Imagine you intended to carry out pre- and post-testing. Half way through the research people will or can no longer take part: this is called drop out.
- *Test-effect*. A test-effect may occur if respondents start to react differently to prompts because they know they are the subject of research (see Text box 6.17).

Box 6.17

Hawthorne effect
A well-known example of a test-effect took place during research carried out in the thirties in the Hawthorne factories. The objective was to investigate the working conditions of the factory	workers. The presence of researchers alone was enough to have a positive influence on conditions in the factory. This became known as the Hawthorne effect.

For experiments, measures are put in place to ensure that validity is as high as possible: subjects are assigned randomly to the experimental and control groups, pre- and posttests are carried out, and experiments are carried out in the controlled environments of laboratories.

External validity

You can also check whether your sample is a correct reflection of the population. The sample must resemble the population in terms of certain characteristics that are relevant to the research. If this is the case, then the sample is representative and you can generalize the results to the population.

This type of validity determines the scope of the research, although low external validity does not always mean that the results have no value (see Text box 6.18 and 6.19). External validity is a concept that is mainly applicable to quantitative research but it is also possible to determine the scope for qualitative research. In this case you focus on the scope of the content, that is to say, the generalizability to other situations (theoretical generalizability, that is). We'll discuss this in Chapters 7 and 9.

population validity

Student budgets
In 1998, NIBUD carried out research among students on the subject of their financial situation. Students who visited the *Intermediair* student website were invited to take part in the research. The	following was said about the results: 'The NIBUD research confirms once again that the reality of the Study Financing Act exists on paper only. To start with, students who live

away from home spend more money per month than the study financing norms dictate, while those who still live at home spend far less than the norm' (NIBUD, 1998). The researchers were also critical about their research design: 'NIBUD themselves would like to make a few comments about the research design. The respondents were all visitors to the Intermediair student website. This means that post graduate students are probably over represented. This would probably explain why one in seven students who took part in the research owns a car. The CBS statistics puts this figure at one in fifty' (NIBUD,

1998). Despite the issues with population validity, the results of this research were generalized to the whole student population, which should never have been done. In 2009, NIBUD once again published research, this time about borrowing patterns among students. Once again, the sample was not selected randomly but from the database of financial institution and from various websites often frequented by students. So this sample had similar limitations to the one in 1998. This time there was no mention of this in the report (NIBUD, 2010).

Box 6.18

Suppose that a small survey among experts and those involved in the organization was held during the research into the organizational structure of the youth orchestra. Suppose a total of thirty interviews were held among this select group of people. This would mean that the results of the research could not be extrapolated to 'all youth

orchestras in the country' and as such it would be invalid. The group being researched is too small, too specific and the sample has been drawn too selectively. But this does not mean that the results would not be very valuable to the organization and as such extremely useful and usable! The external validity of this research is not a goal in itself.

Box 6.19

Construct validity

Another kind of validity is *construct validity*. Construct validity has to do with the measurement instruments that are used in the research. In general terms what it means is that you assess whether you are 'measuring what you intend to measure'. You measure length in centimeters and weight in kilograms: these are exact measurements because the units of measure are always the same, wherever you are. Not only that, you only need to ask one question to find out the measurement: 'How tall are you?' is enough.

When it comes to measuring concepts, it's much more difficult, particularly when the concepts could be subjective or unclear, such as insecurity, determination, satisfaction and so on. These concepts first have to be well-defined and then turned into questions – a measuring instrument – that then actually measure the concepts. Normally you need more than one question to measure an abstract concept. But sometimes the questions are badly formulated, and the construct validity is threatened. For instance, you may want to conduct research into the general level of education at a particular college. You can ask people what they think of the level of education, but you'll get various answers because the question hasn't been formulated properly. Respondents will think of various aspects of 'level of education', which is why it is better to name each aspect separately and to ask separate questions about each. This will strengthen the validity of the concepts. A way to assess this is to test the hypotheses of your theory. In Text box 6.20 you will find an example of construct validity.

Performance of elderly drivers

Elderly drivers are half as likely to see pedestrians on the sidewalk due to a limited field of view, and compensate in part by driving more slowly. Many states have special requirements for senior citizens to renew their licenses. Sometimes they have to apply for a renewal more frequently. In some states, they need to retake road or vision tests or renew their license in person. However, the test is usually done by a GP that does not personally know the driver, and hearing and vision tests are usually perceived in a different way when taken in the doctor's office than when people are actually driving. Hence, the validity of the test is under pressure. The National Institute on Aging (NIA)/National Institutes of Health (NIH) propose the use of the Useful Field of View Test for Older Drivers, a reliable and valid measurement of the visual function of elderly drivers that actually tests the way in which they process visual information while driving.

Source: www.aging.senate.gov

Box 6.20

Alongside the difference between internal and external validity, various other kinds of validity are described on the website. You will find references for further reading on all these kinds of validity in the section entitled 'Chapter 6' (tab Extra material).

WEBSITE

6.5.3   Usability

How usable are research findings? What should you do with the results? Is it safe to extrapolate the conclusions to the population? Can you be sure that your research is sound? Will it produce similar results if repeated?

No, not always. Depending on the design, the results of various research projects into the same subject may well be different. Start by looking at the sample. You want the sample to be representative. Each time you draw the sample you'll get a new, randomly selected sample with slightly different results. The data collection method is also crucial: if you conduct interviews by telephone you'll get different results to those you will get if you conduct an Internet survey. There are both random and systematic circumstances that can threaten the reliability and validity of the research.

If validity and reliability are your yardsticks, then a lot of research can go straight into the bin. This doesn't happen because clients can use the results regardless, to improve their organization (see Text box 6.21). This means that although reliability and validity are often not quite up to scratch, usability is still adequate.

instru- Research results can sometimes be used to help plan policy for the coming
mental and years. This is what is known as *instrumental usability*.
conceptual When research results are used in discussions about specific subjects or
usability issues (Boeije et al., 2009) it is known as conceptual usability.

Research for youth orchestra is usable

The research into the organizational structure of the youth orchestra has its limitations in terms of validity and reliability. The sample is small and non-random, questionnaires were not administered under the same conditions, and so it goes on. Despite these restrictions, the usability for the organization is good: the organizational structure had not been researched before and the orchestra can use the recommendations from the research to map out their policies for the coming years. Not only that, being able to extrapolate the results to, say, 'all' youth orchestras in the country is not in question because they are all differ too much in terms of set up and composition. The researchers tried to safeguard the reliability of the research as much as possible by:

- studying the research question from more than on perspective (triangulated approach), by carrying out a study of the literature and by administering a questionnaire and several in-depth interviews;

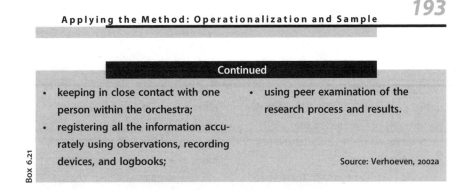

Continued

- keeping in close contact with one person within the orchestra;
- registering all the information accurately using observations, recording devices, and logbooks;

- using peer examination of the research process and results.

Source: Verhoeven, 2002a

Box 6.21

In order to ensure that the results of applied research, in particular, are usable, it is important to involve the client every step of the way (Boeije et al., 2009). If you do so, you'll ask the right questions (operationalization) that are relevant to the client's situation. Also, the client may well have experts on their staff who can help you with your research. Establishing who is the right contact person within the organization, for information and collaboration, for making appointments and thinking things through, also contributes to the research. Finally, working closely with the client not only has a positive impact on the usability of the research, but also on its reliability.

In summary: the quality of research is determined by validity, reliability and also its usability. That research firms don't always carry out good quality research is illustrated by the example in Text box 6.22 and Figure 6.5. The results of this research were however used to stimulate discussions about parliamentary elections. Conceptual usability, in this case!

Predicting election results (2)

In the Netherlands, as in most countries, parliamentary elections are surrounded by a lot of speculation about the results. This happened in 2003, and again in 2006 and 2010. Several leading research bureaus were commissioned by the media to conduct research into the expected results. The research results varied quite significantly. This had to do with the way the samples were structured, the way the research was conducted and how the findings were reported.

The research projects differed in four aspects:

- *Sampling methods*: these varied from a random sample drawn daily from 25,000 e-mail addresses, to a fixed panel, to a random sample drawn from telephone numbers. Panel members had signed themselves up to take part in the research out of interest in politics. They also all had Internet connections.

Continued

- *Sample sizes*: These varied from 1,000 to 4,000 people. This means that the margins of error varied too, which impacts on the accuracy of the predictions.
- *Data collection methods*: these were done using the Internet or telephone. When surveys are conducted by phone, it may be that people are not at home, or you only get those who are unemployed, or those within a certain age group, and so on. On the Internet, the respondents themselves decide whether, and if so, when they want to respond.

Using different methods results in differences in the response rate.
- *The period*: the research project was done either on a daily basis, weekly basis, or every two weeks. During election campaigns, things change quickly, so it makes a difference whether you gauge opinions every day, every week or even less frequently.

Let's just say that the opinion polls reflected trends in voter behavior (*NRC Next*, 3 and 10 June, 2010).

Box 6.22

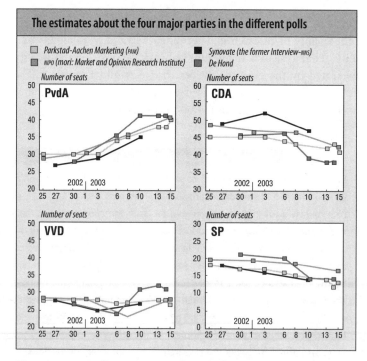

Figure 6.5   Differences in predicting election results from four research bureaus

6.6   Glossary of Most Important Terms and Their Meaning

Operationalization	Turning concepts into measurable instruments.
Likert or multiple item scales	Composite measuring instrument used to measure complex concepts using sub-questions (items).
Multiple item *response* scales	Response scales in ascending order with a limited number of options.
Double-barreled questions	Two questions in one.
Routing	The logical sequencing of questionnaires.
Filter questions	Questions that filter the respondents according to certain criteria.
Sequence effect	The sequence of the questions impacts on how they are answered.
Exhaustive responses	When all possible responses are noted.
Exclusive responses	When no overlap in responses is possible.
Multiple responses	More than one response is possible using dummy variables.
Topic list	List of subject that is used in in-depth interviews.
Population	All the elements that you want to make statements about, i.e., the domain.
Operational population	Demarcated section of the population based on a particular attribute.
Pilot study	Test research for surveys. In in-depth interviews, known as test interviews.
Sampling frame	Database that can be used for drawing the sample.
Random number generator	Instrument for generating random numbers from a series (database).
Probability sample	Randomly selected part of the population that you want to research, drawn according to specific rules. Each unit has an equal chance of being selected for the sample.
Simple random sample	Randomly selected sample from the whole population.

Systematic sample	The sample is drawn systematically from the population by choosing every n^{th} unit from a random starting point.
Cluster sampling	A number of *whole* groups of people are drawn from existing groups within a population. If the sample is structured, then respondents are selected randomly within the groups.
Stratified sample	Sample is drawn randomly from a number of strata (sub-samples) within the population.
Multi-stage sample	Various sampling methods from different layers of the population, starting from clusters.
Non-probability sampling	Non-random sample drawn from the population, using specific rules.
Quota sampling	A given number of respondents selected according to specific attributes.
Self-selection	Sample comprises people who sign up for a study themselves.
Purposive sampling	Sample chosen on basis of specific attributes, normally to do with expertise.
Convenience sampling	Sample in which everybody that falls within the research setting can be used.
Snowball sampling	Sampling that starts with a small network and grows by including the networks of the respondents.
Level of confidence	Indicates the range (for instance 95%) within a population that a given characteristic occurs.
Reliability	Safeguarding against random errors.
Validity	Safeguarding against systematic errors, accuracy.
Intersubjectivity	Extent to which there is agreement among the researchers.
Internal validity	Extent to which correct conclusions can be drawn from the results.

External validity or population validity	Extent to which a sample resembles the population in terms of relevant attributes; determines the generalizability of the research.
Construct validity	Extent to which you are measuring what you want to measure.
Instrumental usability	The results are used to draft policies.
Conceptual usability	The results are used to start a debate.
Survey fatigue	People are no longer interested in taking part in research because they get approached too often.
Test-effect	Research participants react differently because they are taking part in research.

6.7   Assignments for Chapter 6

1 Describe the following concepts:
   a dichotomy;
   b routing;
   c Likert scales;
   d test effect;
   e filter questions;
   f conceptual usability.
2 What is the difference between a population, an operational population and a sample? Give examples.
3 Here are a few research samples. Indicate which methods were used to select them.
   a In research into support for the conception of a nuclear power station, you interview a few of the local town councilors.
   b You also want to know what the local residents think. First you select a number of suburbs; then, from this set, you draw your sample randomly.
   c A large chain of supermarkets commissions you to do research into a price war. They're expecting shoppers to be queuing at the doors. The intention is to interview as many men as women, older people as younger people.
4 Read through the example in Text box 6.18
   There were several ways that students could take part in the research: a letter from the study finance department invited them, as did pop-up

menus on various websites. What sampling method did they use? Describe the advantages and disadvantages of this sampling method.

5 What is the difference between a multiple response question and a scale? Give an example of each.

6 Suppose you are researching the function and perceptions of the new community centre in your local town. What would be the best way to demarcate the sample? Put together a proposal for the sample selection. Take into account the representativeness of the sample. Which groups should the sample represent?

7 Operationalize the following concepts:
   a quality of service for student grants;
   b concentration during lessons among primary school pupils;
   c student spending patterns;
   d satisfaction with patient care at the emergency rooms of Mercy Hospital.

8 Suppose you have to gauge opinions about the upcoming student body elections at your college. These are the aspects that you need to take into account: the election results, composition of the student board, forming sub-committees, opinions about how the student body should address the issue of violations of the 'no guns on campus' regulation.
   a Formulate a few questions to elicit opinions about these aspects using dichotomous response options.
   b Now use these same questions with five ascending response options.
   c The same again except this time in four ascending categories.
   d Which of these three categories would you choose and why?
   e Discuss the results with your fellow students. What did they choose and why?

9 Read Text box 6.23.

New: study among members of parliament

A study was conducted among members of the European parliament. Of the 736 members, 404 filled in the questionnaire (54.9%). The highest response rate came from the Christian Democrats (40%), followed by the Socialists (20%) and the Democrats (14%). They form 36, 25 and 11.4% of the Euro-parliamentary population respectively. The lowest response rate came from the Conservative Party, with a 3% response rate (they form 7% of the parliamentary population). Many female representatives filled in the questionnaire (45%), while in fact they only make up 35% of the Euro-parliament.

Source: www.europarl.europa.eu

Box 6.23

a What can you say about the population and the sample?

b Look at the demographics of the people that responded. Can the results be generalized? Motivate your answer.

10 Below is a description of a population and sample. Put them into the correct order and describe each part in terms of population and sample.

a all freshmen students in the State of California;

b student administration of Berkley University;

c every tenth student;

d the first student was selected randomly;

e all social science students in the State of California.

11 Text box 6.9 contains an example about research into the perceptions of kidney patients. What sampling options are there? Why?

12 What is the best way to assess the quality of research? What aspects are studied to assess quality? Describe the various aspects.

13 Students are sitting their stats exam. They are divided into two groups: those that sit the exam in the afternoon and those that sit it in the evening. In the afternoon they are busy fixing the sidewalk right outside the room where the exam is taking place. The workmen are using jackhammers and the students are disrupted by the noise. If this noise had interfered with research, what kind of interference would it be?

14 Read the article in Text box 6.20 carefully.

a What are the quality aspects involved in medical assessments for the elderly? Discuss these aspects in terms of the research.

b What aspect is the most important: that research is reliable, that it is valid or that it is usable?

15 Read the article in Text box 6.24.

People suffer from exhaustion

In 2003, as was the case in 1988, a healthcare survey into exhaustion was carried out. The findings showed that people suffered more from exhaustion in 2003 than 15 years previously. This increase was evident among men (from 24 to 33%) as well as women (from 38 to 50%).

It is striking that it is particularly younger women with a college or university degree that suffer from exhaustion. Single parents also suffer relatively speaking more than their peers, particularly women taking care of children under the age of 6. The extreme cases are women with disabilities (81%). Fifty-nine percent of the women who combine working with taking care of children are frequently tired, among men this category was 34%. The percentage of househusbands who tend to feel tired was also higher than men on average (39%). What tiredness is exactly was not defined, nor were people asked

Continued

whether they distinguished different degrees of exhaustion. What is clear from the results is that exhaustion is not an isolated problem.

People who suffer from exhaustion are a burden to the healthcare system while doctors and other carers find it difficult to sympathize. It is ironic, according to *Medical Contact*,* that 'it is particularly those that suffer the most

that are given the least attention by those in healthcare'. Exhaustion is a problem that deserves priority because an increase in the problem leads to an increase in sick leave, permanent disability and costs to society.

* *Medisch Contact*

Source: Bensing & Van Lindert, 2003

Box 6.24

a What method of data collection was used?

b A comparison is made with fifteen years previously. Why?

c Mention some operationalizations of concepts and variables.

d What can you say about the quality of the research? Which aspect of quality are mentioned in this text?

16 Below are a number of situations that influence the validity of research results. Which aspects are discussed?

a In September 2001, research is conducted among members of the New York Stock Exchange. On September 11, an attack on the Twin Towers takes place.

b You are researching changes in sexual behavior among freshmen at your local college. After some initial analysis you decide that you have to adjust the questionnaire. You then continue the fieldwork using the new questionnaire.

c A member of a three monthly advertising panel can't take part in the scheduled research.

d For research into overland travel through South America, you put an advert in the paper to recruit people who recently undertook this kind of travel.

WEBSITE

In the section 'Chapter 6' (tab Assignment solutions) you will find the solutions to the assignments in Section 6.7. You will find information about the design cases under tab 'Design cases' in the section 'Chapter 6'.

Data Collection

7

Chapter 7 deals with setting up the fieldwork, in other words conducting interviews for surveys and in-depth interviews. In your research plan, you will have decided which is the best method to get the answers you want, but that doesn't mean there are no more decisions to be made. These decisions will dictate the way you will carry out the fieldwork, how you will approach the respondents, aspects such as the costs, timing and so on. You also anticipate the results that you're expecting your research to deliver in terms of the response rate. You need to take this into account when setting up your sample. To give you an idea of issues you may be confronted with when you start your fieldwork, we'll be discussing two types of data collection methods in this chapter: those for surveys and in-depth interviews.

Learning objectives

By the time you get to the end of this chapter, you will be familiar with several aspects of fieldwork, namely: the way you conduct interviews for surveys; how to approach respondents; how to get people to co-operate with your research project; how to get as many people as possible to take part in the research; and how to build rapport with the respondent during face-to-face, open interviews. After studying this chapter, you will also know how to make your interviews as informative as possible.

Box 7.1

7.1 The Research Setting

Now that the questionnaire is ready, it's time to start collecting the data. Make sure you've set aside enough time for this! Experience shows that data collection is a long-drawn-out process, and it often overruns the schedule, for instance when a lot of questionnaires start coming in after the cut-off date, questionnaires that you'd like to include in the analysis. In-depth interviews and surveys can be conducted in many different ways.

Surveys:
- by post;
- electronically (Internet, e-mail);
- by telephone;
- face-to-face.

In-depth interviews:
- by telephone;
- face-to-face (at a venue that suits the respondent).

When it comes to deciding which way to conduct the interview, the content of the interview may influence the decision, but circumstances and restrictions imposed by the client may also influence the method you choose. We will discuss these circumstances and restrictions in the sections to come.

back to the research plan Before you start planning how to organize the fieldwork, it's a good idea to go back to the research plan. You go over the problem and objective: What was the main issue again? This is a good time to look back over the plan because it's not too late! You can compare your questionnaire with the central question and make sure they correspond with each other. Are you sure the questions will cover all the aspects of the research objective? Once you've collected the data it won't be possible to go back and do it again because there's an oversight.

This is also the time to catch up on your notes in your logbook. The information in this chapter will enable you to describe how you arrived at your choice of method; how it went when you approached the respondents; how you demarcated the sample, and how you set up the fieldwork. In your final report, this section will be entitled 'Methodology'.

7.2   Going into 'the Field' or Not?

There are all kinds of arguments to support the method you choose to conduct your interviews or distribute the questionnaires. We discussed theoretical and content related arguments in the preceding chapters. There are, however, a number of *practical* arguments that may support your decision.

You could decide to conduct the interviews yourself, be they full-length questionnaires or in-depth interviews. You could conduct telephone interviews, or send your questionnaires by post or via the Internet. The decision is often based on considerations to do with time, money, manpower, aspects of the sample and so on. Table 7.1 lists these aspects. We'll first explain them in brief.

Time

Conducting a postal survey is a time-consuming business, particularly when it comes to waiting for the questionnaires to be returned, sending out reminders and carrying out a second, follow-up round. Personally conducting interviews also takes a lot of time. You first have to know how to find the people, make appointments and then go out, together with other interviewers, to conduct the actual interviews. The same is true when it comes to in-depth, open interviews.

If you don't have the time you may opt for telephone interviews. Within a short space of time, a large number of people can be approached at home and asked whether they would be willing to take part in your survey. You can use a *call center* to do this for you. For example, you can arrange to have them call, and call back, as many people as possible within a ten day period. Call centers have enough *facilities* and *people* to reach lots of people by phone and conduct a large number of interviews. After ten days you check to see how many interviews have been conducted.

call centers

Money

In applied research you have to take into account your available budget. If you decide to try and reach as many people as possible within a short space of time (for example, a telephone survey), then the costs will be high. Lots of callers have to do the work and the larger the sample, the higher the variable costs. Sometimes, because of this, it is better to do a limited number of interviews of a more qualitative nature. But bear in mind that it takes a long time to process open interviews, and that this needs to be taken into account in the planning! This involves higher costs too. For you the researcher, this may not tip the scales because arguments to support decisions of whether or not to do a survey or open interviews will be more important. But the available budget will also be an argument for restricting the sample size.

Expected response rate

A third consideration when deciding which method to use is the number of respondents taking part in the research. We discussed this aspect in Section 6.4.2. The *expected response rate* (see Section 7.4.3 also) is an important factor when deciding which method to use. Many different views exist about expected response rates. Generally speaking you can expect a lower response from written surveys than from telephone surveys. You may get back as little as 20 to 30% of the questionnaires that you send out. Apart from the issue of whether people are easy to reach or not, approaching them in person (either face-to-face or by phone) is generally the most successful way.

Besides time, money and the expected response rate, the following aspects can play a role in your choice of data collection:

- It could be that your questionnaire contains sensitive questions, to do with income, say, or about intimate relationships. Respondents may give you a *socially desirable answer*, in other words, the respondent is tempted to give the answer they feel would be the most socially acceptable or give them some kind of status. If your questionnaire contains a lot of these kinds of questions, and you want to avoid socially acceptable answers, then the best thing to do is telephone interviews. Respondents are much more inclined to give honest answers over the phone than they are when they are face-to-face with the interviewer. This is also the case with self-completion questionnaires.
- If the questions are open and there are *few closed questions*, then open interviews would be your method of choice. If the questionnaire is *short*, then you can conduct the interview by phone. If it is *long*, then telephone interviews are not suitable and you'll have to send the questionnaire by post or interview people face-to-face.
- You can't use telephone interviews if you have to show the respondents show cards or pictures from which they have to choose.
- If the *relationship* between the interviewer and respondent is important to the research, then face-to-face interviews should be used. This will be the case for subjects of a personal nature.

Table 7.1   Practical aspects of survey methods

Arguments	Self-completion	Telephone	Face-to-face
Time	a lot	a little	varies
Money	varies	expensive	varies
No of questions	a lot	few	a lot
Nature of questions	closed	closed (a few open)	open
Pictures/show cards	yes	no	yes
Expected response rate	not very high	quite high	quite high
Risk of social acceptability	not very high	not very high	quite high
Rel. interviewer-interviewee important	no	not very	very

7.3   Online Research

More and more research these days is being done without interviewers, for instance via the Internet (e-mail or websites), and even by mobile phone. The same arguments count when opting for these methods as for more conventional methods. The problem with this kind of research is the validity and reliability of the sample, and with it the results. The first results into these aspects are starting to come in (see for example Text box 7.2). Not much is known at the moment about research using mobile phones, but we expect this to change with time. Online research has been significant for a while now. Table 7.2 gives the pros and cons of online and mobile research.

Table 7.2   Arguments for online and mobile phone surveys

Arguments	Online research	Mobile phone research
Time	varies	little
Money	not very expensive	expensive at the moment
No of questions	a lot	few
Nature of questions	closed (limited open)	closed (limited open)
Level of acceptance	varies	low
Pictures/show cards	yes	no
Expected response rate	quite high	low
Risk of social desirability	not very high	not very high
Relationship interviewer-interviewee important	no	no

Likelihood of responding

Motivaction conducted research into the response of panels to being invited to take part in online surveys. It is known that panel research, especially online, does not produce representative databases because some panel members are more likely to respond to invitations than others. Motivaction carried out an experiment that involved invit- ing those that were less inclined to respond more often to see if this resulted in a more balanced representation. The results showed that this method resulted in higher response levels and thus a more balanced spread, which in turn improves validity (Huizing, Van Ossenbruggen, Muller, Van der Wal & Lensvelt-Mulders, 2007).

7.3.1   Online Surveys

Research bureaus are offering the possibility of carrying out research via the Internet more and more often. Bureaus that offer questionnaire design via the web are also popping up all over the place. The following options are possible.

- You open a website and a *pop-up screen* appears asking if you'd like to take part in research.
- You receive an e-mail with an invitation and a *link* to a website with a questionnaire.
- You receive an e-mail with a download (e.g., a *pdf file*) that you can complete and return (generally via e-mail).

It is relatively simple to design an Internet survey as witnessed by the many software programs that are available for this, for example SurveyMonkey, NetQ, Freeonlinesurveys, Zoomerang, CheckMarket. Some you have to pay for, others are freeware. Some colleges are licensed to offer their students the option of using this software.

If you complete a questionnaire on the Internet and send it back via a link, then the data is fed straight into a file (normally Excel), so that data capture errors are very unlikely to occur and analysis can start straight away. This has huge advantages, as well as saving both time and money (see Text box 7.3). They can also be cheaper depending on the length of the questionnaire and the kinds of questions. Screening questions, routing and longer lists, as well as open questions, are all possible.

Not only the Internet but also intranets can be used for sending out survey questionnaires. Colleges and universities, for example, are increasingly making use of this so-called *electronic learning environment*. Students are sent study material, assignments, exam marks and advice through this learning environment. Evaluation forms are also distributed using intranets.

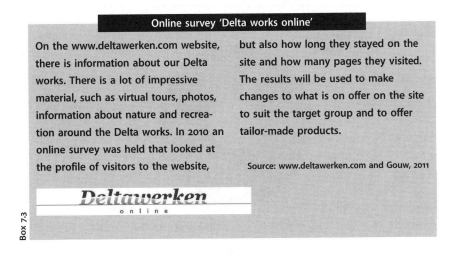

Box 7.3

Online survey 'Delta works online'

On the www.deltawerken.com website, there is information about our Delta works. There is a lot of impressive material, such as virtual tours, photos, information about nature and recreation around the Delta works. In 2010 an online survey was held that looked at the profile of visitors to the website, but also how long they stayed on the site and how many pages they visited. The results will be used to make changes to what is on offer on the site to suit the target group and to offer tailor-made products.

Source: www.deltawerken.com and Gouw, 2011

Deltawerken
o n l i n e

Are there no disadvantages to this method? Yes, there are.
For a start you can only access people that have an Internet connection. Although most people in First World countries have access to Internet, some sources of information about this (such as Internet providers) are unclear. There are still groups where Internet access is not as high as the average. Those with lower levels of education, people on social welfare, people living alone and the elderly are underrepresented when it comes to having access to the web (see Figure 7.1). Research that targets these people will have to be carried out in another way. Also, you only access people that visit the website. You can't gather any information from people that don't visit the site and you will never find out why they don't.

Another issue is access to e-mail addresses. People often have more than one address, they change addresses frequently and addresses become obsolete. Also, there's no proper directory of e-mail addresses, which is not the case with telephone numbers. You'll soon find that your address database is out of date and incomplete. Before you start the survey, you need to *update the database*. You can do this using a call center and approaching the people by phone. And if that's the case you may as well conduct the interview. If in the future there's a better registration of e-mail addresses, then Internet surveys will become one of the most important ways to collect data.

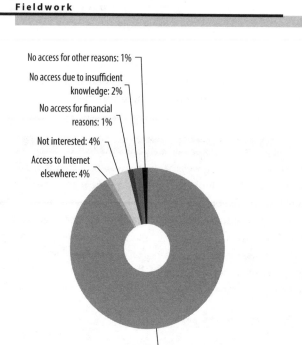

No access for other reasons: 1%

No access due to insufficient knowledge: 2%

No access for financial reasons: 1%

Not interested: 4%

Access to Internet elsewhere: 4%

Has Internet access: 91%

Figure 7.1   Internet usage

7.3.2   *Wireless Research: Mobile Phones*

A new type of 'wireless' research is conducting surveys using mobile phones, also known as 'mobile research'. Via SMS messages panels are asked questions, or people are approached while they are on the Internet when using their mobile phones. Initial feedback about these methods indicates that the response varies: sometimes it's higher, sometimes it's lower than online and telephone surveys. Some researchers think this makes sense (Roy & Vanheuverzwyn, 2002) because mobile phones are people's own personal possessions. As opposed to fixed phone lines, you always have your mobile phone on you. But you're not always up for a phone call because the situation or environment is not conducive. While the initial response (answering the phone) maybe higher than fixed lines, the response rate or '*level of acceptance*' (the number of people that actually take part in the research) will probably be lower. Table 7.2 lists the arguments.

This new kind of research comes with a lot of disadvantages. In some countries people have to pay for messages themselves because there is no reverse billing system in place. Also, the same limitations that we mentioned for online research apply here too: those that don't have mobile phones can't take part in research and there are no mobile phone directories so lists of numbers are inaccurate or incomplete. This raises problems for sample selection (see Roy & Vanheuverzwyn, 2002). Generally speaking adequate databases for mobile phones don't exist. To overcome this, the best thing to do is use a *random number generator* to select the numbers (see Section 6.4.3). In Text box 7.4 you'll find an example of research done using mobile phones.

Interview-NSS is going to do mobile interviews

'Interview-NSS is going to start research using SMS messages from next month onwards. This interviewing technique apparently gets a better response rate than telephone or online research. For this service, Interview-NSS will be working together with Wireless Opinion, a Swedish company that has designed the technical system to support it. According to Robert Schueler, manager of New Media Research at Interview NSS, research using SMS has already proven itself in Sweden. "Telephone research usually gets a response rate of between 30 to 50% on average. For online research the response rate is between 40 to 50%. In Sweden, SMS research achieves a response rate of between 60 to 80%." How will the service work exactly? Interview-NSS will send questions by SMS to all members of the panel. They respond directly to the questions by typing in codes. The answers go by SMS to Wireless Opinion's gateway in Sweden.'

According to Schueler, there are costs involved for the participants. 'In the future it will be free, but at the moment you still have to pay the usual charges for sending messages.' In order for the sender to pay for responses to SMSes, you need a so-called reverse billing system. According to Schueler, Wireless Opinion has not yet reached an agreement about this with the large telecom companies in the Netherlands. Prepaid phones will, however, be able to take part in SMS research.

Schueler says that, for the time being, he still sees the technique as a supplementary medium despite its high response rate. Mobile phones are not suitable for extensive research because of their limited screen capacity. Schueler: 'On the other hand, for short assessments they are ideal. At events and expos you can get respondents to vote directly about a given subject' (Mulders, 2002).

Box 7.4

7.4 Respondents and Surveys

7.4.1 *The Real Fieldwork Begins*

pilot survey To ensure that your survey goes well, you can test your questionnaire (verbally). A pilot study like this has several advantages, as we have already noted:
- You can sift out the mistakes: for instance, you can change sentences that don't flow well.
- You can change the structure if necessary; as good as it may be in theory, sometimes you need to adjust it.
- Practising with the questionnaire will ensure that it goes smoothly later.
- This will enhance the reliability of your results.

lay-out Sometimes it's difficult to read questionnaires, they look messy or it's not easy to find the correct answer. This happens because not enough attention was paid to the lay-out, and this is an important aspect of questionnaire design. It is unprofessional to present the respondent with an untidy questionnaire, and this will impact on the validity of your research. Apart from anything else, it will irritate the respondents. There's a danger that respondents will refuse to take part in the research or that they won't fill in the answers correctly.

recruiting respondents These days respondents are often, too often perhaps, asked to take part in research. To motivate them you need to design a catchy invitation that inspires confidence. For telephone surveys, Internet surveys and even surveys on the street, it is important that you make it immediately clear what the objective of the research is, what the questions are about and how the questionnaire is structured. The most important thing is to make it clear to the respondents that their contribution is of interest to the research and that their opinion will make a difference. And of course you must always inform them that everything they say will be treated with the strictest confidence!

One thing you can't do in a street interview, but you can in surveys using the Internet, post or phone, is send more than one invitation to take part in your survey.

reminders Normally self-completion questionnaires have a 'due date', and a request to return the questionnaire before the date expires. If you are doing a postal survey and the date expires, then you can send a reminder, accompanied by another questionnaire in case the first one got lost. Do this after a reasonable space of time. What is reasonable depends on a number of factors: the original period of time, but also the method that you are using, the subjects, the length of the questionnaire, the client's deadline and so on. Whatever you do, don't get pushy on the phone the day after the first deadline has passed. Their co-operation is voluntary and forcing the issue is not going to help, it's more likely to annoy them in fact.

In telephone surveys sometimes the respondent isn't home the first time you call, or it's not convenient, or they just don't feel like answering questions at that point in time. You can try calling back or making an appointment to call back. Another way to do it is to offer to send a self-completion version of the questionnaire by e-mail or by post, with the obligatory self-addresses envelope plus postage. The respondents can then fill in and return the questionnaire at their leisure. Whatever you do, always ensure that your rapport with the respondent is good. They are doing you a favour after all! Don't take the hard sell route because you'll only get their backs up.

7.4.2   Incentives

Nowadays it is becoming more and more difficult to get people to take part in research. People are getting 'survey fatigue', they can't see the point of yet another questionnaire. This is because way too often they are asked to co-operate with research that doesn't seem to be very relevant to them. Often research asks a lot of them without them ever getting to know what the outcome is. Not only that, telephone surveys often end up being a sales pitch for insurance or some other product that they can well do without.

The least you can do as a researcher is compensate participants for their costs. It goes without saying that you make sure that the research doesn't actually cost the respondents anything, apart from the time and energy that it takes to answer your questions. This means that if it's a postal survey you must send a self-addressed envelope and stamp (or use a freepost address). If it's a telephone survey, they shouldn't have to call you. Sometimes it's not possible to avoid costs, for instance if the respondent has to take time off work or if they use the Internet to respond.

The best way to reward the respondents for their participation is if the results of the research benefit them. Greyhound, for instance, promises respondents that their co-operation will result in improvements to service, and passengers like the thought of this (see Text box 7.5).

Greyhound uses 'Mystery Travelers' to assess their service. Travelers can sign up for this survey by ticket number. After signing up, they take the trip. Under no circumstances are they to reveal to the personnel on the bus that they are evaluating their services. After arriving at their destination, the travelers have 7 days to send in the completed questionnaire. Upon receipt, the Greyhound Company will give the traveler a 50% discount via their credit card. This particular incentive motivates many travelers to participate, the methodological downside being that the sample is self-selected, and this threatens external validity.

Source: www.ibiblio.org

Box 7.5

The best way to let people know that you value their opinion is to use the results and adjust company policies. There are other ways of thanking respondents for taking part in your research. Research bureaus have become very good at coming up with so-called incentives to encourage people to take part in research. Here are a few examples:

- Respondents are given a small *gift* or *gadget*, for example a pen.
- People are given free tickets to a game, a museum or the movies.
- To encourage people to think that they are helping a worthy cause, the research bureau (the client, in fact) promises to give a small donation to *charity* for each person taking part (see Text box 7.6).
- A raffle among participants is organized, the prize being a dinner out, a book voucher or an evening out (sometimes even weekends away are promised!). The respondent number is then used in the draw. This does raise the question of why the respondents are taking part: because of the raffle or because they are interested in the research subject?

Unicef

On the website for Unicef (United Nation's children and education fund), there is a special page for 'research donations':

Contributions on behalf of research respondents
More and more often companies are being confronted these days with high non-response levels for surveys and research. Motivate your research group by offering to contribute to a Unicef project in exchange for their response.

Source: www.unicef.kpnis.nl

Box 7.6

7.4.3 Survey Response

There are many factors that influence the survey *response rate*. By response, *response* we mean that proportion of the questionnaires sent out that come back *and non-* completed and that actually contain relevant information. The proportion of *response* questionnaires that come back incomplete or not at all is called *non-response*. Reasons for non-response could be:

- people are not at home (on vacation, at work or elsewhere);
- people are not able to take part (through ill-health, a handicap or something similar);
- people just don't feel like taking part, for whatever reason.

Because of this non-response, there is a chance (or rather: a risk) that the *random or* completed questionnaires do not represent the target group. If this is because *systematic* of coincidence (for example if the respondent just happens not to be at home), then it is what is known as a *random sampling error*. If people choose not to take part, then this is known as a *systematic sampling error*. These errors in the sample jeopardize the generalizability of the results, particularly in quantitative research. You will have to assess the extent to which the sample still has similar attributes to the population that is relevant to your research. If the sample does not resemble the population in terms of these attributes, then you will not be able to extrapolate the results of your analysis to the population. The results will not be generalizable because the sample is not representative of the population. Whatever the case may be, you will have to investigate the reasons for this non-response and mention it in your report. This kind of non-response also happens in qualitative research. Given that statistical generalizability is not an objective, it is considered less important. What is important is theoretical generalizability (see Section 6.5.2 as well).

Partial non-response also happens. The questionnaire in this case is incom- *item non-* plete, one or two questions are skipped. This so-called *item non-response* *response* often has to do with the way questions are phrased. It can occur because:

- the respondent doesn't understand the question;
- the question doesn't apply to the respondent;
- the respondent doesn't feel like answering the question;
- the respondent doesn't know the answer to the question, or has no opinion on the subject;
- the respondent hasn't seen the question (for example because it is on the back of the page).

This kind of non-response affects the reliability of the results. If the respondents deliberately skip questions, then it will impinge on the validity of the research.

Gossip magazines a hit, and not only at the dentist

Newspapers have far greater readership than previously thought, and the same goes for porn and gossip magazines, whereas respected current affairs and business magazines, on the other hand, do not. This has emerged from the first readership results from research undertaken by publishers and advertisers. For the old advertising and media research, people were contacted by phone. The data for this research was gathered by giving the respondents a laptop and asking them to complete the questionnaire electronically. Now that interviewers are no longer involved, the readership of gossip magazines has almost doubled. Porn magazines shot up by a third. Director of the research bureau, Costa Tchaussoglou, calls this the embarrassment effect: 'If there's no interviewer involved, then people aren't afraid to admit that they're interested porn and gossip magazines.' And because they don't have to impress the interviewer with their readership of expensive management magazines and intellectual current affairs publications, readership of those has taken a nose-dive.

National newspapers have also done better in this new set up because a lot of newspapers are read along the way. When under pressure by the interviewers, many respondents forgot to mention the newspapers that they read. Respondents are also more inclined to mention their regional papers because they can take their time with the new method. Sport, interior and gardening glossies are also read much less than previously assumed. This is because when people are interviewed by phone they often confuse these magazines. Director Bart Soels of media research bureau OMD thinks that the new figures will not be lost on the advertising industry. 'Particularly those magazines that have a lower readership than previously thought will notice. That was a finding that that market did not see coming.'

Source: Reijn, 2002

Box 7.7

The article about the research into the popularity of gossip magazines (Text box 7.7) illustrates a few things. In the first place it shows the impact of interviewers and what happens if interviewers are not physically present when the questions are asked. The subject of this research, in some cases, is somewhat sensitive. The interviewer would like to know if the respondent reads porn magazines. In the presence of an interviewer, the respondent is not that likely to answer the question truthfully. If there's no interviewer then the respondent will feel less restrained. In this readership survey, *social desirability* in the answers is also avoided in the same way. The respondents fill in the questionnaires themselves. There is no interviewer to impress by claiming to read management magazines. The respondents also don't feel they need to skip sensitive questions. Secondly, the article also demonstrates what IT can mean for research methodology. The respondents can complete the questionnaires on their laptop, at their leisure. Because they don't feel under any pressure from the interviewer, they can take their time to recall all the newspapers and magazines that they read. Thirdly, the article shows what the consequences of this approach will have for the clients of this readership survey (gossip magazine publishers): higher response in general, higher item response and moreover reliable and valid results.

7.4.4 Tips & Tricks

We'll close this section with a few tips and tricks to ensure that the survey goes as well as possible (Text box 7.8) because as the researcher, but also as the client, you want the response rate to be as high as possible, and you want to keep the respondents and interviewers happy as well.

Tips & tricks for a survey that goes smoothly

- Test your questionnaire first!
- Make the questionnaire as short as possible and as long as necessary!
- To ensure that the response rate for telephone surveys is as high as possible, take the following into account: vacations, working hours, age, marital status and so on.
- If you are drawing your sample from a specific neighborhood, then first investigate what the demographic profile is so that you can get a sample that is as representative as possible in terms of:
  - level of education;
  - employment levels;
  - ethnicity;
  - state of buildings and infrastructure;
  - socio-economic status (the status of one person in relation to another within the environment based on education, occupation, income and housing).
- Always write an introduction letter.
- Keep the tone of the letter personal.
- Assure the respondent that their information will be kept confidential.
- Pay attention to the layout of the questionnaire.
- Send reminders at the appropriate time.

7.5 Interviews: Working on Rapport

Everyone has taken part in an interview at some point. Be it in daily life or as part of research, the goal is to collect information. It could be that you have a discussion with your tutor to see how your internship should be structured, which steps you need to take and how you will write your report. You may go to a travel agent and sit down with them to gather information about your travel destination. The same applies to research: you question employees about their perceptions of the work climate; you interview couples about their relationships and what they think about marriages of today, and so on. But don't take interviewing too lightly! The respondent may clam up if the tone is wrong, you ask an unexpected question or they get a confrontational reaction, and you won't get any more information from them. After that, you can just forget it! The most important aspect of a good interview is to work on the rapport with the respondent! You start your conversation in this way and it is the thread that you follow throughout the interview. The questionnaire structure is also important, and last but not least, the questions have to be relevant. Here are a few tips to ensure that the interview goes as smoothly as possible.

interview structure for in-depth interviews

1 Your interview should have a beginning, a middle (the core) and an end:
   a Introduction:
      • introduce yourself;
      • the objective of the interview;
      • the structure;
      • estimated time it will take;
      • how much their participation is appreciated;
      • how important their contribution is;
      • what will happen to the information;
      • assure them that their information will be treated with the strictest confidence.

b You then get to the heart of the interview, where you introduce aspects of the main subject.

c After the interview, wind down properly. Summarize what has been said and give the respondent the opportunity to add information or comments. Make sure that they are satisfied with how it went.

2 Use a list of subjects: it will give structure to your interview.

3 In order to process and analyze all the information properly, tape the interview (you can record it on video but normally this is done using audio tapes). Always ask permission first!

4 As the interviewer, your attention should be on the respondent. You empathize with what they have to say, you stimulate them so that they give you the whole story, without losing sight of the subject.

5 You have to be a good listener.

6 You should have a few techniques at your fingertips to help get the information. These techniques are instruments that you can use if the discussion is not going well, if you're not getting the right information or if it's incomplete. If the interview is going well, then you don't need to use these techniques, in fact you shouldn't! Don't turn it into a contrived situation!

7 You don't become a participant in the discussion; as the interviewer you remain as objective as possible. As the researcher, you stay on the sidelines, you observe, you register and you take notes. In addition you stick to the 'thread' (the main theme).

In the sections below we will be talking about the following subjects: how to recruit respondents, the flow of the interview, discussion techniques that you can use, and the issue of how to close the interview properly. We round off by talking about a few pitfalls or 'wrong moves' that can send the interview into a tailspin. We will be discussing these subjects using an on-going case: research into the delegation of household chores (see Text boxes 7.9 to 7.15).

Delegating household chores (1)

You study the delegation of household chores. For this you conduct a few paired interviews: interviews with couples who share the same household. The main subject of the interviews is about their ideas to do with task sharing in the household. The following topics will be dealt with:

• How are the tasks divided? (Thinking of things like: shopping, cleaning, washing and ironing, taking care of the children, maintenance in the house, gardening, and so on.)

- What do the respondents think of this division of tasks? (This is a question about perceptions of how chores have been delegated by the partners.)
- What should stay the same, change and stop? Why should this happen and how?

- How do the respondents see task allocation in the future?

This is a very open interview. As the interviewer, it is up to you to decide how you will introduce the questions and which ones you ask, as long as you cover the subjects mentioned.

Box 7.9

7.5.1   Recruiting Respondents

Recruiting respondents takes more time than you'd expect. You have to phone them or make an appointment to see them, you have to explain what the interview is about and emphasize that confidentiality will be safeguarded. Not only do they have to be interested in taking part, they have to have enough time to do so. They also have to something to say on the subject. Experience shows that people are often reluctant to take part in interviews, regardless of the subject. Be cautious, polite and forthcoming, and whatever you do, don't be pushy! You are not a door-to-door salesman!

A good way to get names and addresses of potential respondents, using a small network of people, is the *snowball method* that we mentioned in Section 6.4.4. This method of sampling is often used for in-depth interviews. By using a small group of involved and/or expert respondents you will find it easier to access other people. Also, the respondents will probably know each other, which makes it easier to get their permission to do an interview. Normally you won't be interviewing large groups of people. If you do between 25 to 30 interviews (which is a lot!) you'll reach your *saturation point*. You may even reach that point after 10 interviews. This means that you are not really getting any new information. The more experienced you become as an interviewer, the easier it will be for you to recognize this saturation point.

Interviewing is an intensive and time-consuming business. You also have to bear in mind the time it takes you to process the interviews. An interview that takes an hour to conduct will easily take a few hours to process (depending on how detailed it needs to be). As we have noted, statistical generalization is not important, but theoretical generalization is! So a limited number of interviews makes sense.

Box 7.10

Delegating household chores (2)

For your research into delegating household chores you start to look for couples who would like to take part. The conditions are that they have a relationship and that they share a household. They may or may not have children. The first thing you do is approach people in your own circles, for instance acquaintances or neighbors. These people may put you onto other likely candidates for you to approach.

7.5.2 *Introduction to the Discussion*

Starting off on the right foot is important. So make sure you are punctual! Also, a good opening (we discussed this at the beginning of the section) clears the way for a smooth interview. The opening of an interview has two elements: to do with the *relation* with the respondent and aspects of the *content*.

interpersonal aspects
However much a person knows about the subject and however experienced they are when it comes to giving interviews, there's often a bit of tension at the beginning of the talk. Starting with yourself: Will the interview go well? Will you get the right information out of the respondent? Will the respondent be happy with the way the interview goes? Often respondents are a bit nervous. They may be nervous types, but maybe it's because you're dealing with awkward or controversial subjects, or because they are afraid that you may ask them a question for which they have no answer. And then there's your undivided attention: a lot of people have to get used to being in the spotlight like that.

To make people feel at ease, it's a good idea to start off with small talk. Have a look around and say something complimentary about their home or offices. You can also try finding a light subject to chat about. You can make a remark about the paintings on the wall, or if they have photos of their family on their desk, you can say something about them. Why does the subject have to be superficial? Because as the interviewer you have to stay objective and independent, you don't know yet how the interview will go. By starting off with small talk you create a confidential atmosphere without giving the impression that you are going to be too involved in the subject. Whatever it is that you chat about, it should not become a subject of discussion because this is too distracting. One last tip: don't forget when you start the interview to thank the respondent for taking part in the research! The whole point of 'working on the rapport' is to win the confidence of the respondent so that you can get more reliable information about the subject you are researching.

content   You start the discussion by offering information: what the subject is about,
aspects   how it's structured (the broad brush strokes, you don't want to steer them too much), how long you think it will take. You also tell them about the core question: that will be the main thread of the interview. During the course of the discussion, you'll divide the main question into a number of sub-questions, or you'll have a topic list that you can tick off after you've discussed each topic.

You also assure the respondent that the information will be handled confidentially and anonymously so that the respondent knows that any information given to you during the interview will not 'get out'.

In order to get as much useful information as possible, you can use a few interviewing techniques. We'll talk about this in Section 7.5.4.

Delegating household chores (3)

You've selected the first couples for your interview, and appointments have been made. Now you can start the interviews. You've already thought about how you will start the first interview. You introduce the research subject and tell them what the aim is: to make an inventory of how household chores are divided between the partners and their perceptions of this. You indicate that the interview should take about an hour. You've made a note for yourself that delegating household tasks between partners can be a source of conflict between partners. If this is in fact the case, then you must make sure that, although you're very understanding of the situation, you don't get caught up in the conflict.

Box 7.11

7.5.3   Recording Interviews

Most interviewers record the interviews, provided they have permission to do this. So you first have to ask. Normally it is an audio recording using a mini-cassette recorder, a mini-disc recorder or an Mp3 player that can record. Sometimes video cameras are used. You can also use your mobile phone, but make sure that the quality of the recording is good enough. You have to be able to hear everything that is said. Taping the interview has several advantages:

- You can give your undivided attention to the respondent and you don't have to write down everything they say. That's not to say that you don't write anything. Writing during an interview is often interpreted as being interested in what is said, that the responses are important for the research. However, that is not the most important reason for writing during the conversation. In these notes you write down key words that you can use for the next question. So always make notes!
- Recordings give you a verbatim version of the discussion, which enables you to make very accurate notes about what was said.
- You can listen to what was said as many times as you like. This also increases the reliability of the results.

You must take into consideration that not everyone likes to be taped, and this may make them a bit reticent during the interview.

Delegating household chores (4)

During the introduction you ask their permission to record the interview. For this you have brought along a mini-disc recorder that can be put inconspicuously on the table between you and the respondents. The respondents want to know why it is you want to tape the discussion? Then don't hold back. In this case you are interviewing two people at once, which is why it would be a good thing if you could record the conversation. The respondents will not only be answering your questions about how they delegate chores, will also be reacting to each other and sometimes talking at the same time. It would be really useful for you to be able to listen to what was said and have a record of how it went.

Make a point of emphasizing that the information given will be kept anonymous and that you'll be wiping the tape after you've written the report! If the respondent isn't happy for you to record the interview, then don't do it! If an awkward situation arises during the interview – say because there's a conflict about how chores are delegated – switch the recorder off and mention that you're doing this. You can then first talk about the emotion or disagreements. Let the respondents calm down first and talk about the conflict. This is all about working on rapport. Only turn the recorder back on when the conversation has returned to the main subject, and mention this again: 'The discussion is about how you share the job of looking after the children. I'm turning the recorder back on.'

Has the conversation come to an end? Then you switch the recorder off and mention it again.

Box 7.12

If you've been given permission to tape the discussion then don't mess around with the equipment. It's very distracting and it doesn't come across as very professional. Make sure you know exactly how it all works so that you can get on with the job. You can do a test before you start just to make sure that you know that it's all working properly.

7.5.4   Interviewing Techniques

Every conversation, or parts of it, should start with an introduction followed by an intelligible question, the main question (either open or closed). If the response is unclear or incomplete, or not to the point, then you can prompt the interviewee (see Text box 7.13). There are also other ways to make sure it goes according to plan.

interviewing techniques Interviewing techniques are tools that are used during interviews. By practicing a lot you can learn them so that you can apply them in interviews. Do interviews generally go badly if you don't use these tools? Of course not, they often go well. These techniques are only meant to give you extra support; for when the interview threatens to go wrong; if you are not getting the information that you need; or if things are getting too emotional. Interviewing techniques can be both verbal and non-verbal. Also, asking questions is not the only skill you need, you also need to be good at listening (listening skills). Some techniques are passive; others are active. We'll discuss a few here.

Bearing and eye contact
Your bearing as an interviewer says something about you. It shows whether you are interested, whether you empathize and whether you're focusing on what is being said. The respondent may not be conscious of it, but it puts them at ease. The best thing to do is to sit sideways at the table, across from the respondent, for example at the corner of the table (see Figure 7.2). Then you don't have to sit directly opposite, staring each other in the face. It's less daunting and therefore much nicer for the respondent.

Delegating household chores (5)

After you've explained the aim and subject of the interview, you start with the first question. You could start by saying 'How are the household chores divided between you and your partner at the moment?' One of the respondents begins. What if he starts giving his opinion of how the tasks are dele-

Continued

gated instead of the actual division of tasks? Then it's your job to make sure that he talks about the actual division and not how it came about or what he thinks of it. You could respond by saying that what he has to say is interesting and that you want to talk about it. You then say: 'Please can you tell me who does what in your home when it comes to household chores?' You repeat the question, as it were, in a slightly different way.

You can also ask the respondents to clarify their answers, or to give you more information about certain aspects. Make sure you don't steer the respondents by asking leading questions. So don't ask 'Don't you hate it when ...?' Instead ask 'What do you think of ...?'

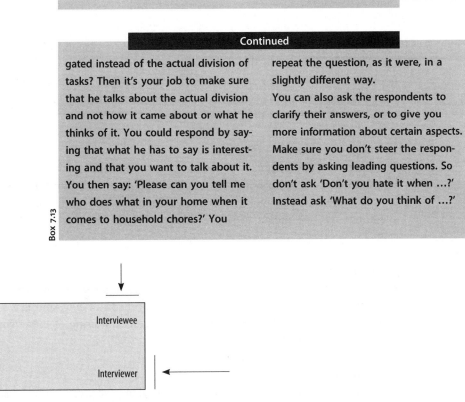

Figure 7.2   Seating of discussion partners

For the rest, it's encouraging for the respondent if the interviewer is paying attention and leaning forward slightly (this is known as *coachman's posture*). It shows that you are interested in what is being said. Never cross your arms or your legs when you listen; it comes across as 'closed' and doesn't encourage the other person to talk.

Nodding
You can support the person you are interviewing by keeping eye contact and nodding every now and then. Eye contact is not the same as staring, which you should try to avoid!

Handling silences
Often in the middle of a conversation it suddenly becomes quiet. Sometimes this is because the respondent has nothing more to say on the subject and is waiting for the next question. It could also be because they are thinking about their next remark. As the interviewer, you should not be afraid of silence. You can put it to use. If you haven't had a satisfactory answer to

your question you can use the silence to prompt. The respondent will think that more is expected of them and will carry on with their story. You can hold the silence for a few seconds, which is known as the 'four-second rule'. Regular pauses in an interview may even ensure that the conversation goes more smoothly (Emans, 1990).

Intonation and volume

The intonation and volume that you use to ask questions and summarize the information given in an interview influence the flow of the conversation. If the intonation of your voice goes up at the end of the sentence you will encourage the respondent to answer. Remember also to speak audibly and calmly.

Acknowledging

If you use words like 'yes, yes, mm, exactly' in the right places this will also stimulate the respondent. This has the same effect as nodding, and is a sign that you are listening. But don't overdo it! A constant string of these words and gestures can be irritating.

Paraphrasing

If an answer is long, you can paraphrase it in your own words to make sure that you understood. You start by saying 'If I have understood you correctly ...' or 'So ...'. At the end of a section of the conversation you can also *summarize* the information you've been given. In this summary you use key words from the respondent's information. A third way to paraphrase the information is to repeat the words they have just said. This is known as *parroting*. You will see that the person will respond by telling you more about the subject (see Text box 7.14).

Delegating household chores (6)

The respondents have told you everything to do with how they decide who is going to do what in their household. Now you want to know what they think about it. You ask what their perceptions are of the division of tasks. In their responses the couples carry on talking about the disagreement between them regarding the way they have divided the tasks. One of them states: 'And that's when we decided we should do it *differently*.' Your response is: 'Differently ...?' And the respondent relates: 'Yes, differently. I wanted to change the way we do ...'

Box 7.14

7.5.5   *Winding Down*

Interviews don't come to a sudden halt. You wind down slowly and work your way towards the conclusion by saying something like: 'I've come to the last question ...' or: 'Is there anything I've forgotten?' Or: 'Is there anything else you would like to add?' The respondent can then add information that may not be directly related to the questions, but that they feel is important. It goes without saying that you thank the respondent for their time and trouble.

Often what happens is that you get extra information after the interview has come to an end and the recorder has been switched off. The conversation can sometimes be more personal than what was said during the interview. Often the information is not meant for the interview itself, but the interviewee wants to talk about it anyway. If the information is useful for your report then you must ask permission to use it. After all, it has been given 'off the record'!

If the subjects have been difficult to talk about or personal, or if the conversation has been emotional, take this into account and make sure you close the conversation properly. This is when you should discuss these difficulties, and pay attention to the emotions. You can also ask the respondent what they thought of the discussion, maybe you should have done some things differently. Then you can bear these things in mind during the rest of the research. In short, if questions or remarks crop up during the interview that are aimed at you personally, then put off reacting to them until the end. Attend to these things once the interview is over, that's when the time is right.

7.5.6   *Tips & Tricks*

Practice makes perfect, and this applies to interviewing too, but you have to work at it. There are a few things that you must take into account:

• Keep *control* of the interview. Sometimes people try to take over: they start asking you questions, they change the structure of the interview, you name it. Don't let this happen. You are in charge. In practice this means that you stick to the interview guide and, by doing so, you will give the conversation structure (Text box 7.11).

• Stay *independent* and *objective*. Don't be tempted to make personal comments. Sometimes you'll be asked 'What do you think about it?' You should say that you'd love to talk about it after the interview.

- Be *empathetic* but not too empathetic. If you don't keep enough of a distance, the conversation will digress or you'll become too personally involved with the respondent.
- Don't be taken off guard. For example, despite having made an appointment, there's a third person there during the interview. Or: it turns out that the respondent has less time than they originally said they would.
- Asking people for their opinion does not mean helping them to give you an answer. Resist making value judgments and asking leading questions. Do not ask: 'Do you hate it when the train is late?', but instead: 'What has your experience with arrival and departure times of trains?' So don't give advice or your unsolicited opinions.
- Closed questions can introduce subjects, like a filter. But don't ask too many closed questions. It gives you support when you're not very experienced but it doesn't lead to a lot of useful information. Ask as many open questions as possible, keep asking questions and so on.
- Probing is a difficult technique. You have to strike a balance: on the one hand, don't be too easy to please; on the other hand, don't go on too much. Keep to a happy medium, as in Text box 7.15.

Delegating household chores (9)

If the respondent says 'It's fine' when you ask about delegating household chores, then that is not enough information. You can probe by asking: 'Can you explain how you've divided the tasks?' or 'You say you're happy with the way you've organized the household duties. Can you explain?' The respondent goes on to say: 'I'm happy with it the way we've divided the tasks, but I told you that already.' Then you don't carry on asking, the respondent has repeated his answer. It may be possible to return to the subject later, in a different context.

Box 7.15

- Only use interviewing techniques if they are necessary to make the interview go smoothly. If the interview is going well, then that's fine. Using techniques for their own sake is not a good idea: it is irritating. So don't exaggerate the nodding, agreeing, parroting etc.
- Don't jump to conclusions. The respondent's opinion is what is important.
- And finally: whatever you do, be yourself.

7.6 Interpretation Errors

For all kinds of unforeseeable reasons, errors can easily occur in your interpretation. This goes for qualitative and quantitative research alike. Circumstances may lead to your sample not being representative for the population, i.e., the group of elements (people, businesses, organizations) that you want to make statements about. Sometimes the sample is deliberately restricted, which jeopardizes the generalizability of the results. Often when the research results are reported on in the media, this restriction is ignored: either it is not mentioned at all, or little is said about it. Newspapers go to great lengths to discuss research that only applies to a small group. The example in Text box 7.16 illustrates this. Research undertaken in 1954 (see Text box 7.17) shows that the incorrect interpretation of non-response can lead to the wrong conclusions.

Busy, busy, busy ...

In 2003, an ad campaign warned the public that children these days are way too busy. This sparked a flood of information in the media. Research showed that this notion probably applied to a specific group of children that are extremely busy: children who are native to the country, who are receiving a higher level of education and who have plenty of pocket money. Children from immigrant parents often have less to keep them occupied than they would like. The qualifier 'too' busy is also a misinterpretation: according to the researchers, children prefer a busy schedule to an empty one!

The research differentiates between the two groups of children. Apparently the characteristics of the first group of children differ from those of the population. It seems as though the children from that ethnic background, who are enjoying a higher level of education, and have enough pocket money are overrepresented, resulting in a distorted impression. The researcher noted that this particular group of children did not resemble the total population of children with respect to these attributes. The journalists made no mention of this.

Source: Vermeulen, 2003

Box 7.16

'Lies, damned lies and statistics'

In his book *How to lie with statistics*, Huff (1991, p. 14) reports on research conducted in 1954 that had remarkable

results, at least that was what was reported in the newspaper: the biggest conversion of all time from the Roman

Catholic Church to the Protestant Church! The *Herald Tribune* reported that 2,219 Protestant pastors had said that they knew of at least one person who had made this conversion. The journalist simply took this figure (from those who had responded) and extrapolated it to the total number of Protestant congregations in the United States and came up with a figure of more than 4 million for the whole country.

Obviously you can't do that. What was really the case? The researcher had sent 25,000 preachers a questionnaire. Of that number, only 10% (2,219) sent the completed questionnaire back. These preachers either thought the survey was useful or recognized the situation because they knew of people in their congregation who had converted to Catholicism. The other 90% said nothing on the subject because they either couldn't or wouldn't take part in the research.

Box 7.17

7.7 Glossary of Most Important Terms and Their Meaning

Online research	Research done without interviewers, via the Internet.
Mobile research	Research done using mobile phones.
Data enrichment	Supplementing incomplete databases by adding the correct addresses for example.
Pilot study	Testing your questionnaire and research design by carrying out a small-scale preliminary study.
Incentive	Offer of a small reward to respondent to encourage them to take part in the research.
Response rate	That proportion of the questionnaires that are completed and returned. The number of people that actually took part in your research.
Item non-response	Those questions that were not completed by the respondent.
Paraphrase	The interviewer repeats the respondent's answer in their own words.
Parroting	The interviewer repeats the last part of the respondent's answer.
Four-second rule	An interviewing technique in which the interviewer uses pauses (silence), by letting it continue, to encourage the interviewer to continue with their answer.

7.8 Assignments for Chapter 7

1 Interviewing techniques.
   a Mention the interviewing techniques that you know.
   b How would you group these techniques?
2 Read the example in Text box 7.18 about the Cycling Challenge research.
   a What can you say about the responses from the men and the women?
   b What can you say about the responses from the athletes who did the 100km and 150km rides?
   c Discuss the representativeness of these figures compared to the total population. Discuss the reliability. Tip: these figures only apply to those who finished the race!
   d What can you say about the representativeness according to gender? In other words, do you think the division by gender is a good reflection of the population (of those who finished the race)?

Cycling is good for you!				

In 2010, a study was conducted into the factors that influence performance during the Cycling Challenge. It looked as aspects such as training, physical characteristics and experience. The population comprised all those who took part in the Cycling Challenge and finished the race.

The following response was recorded:

150 km men	Total completed	855	sample	120 (14%)
150 km women	Total completed	34	sample	6 (17.6%)
100 km men	Total completed	473	sample	41 (8.7%)
100 km women	Total completed	44	sample	2 (4.5%)

Source: cyclobenelux.com

Box 7.18

3 'Wireless research' (Section 7.3.2).
   a What are the limitations of research using mobile phones?
   b How would you draw a random sample from mobile phone numbers?
4 Read the example about the Motivaction research in Text box 7.2.
   a Mention the pros and cons of panel research.
   b What are the solutions to the problem of selective non-response?

5 Read the example about the study into gossip magazine readership in Text box 7.7 closely.
Discuss the problems to do with the response rate in terms of reliability and validity.

6 Read through the case about delegating of household tasks once more (Text boxes 7.9 to 7.15). Draw up a topic list that you could use for this in-depth interview.

7 Using the household tasks case as a guide, suppose you conduct an interview in which the couple does not agree with the way in which the tasks in their household have been delegated. They both answer your questions at the same time and they no longer address you as the interviewer, instead they address each other. They clearly don't agree with each other. What should you do about it? How do you respond as the interviewer?

At the agreed time, the interviewer arrives at your home and rings the bell. You open the door. You are a bit nervous. Giving information to a stranger is no easy feat. You hang up his coat and ask if he'd like some coffee, and tell him to take a seat. He looks around, with a friendly smile, and tells you that he's seen the film on the poster in your hall. You chat a bit. You make coffee; the interviewer sets up his cassette recorder on the dining room table, and sits down across from you, a bit to one side. He leans towards you and starts. His names in Frank Schover, he is an interviewer working for research bureau BOTS. He tells you what the interview is about, how long he thinks it will take and how it is structured. He says how much he appreciates it that you are prepared to give him so much information. You start to feel a bit more at ease.
The interview starts. Every now and again, you hesitate. He carries on looking at you and waits for your answer. Every now and again he nods in agreement. You don't immediately have an answer to a question he asks your opinion about; he rephrases the question and suddenly you've got the answer! It's as though your answer is a waterfall of letters and words. Fortunately the interviewer knows how to paraphrase your answers in one sentence. He seems to really appreciate your information. He encourages you to say more, waits until you've finished, repeats some words to emphasize what you've said.
At the end of the interview you've given him all you've got and you're satisfied. He thanks you once again. Is there anything you'd like to ask? Is there anything more you'd like to add? You ask him if he'd like another cup of coffee. Relieved and satisfied, you say goodbye after an hour and a half. It's fun giving an interview!

Box 7.19

8 Which verbal and non-verbal techniques did the interviewer use?

9 In these times of financial crisis, there have been a lot of cutbacks in spending on cultural facilities, and your city is no exception. To ensure that the reductions are done as efficiently as possible, the district offices commission research to find out which facilities are used and valued the most by the residents of the region. The budget for research is limited and the researchers have been given four months to complete the research and present the findings. The sample must be representative of the region's residents in terms of given attributes. Using a questionnaire, information is gathered about awareness and appreciation of cultural facilities in the region. Pictures are used to gauge awareness of the facilities. You can choose from the following methods:
- postal survey;
- Internet;
- telephone;
- face-to-face interviews.

a Which method would you use and why?

b Why would you not use some of these methods?

c How can you ensure that the response is as high as possible?

10 Read Text box 7.16 ('Busy, busy, busy ...') carefully. Discuss which mistake may have been made and what the consequences would be for the quality of the research.

In the section 'Chapter 7' (tab Assignment solutions) you will find the solutions to the assignments in Section 7.8. You will find information about the design cases under tab 'Design cases' in the section 'Chapter 7'.

WEBSITE

Part III
Analysis

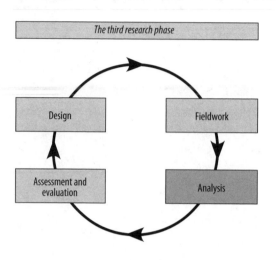

Part III of this book is all about analysis. You've collected the data and from this pile of information you have to distill your results. We will be dealing with questions like:

- What does the research group (sample) look like?
- What is the answer to my research question after I've analyzed the information?
- What results will I find in the material I have gathered?
- Are these results also valid for a larger group of people?

Chapter 8 deals with quantitative analysis. We will talk about levels of measurement, inferential statistics, and processing survey data. We will also discuss some simple descriptive statistic techniques. You will also be given information about how best to go about presenting your results, and which graphs and charts you can make for this.

Chapter 9 gives an introduction to qualitative data analysis: analysis of data from open interviews, observations, documents and so on.

8

Processing Quantitative Data

Chapter 8 is about quantitative data analysis. This phase starts once the data collection is complete. How do you approach it? How do you process the pile of answers that you have gathered? How do you turn it into a table or a graph, how do you extract the results? Which techniques should you use in your analysis and what do you have to take into account? This is what this chapter is about. Qualitative analysis is not discussed here; it follows in Chapter 9.

For quantitative analysis, software programs such as SPSS, STATA, R, S-plus, SAS, AMOS and LISREL are all used. Excel, too, has a lot to offer in terms of statistical analysis. You can buy a support program called XLstat that gives you access to extra statistical functions within Excel. In this chapter about analysis, we'll be using SPSS (from version 17 onwards, the name PASW is also used, but SPSS is the name most commonly used for this program). The makers of this software launch a new version every year. In 2011, version 20 will appear. This book refers to version 15. More recent versions differ in terms of layout but not so much in terms of program content.

SPSS or PASW

PASW® Statistics 18

Install PASW Statistics 18
Install Amos 18
Install SPSS Inc. Data Access Pack
Install PASW Statistics 18 Python Essentials
Install PASW Statistics 18 R Essentials
Install PASW Reports for Surveys Components
Install PASW Smartreader
Installation Instructions
Browse the DVD
Exit

www.spss.com

In addition to the SPSS examples given in this chapter, you will also find a short introduction to SPSS on the website. Several principal functions are explained in the file entitled 'Introduction SPSS'. For more information about SPSS you can consult one of the extensive manuals that have been published about this program. You'll find references to literature and web links on the website. Look in the section entitled 'Chapter 8', under the tab Extra material.

content and In this chapter we will only be discussing the most general statistical techni-
objectives ques. You will find information about how to describe two characteristics, namely univariate analysis (Section 8.3) and bivariate analyses (Section 8.4), divided into the differences and similarities between attributes and how to present them. The aim is to introduce you to the possibilities of quantitative analysis, and to teach you how to make the right decisions. You also have to interpret the results in the correct way. In practice you'll be using these general statistical techniques the most. Only very rarely will it be necessary to delve deeper into your analysis and compare or assess more than one variable at the same time, or come up with a *causal model* – the effect of a number of attributes (predictors) on variables (outcomes). These subjects are beyond the scope of this book.

WEBSITE For students who want to explore specific statistical topics at greater length, or researchers that need to use them, there are references to literature in the section entitled 'Chapter 8', under the tab Extra material.

Learning objectives

By the time you get to the end of this chapter, you will be familiar with several simple descriptive analyses, involving one or two variables, be able to carry out such analyses and interpret the results. You will also be able to recognize hypotheses and know how to formulate them. You will also be able to illustrate your results using graphs, tables or charts. You will be familiar with several properties that summarize these variables. You will also know how you to derive (calculate) these properties, for example, averages and means. Finally, after studying this chapter, you should be able to process a few basic statistical techniques using SPSS.

Box 8.1

8.1   Terms Used in Quantitative Analysis

In this section we will describe a number of terms that are used in quantitative analysis. Some of these terms have already been mentioned in previous chapters, we'll elaborate a bit more here. The concept 'level of measurement' will also be introduced. You will need this concept in order to make the right decisions for your analysis.

8.1.1   *Terminology*

A *data matrix* is a rectangular sheet, similar to an Excel spreadsheet, with *data matrix* rows and columns, containing all the data you have collected. In the cells, you can insert all the information that you have collected per unit (case). Generally speaking, data matrices are generated by computers.

On the website, under 'Introduction SPSS', you'll find an example of a data WEBSITE matrix.

A *variable* is a characteristic of an object, for example, an attribute of a per- *variables* son that has taken part in your research. These variables can have various values. For example 'age' is a variable. A person could be 49 years old, or 12. Roughly speaking there are two types of variables:
- *Independent variables*: also known as predictors because they influence situations. The independent variable itself is fixed, but it causes a change.
- *Dependent variables*: these are variables that change under the influence of independent variables. They are also known as effect variables or cause variables.

Variables come in *categories*, i.e., all the values that the variable can have. *categories* Age, for example, may be registered in whole years. Temperature could be reflected in degrees (Celsius, for example). Opinions may range from 'completely disagree' to 'completely agree'. If a person says he's 49, then that's his *score* for the variable 'age'.

Variable categories are reflected in digits. For example, for the variable 'gender', men may be '0' and women '1'. For 'age', if someone is 39, you would enter '39'. For 'level of education' you could give primary school a '1', secondary school a '2', college a '3', university bachelor degree '4', master's degree '5', PhD '6'. What do these variables mean? Is someone who has a degree twice as educated as someone who has completed high school? Of course not!

8.1.2   Measurement Levels of Variables

definition The *measurement level* of a variable indicates the degree to which you can use the values (that you have assigned to the categories) in calculations. There are four measurement levels that can be used to measure variables, from low to high: nominal, ordinal, interval and ratio. When you process the information statistically, the measurement level is the deciding precondition for choosing your analysis technique (descriptive and inferential). The same goes for choosing graphs. We will now talk about these different measurement levels, one at a time.

Nominal

Variables with a nominal measurement level are made up of separate categories. There are no other values between two categories; they are what are known as *discrete* categories. Categories using nominal variables cannot be used for calculations, but that is not their purpose anyway: the assigned digits are merely codes. They are also called qualitative. Examples of nominal variables would be respondent demographics, such as level of education (primary school, high school, bachelor's degree etc., see Table 8.1), gender (male/ female), state of residence (Alabama, Alaska, Arizona, Arkansas etc.) and marital status (single, married, divorced, widowed).

Table 8.1   Nominal measurement level: State of residence

State of residence	Category
Alabama	1
Alaska	2
Arizona	3
Arkansas	4
California	5
Colorado	6

dichotomous Gender has a special place as a nominal variable. This category can only ever have two values, namely male or female. For this reason it is also known as *dichotomous*.

dummies Sometimes survey questions can have *more than one answer*. The way these are coded is to use dichotomous variables: if the response option has been ticked, then it is noted as a '1', if not, then it is noted as a '0'. In this case, the dichotomous variable is called a *dummy*. We talked about this in Section 6.2.5. Table 8.2 illustrates an example of these dummy variables.

Table 8.2   Dummy categories for multiple responses

Favorite entertainment venue	Category
restaurant	1 = yes, 0 = no
bar	1 = yes, 0 = no
movies	1 = yes, 0 = no
night club	1 = yes, 0 = no
theatre	1 = yes, 0 = no
concert	1 = yes, 0 = no
sports game	1 = yes, 0 = no

Ordinal

Even if you can't calculate with the value of some categories, the variables may be ranked. Examples of these are level of education, socio-economic status, level of satisfaction and opinions about specific subjects. These are variables with ordinal measurement levels. They have the same properties as nominal variables plus one new property. These variables will also not have many categories and are qualitative (discrete), but because they reflect a ranking, they are measured at a slightly higher level: ordinal (see Table 8.3).

Table 8.3   Ordinal measurement level: level of education

Level of education	Category
Primary school	1
High school	2
College	3
Bachelor's degree	4
Master's degree	5
PhD	6

Interval

Variables at interval level can be used for calculations: they are quantitative. The intervals between two categories (or values) are *equal*, the codes assigned to the values are numerical and the values are continuous, which means that any value between two points is possible (see Slotboom, 2008). Examples of interval variables are temperature and IQ. There are two restrictions that limit these variables from being measured at the highest level:

- Firstly there is no '*meaningful zero point*'. Take temperature in degrees Celsius. At some point it was decided that 'zero degrees Celsius' was the zero point given that water freezes at the temperature. This zero point is therefore artificial: it is based on an agreement.
- The difference in temperature between 5 and 10 °C is equal to the difference between 10 and 15 °C: the intervals are therefore *equal*. However, it is not possible to claim that 20 °C is twice as hot as 10 °C. People do say this, but statistically speaking it is not true that 20 °C is twice as hot as 10 °C.

Likert scales In special cases we assign an interval measurement level to variables that were originally measured at ordinal level. This is the case with Likert scales, for instance. Suppose you want to assess opinions about a particular subject using statements or items, such as those about being environmentally conscious (Table 8.4). You then aggregate the items into one factor by adding the scores of each statement (the so-called sum of the scores). This aggregated factor is then analyzed at interval level.

Table 8.4   Likert scale questions about how to best protect the environment

To protect the environment, it is necessary to:	1 Agree completely	2 Agree	3 Disagree	4 Disagree completely
Take public transport more often	☐	☐	☐	☐
Separate garbage	☐	☐	☐	☐
Use ozone depleting gasses as little as possible	☐	☐	☐	☐
Reduce carbon emissions	☐	☐	☐	☐

Ratio

Variables with a low measurement level, such as nominal and ordinal variables, are restricted when it comes to applying certain analysis techniques. Interval and ratio variables (the highest measurement levels) don't have these restrictions. Examples of ratio variables are: hours worked, income in dollars or age in years. Variables at this level are numeric, the values can be used for calculations, i.e., they are quantitative. Not only that, they have absolute zero points and *equal, meaningful* relation to each other; and they have the properties of interval measurement level. These are all properties that allow calculations, i.e., they can be counted (numbers). Because the intervals and the relationships between them are equal, and they have a zero point, it is possible to calculate proportions between two values. This means that these proportions are meaningful. So someone who is 30 is in fact three times as old as someone who is 10. If the number of hours worked is 0, then it means that that person has not worked, and so on.

You have to bear in mind that these measurement levels can change as soon as you manipulate the variables. If you subdivide age or income into groups then the measurement level is no longer ratio, but ordinal. This is because the groups are ranked, which means that the original relationships (proportions) disappear.

In Figure 8.1 we give an overview of all measurement levels.

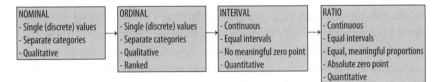

NOMINAL	ORDINAL	INTERVAL	RATIO
- Single (discrete) values	- Single (discrete) values	- Continuous	- Continuous
- Separate categories	- Separate categories	- Equal intervals	- Equal intervals
- Qualitative	- Qualitative	- No meaningful zero point	- Equal, meaningful proportions
	- Ranked	- Quantitative	- Absolute zero point
			- Quantitative

Figure 8.1   Diagram showing measurement levels

The last column in the Variable View window of Data Editor gives you measurement level options for the variables. In SPSS you have three options:
- NOMINAL for nominal variables;
- ORDINAL for ordinal variables;
- SCALE for interval and ratio variables. Why have these two been combined? Because anything from interval level and above normally use the same analysis techniques. Have a look at Figure 8.2.

Assigning measurement levels in SPSS

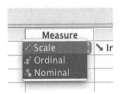

Figure 8.2   Data entry screen measurement levels in SPSS

On the website, under the Introduction to SPSS, you'll find more information about using measurement levels in SPSS. We strongly recommend that you read through this introduction before you start using SPSS.

8.2   Preparing for the Analysis: Formulating Hypotheses

definition of hypothesis

When you start your research project, you most probably have *expectations* about the results. You can define these expectations in the form of hypotheses. Hypotheses are assumptions about the results of your analysis, to do with the research population that can be tested. Take note: we are talking about statistical hypotheses here! In everyday language: based on your theory, you predict answers to your research question and using quantitative analysis you demonstrate that the results of *this particular* study (for this *population*) are correct. Needless to say these assumptions should not be completely baseless; you have to support them with the right arguments. For this you turn to the literature, normally in the form of articles from previous research results and theories.

confidence interval

When can you establish that you were right, that your hypotheses were correct? You can only do that once you are confident that you can show that your statements are valid for your sample. How sure do you have to be? You are sure when you can prove that your results are not founded on coincidence. What is the level of coincidence then? What is the margin of error? In most cases you have to be 95% (or more) certain (confident) that the results are not based on coincidence: a negligible probability. How small is that? Generally speaking this probability should be less than 5%. This is referred to as the *significance level*. You then have a maximum degree of 'uncertainty' of 5%, i.e., that is the risk that you have drawn the wrong conclusion. If you carry out a test 100 times, and you come up with the same result 96 times, then the chance of coincidence is 4%, which is insignificantly small.

significance

How do we get to a confidence interval of 95? This is a question that the researcher has to answer before the research starts. Sometimes you can opt for a different confidence interval: you could opt for 90 (for smaller samples) or 99 (for larger samples). For the rest it is determined by all sorts of factors, such as the issue of how precise the findings have to be for that particular research group. Most researchers opt for a 95% confidence interval. You calculate this 'confidence' using formulas. If the results are not based on coincidence, then they are *significant*.

Statistical hypotheses normally consist of two parts:
- A null hypothesis: the *basic assumption*, also known as H_0, is upheld as long as there is insufficient evidence for an alternative. The assumptions are mostly things like 'no correlation', 'no difference' or 'no effect'.
- An alternative hypothesis: the *alternative assumption*, or H_1. These are normally the hypotheses that assume a correlation, a difference or an effect.

Text box 8.2 gives examples of hypotheses.

Box 8.2

Examples of hypotheses

H_0 : there is no correlation between level of education and income.

H_1 : there is a correlation between level of education and income.

H_0 : there is no difference in music preference between older and younger people.

H_1 : there is a difference in music preference between older and younger people.

H_0 : men and women enjoy equal levels of income.

H_1 : men enjoy a higher level of income than women.

H_0 : work experience has no effect on level of income.

H_1 : work experience has a positive effect on level of income.

If you can prove that your findings, based on quantitative analysis, are not based on coincidence, then you reject the null hypothesis in favor of the alternative hypothesis. You only do this once you are certain about the results, i.e., that they are significant.

You will find more about hypothesis testing theory (inferential statistics) on the website, under the tab Extra material, in the section 'Chapter 8'.

8.3   Univariate Analyses

Descriptions of one variable at a time are also known as *univariate analyses*. What exactly do we analyze? We analyze data: information! A dataset comprises variables from a set of cases. By 'cases' we mean the number of participants (respondents) that have taken part in your research, or the set of completed questionnaires, the observations, research elements, the sample and so on. These datasets are what we base our analysis on.

You can present univariate descriptions in several different ways. We'll talk about three of them here:

- *Frequency distributions* of attributes. This is when you indicate how often a category (of an attribute) occurs, for example in proportion to the total number of cases.

- *Graphs* (charts) of an attribute.
- *Parameters.* A parameter summarizes an attribute in terms of one specific characteristic. For example, you could look at the central tendency in the dispersion or at the range across which all the observation are located, which is known as the dispersion of the variable. There are two kinds of statistical indicators: *central tendencies* and *measures of variability.*

WEBSITE In this section we will only be dealing with descriptive statistics. For a short introduction to inferential statistics, we refer you to the Extra material for Chapters 3 and 8 on the website.

8.3.1   *Frequency Distribution*

Variables are normally presented by indicating how often the scores occur. You can do this by presenting them in tables showing the frequency distribution. You need to know how these tables are generated before you know how to analyze them. Frequency distributions can be very simple (see Text box 8.3).

Example of frequency distribution	
marital status	**number of observations**
married	6
single	4
divorced	1
widowed	1

Box 8.3

Text box 8.3 only gives information about occurance of a score per category. You can give more information by giving the percentages relative to the total number of cases. By doing so you will be giving a *relative* frequency table (see Figure 8.3). We will now discuss how this table is compiled.

Marital status

		Frequency	Percent	Valid Percent	Cumulative Percent
Valid	married/living together	6	50.0	50.0	50.0
	single	4	33.3	33.3	83.3
	divorced	1	8.3	8.3	91.7
	widow(er)	1	8.3	8.3	100.0
	Total	12	100.0	100.0	

Figure 8.3   Relative frequency distribution of marital status

You need percentages to work out relative frequency. When you percenta- *percenta-*
gize incidence, you express the number of observations in relation to the *gizing*
total number of observations, as a percentage that is. In Figure 8.3, 6 of the
12 respondents were married or living together. The relative frequency is
therefore 6/12 → 0.50 or 50% of the total number of cases. Written as a formula, it looks like this:

$$Percentage = \frac{frequency}{total} \times 100\%$$

Relative frequency tables in SPSS

To create a relative frequency table in SPSS, you give the following command: Analyze → Descriptive Statistics →

Frequencies → in the dialogue box (see figure) select the variable in the 'Variable(s)' box. Click OK.

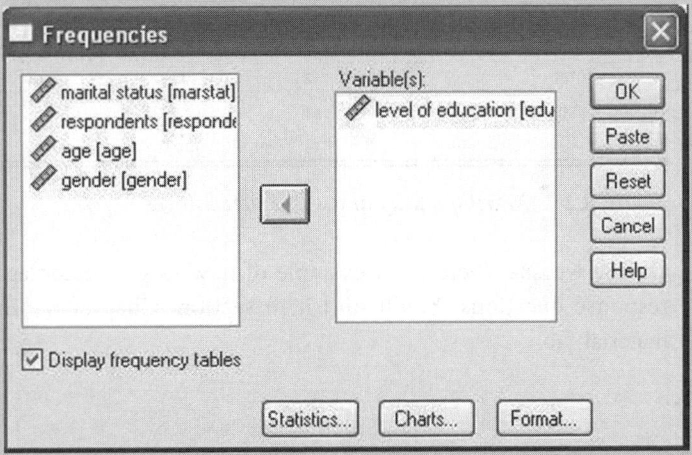

Dialogue box Frequencies in SPSS

Box 8.4

Figure 8.3 was generated by SPSS. Text box 8.4 shows the relevant commands. On the far left, you'll see 'valid', 'missing' and 'total'. We'll talk about those later. The category descriptions are also given ('Value Labels' according to SPSS).

Figure 8.4 contains four columns containing figures:

1 Under 'Frequency' you'll find the number of incidence per category.
2 Under 'Percent' you'll find the percentage per category of the total number of incidence, including missing cases.
3 Column 'Valid Percent' contains the number of *valid* incidence in relation to the total. The table has two totals (2 × total). The total at the bottom is 13. There are 13 people in the sample. The total above that one is 12 and it reflects the total number of valid recordings. One person did not fill in their marital status. The percentage is calculated over the total number of *given responses*, and the non-response is not included. That answer is called 'missing' in SPSS language.
4 On the far right you see the 'Cumulative Percent': the sum of all observations is 100%.

Figure 8.4 gives the results.

Marital status

		Frequency	Percent	Valid Percent	Cumulative Percent
Valid	married/living together	6	46.2	50.0	50.0
	single	4	30.8	33.3	83.3
	divorced	1	7.7	8.3	91.7
	widow(er)	1	7.7	8.3	100.0
	Total	12	92.3	100.0	
Missing	System	1	7.7		
Total		13	100.0		

Figure 8.4   Marital status and valid percentages

On the website, there is an example of how to get percentages for multiple response questions. You'll find it in section 'Chapter 8', under the Extra material tab.

8.3.2 Graphs for One Variable

One way that researchers often use to display their results is by putting them into charts (or graphs, plots). Charts have the added advantage that they make the results clearly accessible to the broader public. Even those who don't know much about statistics and figures find it easy to read graphs, provided you choose the right type of graph of course. Your choice will depend on two things: your aim (what aspect of the variable are your trying to show?) and the measurement level for that variable. We'll illustrate this using the following types of graphs: pie charts, bar charts and histograms, line charts ('ordinary' and 'cumulative'), box plots and scatter plots (see Figure 8.5).

The most important function that a chart has is to illustrate clearly your results. There is no point in illustrating two values in a graph, for example gender. If you know how many women there are in a sample, then you automatically know how many men there are. Start with variables that have three or more categories.

Pie charts
Pie charts are an effective way of showing the *relative size* of the various categories. At a glance you can see which has the smallest share, and which has the largest, but it only works for those variables that have a few categories at most, such as marital status. If you tried to display age in a pie chart, it would just be confusing. This is why pie charts are only really useful for variables with a low measurement level, i.e., nominal or ordinal.

Bar charts
The same criteria that we have just mentioned apply to bar charts: low measurement level, to illustrate the relative size of the various categories, and only if there are a few categories. Each value gets its own bar. You can easily see which categories have a higher number of observations than others: the 'tallest' bar.

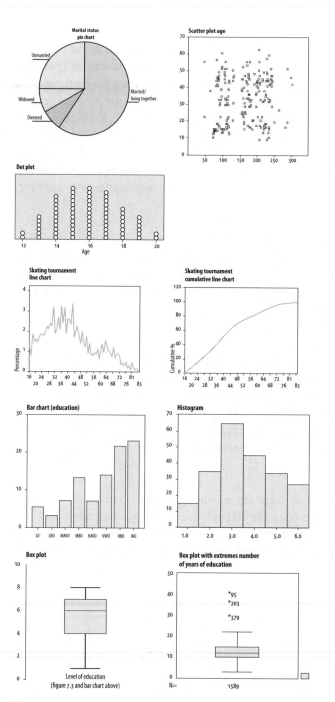

Figure 8.5   Overview of the various types of graphs in SPSS

Histograms

If the attribute has a higher measurement level, i.e., interval or ratio, then histograms are a good way of illustrating the results. This kind of chart is used to illustrate the *shape* of a distribution. It is really a bar chart for continuous variables (Huizingh, 2008). To reflect the continuous character of the variables, the bars are right next to each other as opposed to those that have a space between each bar. The boundaries of each category are adjoined. The shape the chart takes may show that the variables reach a peak in the middle bar, sloping down on either side. This kind of distribution is also known as a 'bell shape' or a 'Gauss curve', and it has special properties. We'll discuss this at greater length in Section 8.3.4.

Sometimes interval and ratio variables are also shown in bar charts, as illustrated in Figure 8.6 (number of children in the family). This data could also have been shown in a histogram because the categories are adjoined. The bar chart was most probably chosen in this case because there are only a few categories and because the figures are well illustrated in this way and can easily be compared.

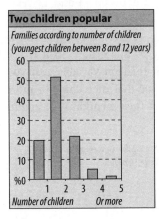

Figure 8.6   Bar chart showing number of children (Source: Volkskrant, February 4, 2003)

Figure 8.7 gives an example of a rotated histogram showing the age distribu- *special* tion of men and women. Statistics bureaus often use this type of chart. They *graphs* are also known as 'population pyramids'. Figure 8.7 shows that there is a 'bulge' between 40 and 60. This is an indication of an ageing population. There's another peak just above 60: the baby boomers that were born just after the Second World War.

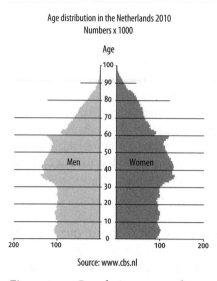

Age distribution in the Netherlands 2010
Numbers x 1000

Source: www.cbs.nl

Figure 8.7   Population pyramid 2010 (source: cbs.nl)

Figure 8.8 resembles a bar chart, but on its side (rotated). It illustrates the results of a study into the lifestyles of those aged between 14 and 18 years (*Volkskrant*, November 25, 2005). It is indeed a rotated bar chart, but illustrating more than one variable. Each 'style group' is given a bar that shows the percentage *of all the respondents* that belong to this group. So it is not one figure, but thirteen figures (one figure with thirteen variables). If you look at the percentages and add them up you'll see that they come to more than 100. If you look at the subtitle you'll see that they mention this: 'multiple answers possible'.

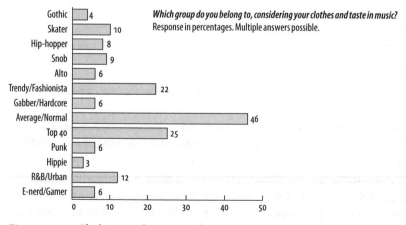

Figure 8.8   Clothing and music style group

Line charts

If you're interested in trends, then line graphs are a good way to illustrate them. Line graphs are used to illustrate variables for interval and ratio measurement levels. The number of categories is unlimited: normally there are many, such as numbers or ages. Developments over time can also be illustrated using line charts. Time would then be an extra variable; we'll discuss this in Section 8.4.2. The line chart (showing age distribution for respondents in a skating competition (Figure 8.5)) shows a changeable situation with a few peaks. Where there are peaks it means that there are a lot of people in this age group. But it is possible that this type of chart does not give a good reflection of the distribution. Cumulative line charts may be a better option. Figure 8.5 first shows an ordinary line chart, giving the age of the skaters, followed by a cumulative line chart. This one starts with 0% and ends with 100% once all the information has been included in the chart. What is noticeable is that the line rises sharply at the point where the ordinary chart shows a lot of outliers (i.e., the highest figures). In other words: the higher the figures, the steeper the line.

Box plots

If you want to show variables at ordinal measurement level, then box plots are a good option. The basis for these is the median, i.e., the observation that lies in the middle (see Section 8.3.3 for an explanation of this concept). You indicate where the middle of the distribution lies (50%) and how the observations above and below are dispersed. Other noticeable aspects are:

- there are vertical lines projecting from either side of the box ending in a horizontal line. These horizontal lines indicate the start (0%) and the end (100%) of the distribution, in other words: the other 50%. Because of their shape, box plots are also known as box-and-whisker plots or diagrams;
- the median is indicated by a thick horizontal line in the distribution: it shows the 50% median of the observations. Above and below this line, the two 'little boxes' both represent 25% of the observations. Figure 8.5 shows the 50% of the median observations in the box (which means in this case that half of the respondents have a high school education, see Table 8.3);
- Outliers are illustrated using dots, as shown in Figure 8.5.

Box diagrams are not useful if you want to show both the middle 50% and the outliers.

Scatter plots and dot plots

Scatter plots are ideal to illustrate the distribution of dependent variable scores (of high measurement levels) and how they relate to one another. Figure 8.5 gives an example of the distribution of age in a sample, i.e., univariate. Scatter plots normally illustrate two variables so that you can compare and analyze their distribution (see Section 8.4.2 as well). Another way of showing the distribution in the score of one variable is to use a dot plot. Figure 8.5 gives an example of a dot plot. Dot plots show you if a variable is unevenly distributed and where the outliers are positioned. You can use dot plots for both continuous and discrete variables.

Table 8.5 gives an overview of the characteristics of the various kinds of charts and graphs.

charts in SPSS and Excel You can generate charts using both SPSS and Excel, with one exception: histograms. In Excel, histograms come standard as a bar chart. Under the charts button, you'll find several types of graphs, including column and bar charts. This distinction is quite confusing since we (and SPSS) use different names for them. What Excel refers to as a column chart is actually a bar chart, just like the bar chart in SPSS. What they refer to as a bar chart is the same as a column chart, but on its side: i.e., rotated. If you want to create a proper histogram, then you need to use SPSS. Look under their menu 'graphs' and choose the right option for what you need. Choosing the right program to generate your graphs depends on a number of factors. Sometimes Excel has the right graph for what you are trying to display, sometimes SPSS is better.

WEBSITE On the website, under the Introduction to SPSS tab, you'll find several examples of how to make graphs in SPSS.

Table 8.5   Characteristics of charts

Type of chart	Characteristics
pie chart	– single categories – nominal (or ordinal) measurement levels – area is total number of cases (100%) – 'slice' is percentage (the relative number) – gives insight into the category shares
bar charts	– single categories – nominal (or ordinal) measurement levels – the height of the bar is the (relative) number of cases per category – gives insight into relationships between the categories
histograms	– limited number of categories – interval or ratio measurement level – categories are adjoined – gives insight into the shape of the distribution
line charts	– unlimited number of categories – interval or ratio measurement level – categories are adjoined – to analyze trends and developments over time
cumulative line charts	– unlimited number of categories – interval or ratio measurement level – categories are adjoined – start at 0% and end at 100% – gives insight into trends and developments over time
box plots	– from ordinal measurement level – ignores outliers – gives insight into middle 50%
scatter plots	– interval or ratio measurement level – normally used to show results of two attributes – gives insight into dispersion of scores in relation to each other

8.3.3 Measures of Central Tendency

Measures of central tendency are statistical indicators that describe the middle of a distribution, of a variable. Below we will describe a few of these.

Mode

The category of a variable that occurs most often is called the mode. The mode can be applied to variables *from* a *nominal* measurement level onwards, i.e., all variables. One advantage is that this measure can also be used for variables that are 'non-numeric'. The category 'married', for instance, is the mode for the variable marital status in Table 8.6 because most of the scores were found in this category (50% married). The notation is: X_{mod}. Text box 8.5 contains numerical examples of modes. The mode is easy to spot in diagrams and charts. Look at the bar chart illustrating lifestyle groups in Figure 8.8. The mode is 'Ordinary/Normalo' because this bar is the longest.

Example of a mode	
Given the following observations:	The mode is the most frequently occurring number, which is 9 because 9 occurs 6 times.
1111222333445666677889999999	

Box 8.5

bimodal distribution Sometimes the distribution produces not one mode, but two. The distribution table in Table 8.6 shows this: both 'married/living together' and 'single' occur most often, both at 34.5%. This is known as *bimodal*, because it has two peaks.

Table 8.6   Bimodal distribution of marital status

Marital status		Frequency	Percent	Valid Percent	Cumulative Percent
Valid	married/living together	10	34.5	34.5	34.5
	single	10	34.5	34.5	69.0
	divorced	4	13.8	13.8	82.8
	widowed	5	17.2	17.2	100.0
	Total	29	100.0	100.0	

Median

The median is the *middle* value in a distribution, or the category that contains the middle value. The median therefore indicates the exact middle of a (sorted) distribution, the point which separates the one 50% from the other (see Text box 8.6). The notation is either X_{mod} or $X_{.50}$. Medians can be applied from *ordinal* measurement level so it is possible to calculate the median for 'level of education'. You can find the median in the category 'High school education' in Table 8.7. How can you tell? By looking at the *cumulative* percentages. The category containing the fiftieth percentile (i.e., the middle value) is the median category. In this case that category is between 38.5% and 53.8%.

Example of a median	
Given the following scores:	Suppose the values were as follows:
11112223334456666778899999999	11112223334456666778899999
In this row of values the median is 6, it is the 14th in a total of 27 values (in this case numbers), an uneven number.	This row has 26 values: an *even* number. The median lies between the 13th and 14th observation, between 5 and 6. The median would then be between the two middle scores: 5.5.

Box 8.6

Table 8.7   Median level of education

Level of education				
	Number	Percentage	Valid percentage	Cumulative percentage
7th/8th grade	2	15.4	7.7	15.4
9th grade	3	23.1	23.1	38.5
10th grade	2	15.4	15.4	53.8
11th grade	2	15.4	15.4	69.2
12th grade (no diploma)	2	15.4	15.4	84.6
High school graduate	2	15.4	15.4	100.0
Total	13	100.0	100.0	

Sometimes separate variable scores are grouped together in classes. On the website, in the section entitled 'Chapter 8' (tab Extra material), you will find more information about how to best go about dividing the scores into classes, and how to calculate the median once you have made this division.

Mean

You calculate the mean by adding all the scores and dividing them by the total number of scores.

arithmetic mean The average is also known as the 'arithmetic mean'. Text box 8.7 shows the formula for calculating the average. The notations is X_{ave} or $\overline{X}$ for a sample. If you are talking about the average for a population, then the notation is σ. Means can be calculated for variables from measurement level interval or ratio. Why is this? Means are only meaningful if you can use the values in calculations. For instance, you could say that the mean life expectancy of people these days is 85, but it's nonsense to say that the mean marital status is 'married'. There is no such thing as an 'mean marital status'! Adverts sometimes say that the candidate should have 'an average level of education'. But we've shown that you can't really speak of an average education because the measurement level is too low. The reason you'll hear people speaking about means is that it is a unit of measure that people are familiar with, one that is used often. Median is a far less familiar term but this of course is not a valid argument for using the term 'average' all the time.

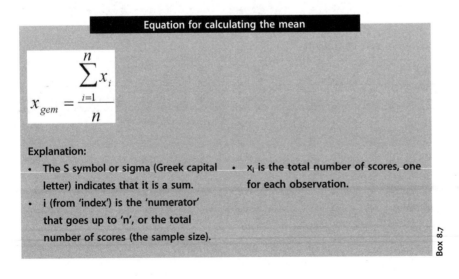

Equation for calculating the mean

$$x_{gem} = \frac{\sum_{i=1}^{n} x_i}{n}$$

Explanation:

- The S symbol or sigma (Greek capital letter) indicates that it is a sum.
- i (from 'index') is the 'numerator' that goes up to 'n', or the total number of scores (the sample size).
- x_i is the total number of scores, one for each observation.

Box 8.7

If you have five people aged 15, 16, 17, 18 and 19, then their average age is (15 + 16 + 17 + 18 + 19)/5 = 17 years. But if there is more than one person per age category, then you have to take this into account: you calculate the average as follows (see Text box 8.8): you take the sum of all the values times the total number of values and divide the result by the total number of values.

The arithmetic median

Suppose you've asked 30 people how old they are. Their responses are given in two columns showing, for instance, that 10 of them are 25 years old. To calculate the average, you first take the sum of all the values:

	Number	Age	Number × age
	2	22	44
	10	25	250
	12	35	420
	6	41	246
Total	30		960

You divided the sum by the total number of observations: 960/30 = 32, which is then the mean age.

Sometimes values don't have the same weight. An example would be your *weighted* final exam result for statistics. The exams would probably count for more *mean* than your assignments. The lecturers would then assign your results different weights (artificially). If you have to calculate the average, then you would take this weighting into account. You do use the same formula, though, as you did for arithmetic mean. Table 8.8 gives an example:

Table 8.8   Weighted mean final mark statistics

Part	Weighting	Mark	Weighting × grade
assignment 1	1x	6	6
assignment 2	1x	8	8
exam 1	3x	5	15
exam 2	3x	5.4	16.2
project report	2x	7	14
Total	10		59.2
Final mark			59.2/10 = 5.92

 On the website, in the section entitled 'Chapter 8' (tab Extra material), you will find more information about how best to go about calculating the mean for a variable that has been divided into classes.

central tendencies in SPSS SPSS can calculate central tendencies for you. There are several ways to do this. For univariate descriptions, the methods used most often are as follows:
- via Analyze → Descriptive Statistics → Descriptives → Options;
- via Analyze → Descriptive Statistics → Frequencies → Statistics;
- via Analyze → Descriptive Statistics → Explore → Statistics.

The average (mean) normally appears automatically in 'Statistics' and 'Options'. You can change this according to the measurement level. Also, many of the SPSS processes give you the option 'Descriptives' in which you can request the various statistical indicators.

8.3.4   Measures of Variability

Sometimes medians don't give enough information. The average number of sick days may not give enough information about how the sick leave is distributed. The organization may need to know what the two outliers are: the minimum and maximum number of days, and how often they occur. For this kind of information, distribution measures would be better because these answer the question of how the observations correlate, in other words, how the scores of the variables are dispersed.

Figure 8.9 shows an Excel graph illustrating the distribution of the variable 'age' (on the y-axis) among 250 people (on the x-axis). As you can see, the distribution ranges from 10 to about 62: i.e., the ages vary from 10 to 62 years.

Figure 8.10 gives the dispersion of sick leave among 250 staff members in an organization. The graph shows that most members of staff take between 0 and 5 days sick leave per six months (there's a black patch of scores at the bottom of the graph). Above this there are fewer scores: the number of sick days increases, but the number of people that are sick for this length of time drops. The distribution of sick leave ranges from 0 to 82, over a period of six months. We will now discuss some dispersion measures.

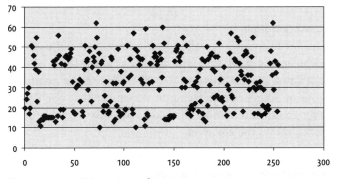

Figure 8.9   Dispersion of age

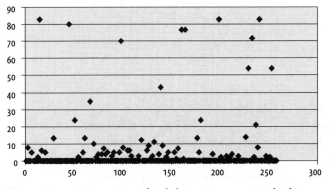

Figure 8.10   Dispersion of sick leave over a period of six months

Range

The simplest way to show the dispersion of a variable is to show the range. Simply put it is the difference between the lowest and the highest scores. You can try to read the range from Figures 8.9 and 8.10, but often it's not that easy. The ages range between 10 and 62 years (the highest score is just above the '60' mark): the range is therefore 52 years. For the number of sick days, the distribution is between 0 and 82: the range is therefore 82.

For Table 8.7 (the distribution of level of education) the range is harder to express in figures. Whatever the case may be, it will be between 7th Grade and High school graduate. It's clear that range is easier to establish for numerical variables.

WEBSITE Another indicator is the interquartile range, the distribution of the middle 50% of the scores. On the website, in the section entitled 'Chapter 8' (tab Extra material), you will find an example of an interquartile range.

Variance and standard deviation
For continuous variables from an interval and ratio level, you can use *variance* as the dispersion measure, or *standard deviation*, a derivative of this. What is variation? It's not an easy thing to describe: *the average quadratic difference from the mean*. Don't bother trying to remember that one! What we're actually talking about here is how the scores are distributed around the mean. Text box 8.9 shows the equation.

Calculating variance and standard deviation

Variation equation:

$$\sigma^2 = \frac{\sum_{i}^{N} (x_i - \mu)^2}{N}$$

Explanation:

- σ^2 (*or* s^2): if the population distribution is known, then the notation σ^2 is used (Greek letter sigma lower case). If the distribution is not known, then the so-called sample variance is used, i.e., s^2.
- The equation between the brackets means that, for each observation, the difference between its score and the mean has to be looked at. The notation for the population is μ, for a sample x_{ave} or $\bar{x}$. We take the

square of the difference. If we didn't do this, then once all the differences were added together, the result would be 'zero', which is not what we want. We want to look at the 'dispersion', at 'absolute' differences.
- The quadratic differences are aggregated, i.e., they are added together.
- The sum of these scores is divided by the total number of observations: this gives the quadratic variation.

Box 8.9

This *variance* is a measure that is squared. The disadvantage is that if the difference is twice as large, then the variation will be four times as large, making this measure difficult to use and interpret. One solution is not to apply the square, but you can't just do this: you have to take the square root of this variation. The square root of the variance () gives you the *standard deviation*.

In the book we show you how to calculate the population variance. On the website, in the section entitled 'Chapter 8' (tab Extra material), you will find an example of sample variance.

WEBSITE

Standard deviation has a few unusual properties:

properties of standard deviation

- If the graph is symmetrical and shaped like a bell, then it is what is known as the *Gauss curve* or the 'normal distribution'. The input used for creating Gaussian curves is the average and the standard deviation. On the x-axis you put all the scores of the distribution, and you put the average in the middle.
- When it comes to interpreting the distribution of the scores in terms of the average and the standard deviation, you can use a few standard rules. Have a look at the bell-shape in Figure 8.11. You can see that the scores are evenly distributed (it is symmetrical), namely:
  - 68% of all the scores are between the mean plus or minus once the standard deviation. Look at the first two lines from the mean (the middle).
  - 95% of all the scores are between the mean plus or minus twice the standard deviation. Look at the second set of lines from the mean.
  - 99% of all the scores are between the mean plus or minus three times the standard deviation. Look at the second set of lines from the mean.

This empirical rule is valid for all variables that have a 'normal' distribution. They are also known as the *1 sigma*, *2 sigma* and *3 sigma intervals* (68.26%, 95.44% and 99.74%). You can generate a graph like this for all continuous variables with a normal distribution. By the way, this also applies if the distribution is not 'normal'.

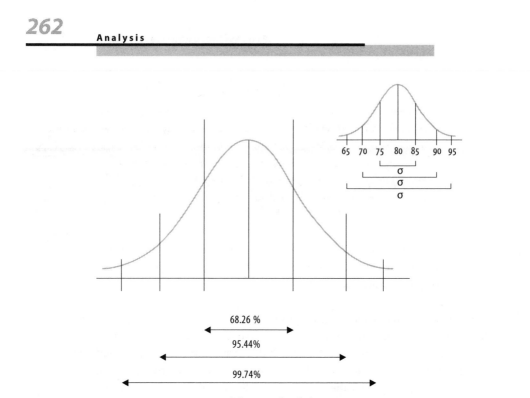

Figure 8.11   Properties of the standard deviation

On the website, in the section entitled 'Chapter 8' (tab Extra material), you will find an example of how to calculate the variation for variables that have been divided into classes.

An example of a variation calculation

Look at the distribution of the variable 'age' in the table below:

Variation in age

Age (X)	n	n.X	(X-$\bar{X}$)	(X-$\bar{X}$)²	n(X-$\bar{X}$)²
10	2	20	-5.6	31.36	62.72
11	1	11	-4.6	21.16	21.16
12	2	24	-3.6	12.96	25.92
13	5	65	-2.6	6.76	33.80
14	11	154	-1.6	2.56	28.16
15	13	195	-0.6	0.36	4.68
16	13	208	0.4	0.16	2.08
17	12	204	1.4	1.96	23.52
18	8	144	2.4	5.76	46.08
19	6	114	3.4	11.56	69.36
Total	73	1.139			317.48
Mean		15.6			4.40

Explanation

The way you calculate variation is as follows:

- First calculate the mean (sum of all the scores divided by the total number of observations). This comes to 15.6.
- Calculate for each score (age) the deviation from the mean: the difference between each score and the mean. So 10 – 15.6 and 11 – 15.6 and 12 – 15.6 and so on.
- Calculate for each deviation (from the mean) the square (this is how you remove the 'minus' from the comparison), i.e., (-5.6)², (-4.6)², and so on.
- Calculate once more the mean of the deviation squared by taking the sum of all deviations and dividing them by the total number of observations, i.e., (31.36 × 2) + (21.16 × 1) + (12.96 × 2), and so on and divide the sum by 73 (total number of observations).
- Result: the variance = 4.4 (and the standard deviation is $\sqrt{4.4}$ = 2.098).

Box 8.10

interpreting
variance
and
standard
deviation

You won't find many references to specific information about variation and distribution in magazine and newspaper articles. What can you say about distribution once you know what the variation is? The higher the variation, the wider the distribution of a variable. A small variation means a narrow range, obviously. This means that all the scores were close to the mean. The only trouble is that the variation is actually a squared measurement. We have already noted that it is actually difficult to interpret. What is 'the square of an age' for instance? Or of 'working hours'? Length in centimeters then becomes centimeters squared (Slotboom, 2008). But this is not the measure we are talking about. Not only that, the variance can become huge because it is 'squared'. If the difference between two scores is twice as big, then the variance will be four times the size (Swanborn, 2010).

Looking at standard deviation gives us a way of assessing the distribution better. We take the square root of the variance so that the s (s) of s^2 (s^2) remains. Look for example at the distribution of 'number of sick days' in Figure 8.10. Suppose you research sick leave in two different departments. The average number of sick days is the same for both departments, but the standard deviation (distribution) is different. The one department has a narrow dispersion, the distribution of the number of days is close to the average. The other department has a much wider dispersion, there are people who have been sick for a very short period of time, and those who have been sick for a long time. The department with a narrow distribution is therefore more homogenous when it comes to sick leave. In the department with a wider dispersion, the distribution is more diverse. Information that is restricted to average number of sick days will not give you the full picture about sick leave in those departments. Looking at the distribution (dispersion) of sick leave is a much more informative way of doing it.

8.4   Bivariate Analyses

Your analysis is based on the description of the characteristics that you have researched. In the last section you were shown how to do, this dealing with one variable at a time. In this section we will be discussing how to go about describing two variables at the same time, such as income levels by gender, annual reports from different departments, level of education by income category, the list is endless. We'll mention a few options. Apart from cross tabulations (one table showing two frequency distributions), we'll also be discussing graphs that can handle two variables. But be careful! Comparing variables is not that useful if you can't test them. What do we mean by this? Well, you have to be sure that the results of your analysis can be extrapolated to the general population. You can only be sure of this if what you find is not coincidental. How sure do you have to be about this? Most researchers want to be at least 95% sure that their results are not random. We spoke about this in Section 8.2.

For more information about inferential statistics, with explanations and examples, visit our website and look in the sections entitled 'Chapter 3' and 'Chapter 8' (tab Extra material). You will also find references to literature on the subject.

8.4.1 Cross Tabulations

A cross tabulation shows incidence for two variables at the same time. It comprises *columns* (from the top to the bottom) and rows (from left to right). Normally the independent variables are shown in the columns and the dependent variables are shown in the rows. Each cell (the block giving the scores) gives the information that applies to both variables.

Table 8.9a shows a cross tab for the variables 'gender' (independent variable) and 'paid work' (dependent variable). The question to the respondent was whether they have a job that pays. Their gender was also noted. Each cell shows the *number of observations* for both variables. So in this cross tab there are 119 men who have a paid job. The last row and column gives the totals for each observation separately: 171 men and 82 women, of which 168 have paid work and 85 people do not.

As is the case with single frequency distributions, you can also reflect the frequencies as percentages. There are three ways to do this:
1 As *row percentages*, i.e., the scores as a percentage of the *row total*.
   You compare the percentages from top to bottom, so *by column* (comparing paid work versus no paid work).
   An example of this in Table 8.9b is: 119 men have paid work. That is 119/168 × 100 = 70.8% of all those with paid work. For men the percentage of total men with paid work is higher than 'no paid work' (61.2%).

2 As a *column percentage*, i.e., the scores in relation to the *column total*. You'll be comparing the percentages from left to right, so *by row* (comparing men and women).

Table 8.9c has an example of this: 119 men have paid work. That is 119/171 × 100% = 69.6% of the total number of men. The percentage of men with paid work is higher than the total of women with paid work (59.8%).

3 As a cell percentage, i.e., the scores in relation to the *total* (Table 8.9d). If 119 men have paid work, then that is 119/253 × 100% = 47% of all the respondents in the sample.

Table 8.9a   *Cross tabulation 'gender' and 'work': numbers*

	Men	Women	Total
paid work	119	49	168
no paid work	52	33	85
Total	171	82	253

Table 8.9b   *Cross tabulation 'gender' and 'work': row percentages*

	Men	Women	Total
paid work	119	49	168
	70.8%	29.2%	100.0%
no paid work	52	33	85
	61.2%	38.8%	100.0%
Total	171	82	253
	67.6%	32.4%	100.0%

Table 8.9c   *Cross tabulation 'gender' and 'work': column percentages*

	Men	Women	Total
paid work	119	49	168
	69.6%	59.8%	66.4%
no paid work	52	33	85
	30.4%	40.2%	33.6%
Total	171	82	253
	100.0%	100.0%	100.0%

Table 8.9d   Cross tabulation 'gender' and 'work': cell percentages

	Men	Women	Total
paid work	119	49	168
	47.0%	19.4%	66.4%
no paid work	52	33	85
	20.6%	13.0%	33.6%
Total	171	82	253
	67.6%	32.4%	100.0%

When you compare the figures in Table 8.9b, c and d, you must make sure that you compare the columns and the rows where they *intersect*, as shown in the figure in dark yellow!

Look at the row percentages in Table 8.9b. Of the people with paid work, 29.2% are women. That is less that the total percentage of women (32.4%), while the percentage of women without a paid job is higher (38.8%) than the total percentage. Among the men, the opposite applies: the total percentage is 67.6%, while 70.8% have paid work and 61.2% do not have a paid job. Men are more likely to have a paid job than women. Now look at the column percentages in 8.9c. Of the people who do have paid work (66.4%), the percentage is higher among men (69.6%) than women (59.8%), while more women than men don't have paid work.

Finally, the group of non-working women is the smallest at 13% of the total (Table 8.9d, cell percentages, which is a comparison of two variables at the same time.

Text box 8.11 explains how to generate cross tabs in SPSS. You will find an example of a cross tab generated and processed by SPSS in Figure 8.12.

On the website, in the section Introduction to SPSS, you will find information about how to create tables and how to adjust them to suit your needs.

WEBSITE

Box 8.11

Cross tabs in SPSS

Select: **Analyze → Descriptive Statistics → Frequencies → Crosstabs**

In the dialog box that appears, select the variables in the left window and move them to the right under 'Variable(s)'. Remember that you also need

to enter the variables into the cross tabs in a fixed structure in SPSS too, i.e., independent variables go in the columns, dependent variable in the rows. If it is not clear what the status of the variables is, then choose the order that gives the best results.

Are you in paid employment? * Gender Cross tabulation

			Gender		
			men	women	Total
Are you in paid employment?	yes	Count	485	359	844
		% within Gender	62.1%	43.8%	52.7%
	no	Count	296	461	757
		% within Gender	37.9%	56.2%	47.3%
Total		Count	781	820	1601
		% within Gender	100.0%	100.0%	100.0%

Figure 8.12   Cross tabs for gender by work

There is an extra assignment about percentagizing cross tabs on the website in the section entitled 'Chapter 8' (tab Extra material).

independent or dependent? The distinction between independent and dependent variables is very important. As you can see from the cross tabs, it determines the structure of your analysis, among other things. Should you want to predict the effect of education level on income, for instance, then level of education would be the independent variable (cause) and income would be the dependent variable (effect). Figure 8.13 illustrates this model: the arrow is the effect that level of education has on income.

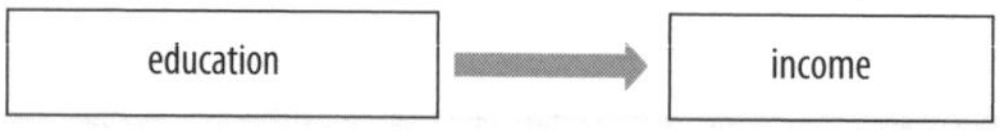

education	⟶	income

Figure 8.13   Effect of education on income

This makes the structure of the analysis clear: the independent variable determines the dependent variable and, in that sense, the one precedes the other (in time). In turn, the dependent variable can manipulate another variable. Have another look at Figure 3.5, Ajzen and Fishbein's behavioral model. Attitude, norms and control (independent) affect intention (dependent), and intention impacts on behavior (dependent); this is what is known as an indirect effect.

It is possible to create a cross tab which reflects the extent to which the correlation between two variables is caused (say 'controlled') by a third variable. On the website, in the section entitled 'Chapter 8' (tab Extra material), you will find information about how to include a control variable. There is also an SPSS example of this. Also, there are several ways in SPSS to carry out analyses of separate groups and to use control variables. In the literature references in the section 'Chapter 8' you will find references to more information on the subject.

8.4.2   Graphs Illustrating Two Variables

Besides presenting two variables in cross tabs, you can also illustrate them in graphs. In the section, we will show you three options: bar charts, scatter plots, and line graphs.

For the examples below, we show you a simple way to create a graph in SPSS using 'Graphs → Legacy Dialogs'. On the website, under the tab 'Introduction to SPSS', you'll find information about using another tool to generate graphs 'Chart Builder'.

Bar charts
Figure 8.14 shows two examples of a bar chart in which two variables are compared, namely gender and level of education. On the left, the chart is a *clustered chart*: separate bars for men and women alongside each other. The tallest bar indicates the largest group. To the right you will see that the bars are on top of each other: this is called *stacked*. In this case it is slightly more difficult to see the difference between the results for men and women. You will find the instructions to how to make these graphs in SPSS in Text box 8.12. In Text box 8.13 (and Figure 8.15) you'll find an example of a clustered bar chart.

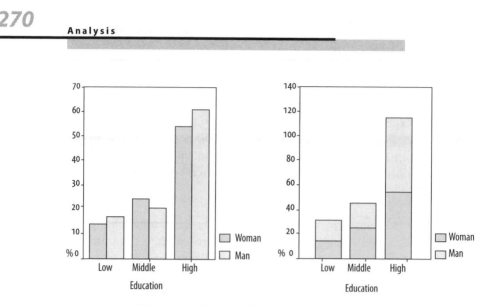

Figure 8.14   Clustered and stacked bar charts

Bar charts in SPSS

One way to generate clustered and stacked charts in SPSS is to use the following menu:

Graphs → Legacy Dialogs → Bar → Clustered (or Stacked) → Summaries for groups of cases

In the dialog window, you enter the *dependent variable* in the y-axis (level of education) and the *independent variable* in the x-axis (gender).

Box 8.12

Many children are poor

According to the Central Bureau for Statistics, many children are poor. Reports claim: 'A little over 11% of all children aged 18 and below grew up with a risk of poverty in 2009. They lived in families with an income of at most 120% of the social minimum. This emerged from figures published by the Central Bureau for Statistics (CBS) yesterday. These figures referred to 382,000 children, which is slightly less

than the 385,000 reported in 2008. Between 2003 and 2008, the numbers decreased by on average 20,000 children per year. But thanks to the financial crisis of the past two years these figures have stabilized, according to the CBS. Children from single parent households are more likely to be exposed to poverty than children who live with both parents.'

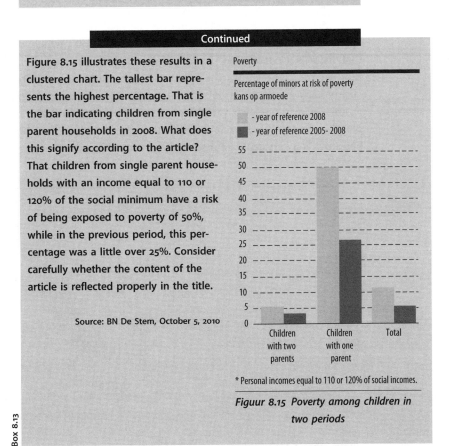

Continued

Figure 8.15 illustrates these results in a clustered chart. The tallest bar represents the highest percentage. That is the bar indicating children from single parent households in 2008. What does this signify according to the article? That children from single parent households with an income equal to 110 or 120% of the social minimum have a risk of being exposed to poverty of 50%, while in the previous period, this percentage was a little over 25%. Consider carefully whether the content of the article is reflected properly in the title.

Source: BN De Stem, October 5, 2010

Poverty

Percentage of minors at risk of poverty
kans op armoede

- year of reference 2008
- year of reference 2005-2008

* Personal incomes equal to 110 or 120% of social incomes.

Figuur 8.15 Poverty among children in two periods

Box 8.13

Apart from using 'legacy dialogs' to generate graphs, you can also use chart builder. Look under the tab Introduction to SPSS to see how this works.

Scatter plots

From interval level and above, the relationship between attributes can be reflected in scatter plots (see Section 8.3.2 as well). Scatter plots are ideal for analyzing the correlation between two variables. Each dot in the plot represents where the attribute is placed in terms of both attributes. This is where the attributes intersect as it were. The more the dots come together (in a cloud), the stronger the correlation between the attributes.

Figure 8.16 shows two scatter plots. The one on the left shows how much time people spend on their hobbies. You can see that respondent number 28, aged 69 years, spends about an hour on his hobby per week and that respondent number 41, aged 68 years, spends 8 hours. The dots are far apart and don't come together in a nice 'cloud of dots', which would indicate that there is a correlation between age and time spent on their hobby. The plot on the right shows the ages of fathers and their children. This one clearly has a cloud: from bottom left to top right. There is definitely a correlation between the two variables (age of the father and age of the child). Needless to say this correlation still needs to be tested. Text box 8.13 shows you how you can generate a scatter chart in SPSS using 'Legacy Dialogs'.

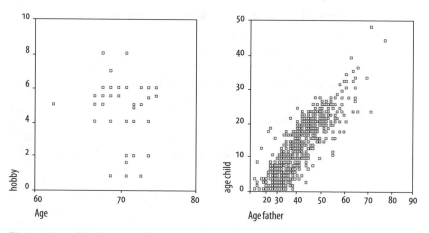

Figure 8.16   Two scatter plots

<table>
<tr><td colspan="2">**Scatter plots in SPSS**</td></tr>
<tr><td>One of the ways to create a scatter plot in SPSS is to use the following menu:

Graphs → Legacy Dialogs → Scatter → Simple → Define</td><td>You enter the variables in the dialog window: the independent variables go in the x-axis and the dependent variables go in the y-axis.</td></tr>
</table>

Box 8.14

Line graphs

A good way to illustrate developments over time, for instance: turnover, is to use a line graph. Time is the separate variable. For example, you may have collected data about turnover at various points in time. Turnover is the dependent variable, time is the independent variable.

Figure 8.17 gives you an example showing more than two variables. During a market research survey, respondents were asked about chewing gum brands.

The results are illustrated by giving each brand its own line. The highest score corresponds with the best-known and popular brand of chewing gum.

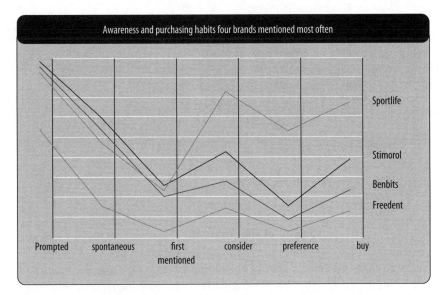

Figure 8.17   *Brand awareness and popularity chewing gum (source: mediatheek.thinkquest.nl)*

If you think there is a correlation between two characteristics, then you can test this by carrying out a correlation analysis. Visit the website and look under the section entitled 'Chapter 8' (tab Extra material) for more information about correlations between variables.

Figure 8.18 gives the results for research into lifestyles for teenagers between *a special* the ages of 14 and 18 years (Lampert et al., 2005; *de Volkskrant*, November *kind of* 24, 2005). It is actually two graphs in one. First you can see how the sample *graph* would be divided if it had been shown in a pie chart. Each 'circle' section shows the percentage of teenagers that belongs to a given lifestyle category. But the sections have been put in a graph that shows two more attributes: the extent the teenagers are 'status oriented' (from left to right) and the extent to which they are inclined to be explorers (from bottom to top), in the sense that they explore and are extrovert.

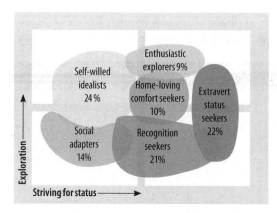

Figure 8.18   Lifestyles among teenagers

8.5   Quality of the Analysis

Testing reliability and validity is an important way to check the quality of your results (see Chapter 6). Having carried out an analysis of a small part of 'reality' (i.e., the sample), you want to check the extent to which your results are 'random', i.e., based on coincidence. Not only that, it is important to know whether you have measured what you wanted to measure, whether your research group (sample) resembles the population that you want to make statements about. In this section we will discuss a few aspects of quality control.

8.5.1   Reliability

One of the most frequently used statistical methods to assess the reliability of a scale is the reliability analysis that you can do using SPSS. This tests the internal consistency (reliability) of your scale. Suppose you have operationalized a concept (for example: motivation to do voluntary work) in a series of scaled questions. In other words, you've used a Likert scale. Using SPSS you can check whether the separate questions together form a homogenous image of a concept. Obviously you can't use SPSS to check whether the *specific* concept (motivation voluntary work) has been formulated reliably. What *can* you do? You can check to see whether all your questions are measuring more or less the same thing: you assess the homogeneity of the items.

Using a complicated procedure that measures the strength in the correlation *Cronbach's* between each item and all the other items, a figure is calculated (from zero *alpha* to 1) that indicates how reliably the questions measure the concept. There are various rules for interpreting this figure. Here we will assume that anything above 0.60 (called *Cronbach's alpha*, after the person who devised it) gives a sufficiently homogenous reflection of the concept. Incidentally, in psychological experiments this measure has to be higher before the reliability is considered to be acceptable. For those sciences, Cronbach's alpha has to be 0.80, or even 0.90, i.e., as close to 1 (being the highest achievable value) as possible, to be considered 'reliable'. Text box 8.15 gives an example.

Sociability

During studies into the social contacts that the elderly have in a residential area, respondents were asked questions about *sociability*: the extent to which a person finds it easy to make social contact with other people. Respondents (those in that neighborhood over the age of 55) were asked to indicate the extent to which they agreed with the following statements:

✓ Starting a conversation with a stranger is easy.
✓ I am a talkative person.
✓ I'd rather do things together with others than on my own.
✓ I enjoy being with other people.

The responses to these questions were analyzed and it turned out that the reliability of the correlation was too low (Cronbach's alpha 0.49). The reliability was not up to scratch. Yet the individual

questions were considered to be measuring one concept, namely sociability. When the study was repeated, they tried to improve the reliability of the instrument (in this case the questions measuring the concept) by operationalizing them as follows:

✓ It is easy for me to speak to people.
✓ I approach people myself.
✓ I build networks with the people around me.
✓ I bring people together.
✓ I talk about personal things to find things that we have in common to chat about.
✓ I am a member of a club.

The expectation is that, if the research is repeated, the reliability will be higher because the aspects being measured are probably 'closer' to each other.

Box 8.15

If the reliability of your individual questions is good enough, then you can consider all the variables combined as one concept for the rest of your analysis. Normally researchers will combine all the variables into one measure and use this for further analysis. Other ways to extract reliable concepts from your variables are factor analysis (which we won't be discussing in this book) and test-retest. Test-retest means carrying out the same test twice but using different groups, after which you check to see whether the results are similar (correlation).

WEBSITE   On the website, in the section 'Chapter 8' (tab Extra material) you will find an example showing how to carry out reliability analysis in SPSS.

8.5.2   *Validity*

Once you've established that your research is reliable, you go on to assess whether or not it is also valid (reliability is a kind of prerequisite for validity). You assess whether you are measuring what you want to measure (construct validity), whether you can generalize the results of your analysis (external validity, or population validity), and whether you have drawn the right conclusions (internal validity). There are several ways to assess validity. Using an example, we will now discuss how you can assess the generalizability of your sample.

generaliz- One of the ways to assess generalizability is to test the extent to which the
ability properties of your sample resemble those of the population. Imagine that you are conducting research among 500 young people of which 225 are girls and 275 are boys. You have more boys than girls in your sample. On the face of it, you could say that the proportion of boys to girls is skewed in terms of gender because the ratio male to female is generally around fifty-fifty. In quantitative research, this observation would not be enough. You have to go a step further and test whether your sample is representative in terms of 'gender'. That is to say that the composition of your sample for this attribute should be similar to that of the population. It could be that in terms of this attribute (gender), the representation in your sample is so different from that of the population that you have to conclude that your sample is not representative for the population when it comes to the attribute 'gender'. 'Gender' is an easy example for an attribute because you can be sure that there are pretty much as many men as there are women.

It is not that easy to assess representativeness for other attributes. How do you establish what is representative for age or marital status? You can do this by comparing your data to data from other research, or with existing stats about population groups. You can consult statistics bureaus on the web. If you have no idea what the population is like, then you can consult the relevant statistics bureau via their website. But if you need information about specific populations, for example athletes, students, pet owners who live in your neighborhood, then these general statistics will not be very useful. Then you need to find out whether there are stats available from a more local source. Generally speaking, though, you'll have to cut your coat to suit your cloth and it won't be possible to establish the generalizability of your data.

Text boxes 8.16 and 8.17 give you two more examples of quality assessment.

On the website, in the section 'Chapter 8' (tab Extra material), you will find some recommended literature for works about how to use and interpret quality assessments. The website also has a short introduction to inferential statistics and explains the concept 'significance' using examples.

Election polls

Box 8.16

The 2003 parliamentary elections led to a lot of speculation about the outcome. Several research bureaus organized polls so that they could predict the results. The various methods that they used lead to different predictions. The aim of this kind of research, of course, is to make *valid* statements, as far as possible, about a large group of people, namely those eligible to vote. It was the selective non-response in particular to the (mostly) telephone interviews that led to reduced validity. Why was this? Among the non-response were a lot of single and socially active people, relatively speaking. The sample did not represent the general population (the Dutch voters) in terms of these attributes, which in turn led to the generalizability being limited. So not only the validity, but also the reliability is an issue in this case which means that you can question the various research methods that were used (also see Text box 6.22).

Source: *de Volkskrant* January 18, 2003

Interpreting research

An article about the quality of the driving fitness test for those above 65 contains the following sentence: 'The question is how valid driving fitness tests for the elderly really are. Is a doctor who assesses someone they don't know really finding out what he needs to know? Or is the doctor assessing things that are not very reliable? The important aspects in these medical examinations are quality of eyesight and peripheral vision. Research into this

8.6   Glossary of Most Important Terms and Their Meaning

Variable	Attribute of an element that is relevant to your research.
Category	Value that a variable can have.
Measurement level	Property of variables that indicates the extent to which you can use the variables in calculations.
Nominal measurement level	Variables with only a few separate categories that you can't use in calculations.
Ordinal measurement level	Variables with a few separate categories in a specific order that you can't use in calculations.
Interval measurement level	Continuous variables, without an absolute zero, in which the intervals between two values are equal. These can be used for calculations.
Ratio measurement level	Continuous variables, with an absolute zero, in which the correlations between two values are equal (and meaningful). These can be used for calculations.
Hypotheses	Verifiable assumptions about the results of your analyses.
Significance	The findings are not 'random' or based on coincidence.
Frequency table	Table that shows how often scores occur (in relation to the total number of scores), in other words: their distribution.
Relative frequencies	The number of observations in relation to the total number of observations.

Percentagize	Expressing relative frequencies in percentages.
Valid percentages	Valid observations relating only to those who responded to that question.
Graphs	A way of illustrating the variables in diagrammatic form. Also known as charts and diagrams.
Statistical indicator	Summary of a variable (attribute) in one property.
Central tendency	Statistical indicator that describes the center of a variable.
Mode	The score that occurs most often.
Bimodal	When two variables are modes (peak).
Median	Middle number in a distribution.
(Weighted) average	The sum of all the scores (times their weight) divided by the total number of observations.
Measure of variability	Statistical indicator that describes the dispersion of a variable.
Range	Maximum minus minimum score.
Variance	Average quadratic deviation of the average.
Standard deviation	Calculated by the variation (square root), in other words the distribution of the variable.
Gauss curve	Bell-shaped form that occurs in graphs showing distributions when they are normal.
Normal distribution	Symmetric distribution in which 68% falls within one times the SD of the average, 95% falls within twice the SD and 99% falls within three times the distribution measured from the centre.
Cross tabulations	Frequency tables of two variables at the same time.
Row percentage	Percentage of the row total.
Column percentage	Percentage of the column total.
Cell percentage	Percentage of the cell total.
Independent variable	Causal variable that can result in a change in another variable.
Dependent variable	Effect variable that changes under the influence of an independent variable.
Cronbach's alpha	Statistical measure to assess the reliability of a scale.

8.7 Assignments for Chapter 8

1 What is the measurement level of the following variables?

   a Place of residence.

   b Opinions about the implementation of a higher rate of VAT in an ascending scale.

   c Total kilometers that you travel for work every day.

   d IQ.

   e Rank in the army.

   f Political parties (Democrat, Republican).

   g Political leanings (left, neutral, right).

   h Income in dollars.

   i Income in categories.

   j Paid employment (yes/no).

   k Your final mark in percent.

   l Your final mark in ascending order from: failed, passed, merit, honors.

2 Read the following conclusions carefully. Which hypotheses have been tested, do you think?

   a 'Students spend more time studying and less time at their jobs. This emerged from the latest Student monitor, an annual study among students' (de Volkskrant, November 22, 2005). This is the result of a comparison between 2004 and 2003.

   b Compared to 'normal walking', Nordic Walking barely relieves strain on the joints, which has been the assumption up until now. 'It is a great way to get fit or to lose weight. It is also ideal for people with certain physical limitations. This is the conclusion of exercise physiologist and movement scientist Wil van Bakel, who carried out his own research into the effects of Nordic Walking on the body' (Tweevoeter, 2005).

3 On television they announce the program 'Weight loss XXL'. They need candidates that must meet a number of criteria, including having a body mass index above 25. A thousand candidates sign up.

   The distribution is as follows: 325 people with a BMI of 25; 200 people with a BMI of 26; 155 with a BMI of 28 and the other candidates are equally distributed between a BMI of 29 and 30. Create a frequency table for these. Show the absolute numbers and the relative and cumulative percentages.

4 Look at Figure 8.19. It shows the age distribution of the 41 respondents that completed the 100 km race, and that took part in the Cycle Challenge survey.
   a What is the highest response in absolute numbers? And the mode?
   b Calculate the response in percentage per age group.

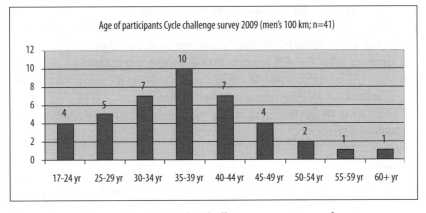

Figure 8.19   Response to the Cycle Challenge survey in numbers per age category

5 Look at the graph in Figure 8.20. It is a pie chart showing ages between 41 and 57 years. Judge the graph in terms of use, readability and results. What kind of chart or graph would you use to illustrate age.

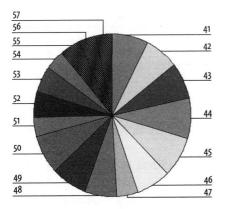

Figure 8.20   Pie chart showing age

6 For Assignment 3 you created a frequency table for the BMI of 1,000 candidates for 'Weight loss XXL'.
   a Where are the mode and the median?
   b Calculate the average.
   c Calculate the standard deviation.
   d What can you say about the properties of the standard deviation, assuming the BMI variable dispersion is normal?
7 There are several ways to determine what the income levels are of a country. You could calculate the modal income or the median.
   a Indicate what the difference is between these two measures.
   b You will often here people talking about 'average income'. Why do you think modal income might be a better measure?
8 Table 8.10 is an age table. Fill in the missing information and calculate the standard deviation.

Table 8.10   *Age table*

Age (X)	n	n . X	X − $\bar{X}$	(X − $\bar{X}$)²	n(X − $\bar{X}$)²
10	10	100	-23		
25	4	100		64	256
55	10	550	22		
40	6	240		49	294
Total	30	990			10,680
Average		33			

9 Study the cross tabulations in Tables 8.9b to 8.9d. Answer the following questions:
   a What percentage of women do not have paid work?
   b What percentage of people without paid work are men?
   c What percentage of the respondents are men without paid work?
10 Mention the variables and values in the following statements:
   a 'Studies show that men are still more likely to have managerial jobs than women are.'
   b 'The working relationship between the students in the project group is excellent.'
   c 'These days children between 10 and 16 years old are fatter on average than children were 15 years ago.'

   d 'To observe role distributions between boys and girls in a nursery school, the researcher organizes several observations of various situations: free play, a simple task and a game.'

   e 'Efforts to operate sustainably have been given increasing priority among businesses in various sectors and among businesses of various dimensions. Research shows that 60% of the respondent companies rated sustainability from "important" to "extremely important".'

   f 'The financial crisis has made spending cuts necessary. That is what the new government has decreed. To what extent do people agree with this? Based on a representative sample of the population, 75% of the people do not agree with spending cuts.'

11 An Internet shop wants to know what their customer profile is and how customers found their website. A study is conducted that records the following demographics: gender, age, income, marital status, and level of education as well as how they first heard or read about the website. Response options for the latter were: via a search engine (1), advert (2), word of mouth (3), other (4). Options for marital status are: married or living together (1), divorced (2), widowed (3) or living alone (single) (4). Level of education is divided into: Primary school (0), High school no diploma (1), High school diploma (2), College diploma (3), University bachelor's degree (4), University master's degree (5), PhD (6). For gender there are two codes: '1' for male and '2' for female.

Look at the dataset in Table 8.11. Enter these figures in SPSS. You should first check to see if they are correct.

Table 8.11   Input SPSS

Resp. no.	Gender	Age	Mstatus	Income	Educ	Website
1	2	18	4	952	2	3
2	1	26	2	1,134	3	2
3	1	134	1	907	2	1
4	2	25	4	862	1	4
5	2	35	1	2,722	7	2
6	2	28	2	2,359	5	2
7	2	25	1	1,542	3	3
8	1	49	3	1,860	4	2
9	2	36	,	,	0	3
10	1	33	1	2,541	7	4
11	1	35	1	2,042	6	3
12	1	999	,	1,179	2	1
13	1	40	1	1,179	3	3
14	2	30	1	680	1	1
15	1	35	2	1,815	4	3
16	F	38	2	1,361	3	1
17	2	60	3	2,405	5	2
18	2	999	2	1,179	6	3
19	1	58	1	2,722	7	4

a   What is in the rows and what is in the columns?

b   Which age group has been marked '999'. What does this mean? What do the commas mean in Mstatus and Inc?

c   There are two errors in the data. Can you point them out? Correct these errors.

d   What does 'Mstatus' stand for and 'Educ'?

Compile a codebook for this data and enter it into an SPSS Variable View window. Enter the data into an SPSS database. Save the file as 'ass8_11.sav'.

12 Which central tendency and distribution measures are suitable for the attributes in 'ass8_11.sav'?

13 Calculate the following parameters using SPSS for the data in 'ass8_11.sav', belonging to the correct variables:

- mode;
- median;
- average;
- variance;

- standard deviation;
- range.

14 Open 'ass8_11.sav'.

  a Make a cross tab for gender and website. Be careful where you put the variables! Calculate the percentages by column and give the percentage of women that heard of the website by word of mouth.

  b Create a cluster diagram for the results of 14a, i.e., a chart that shows gender and the way they heard about the website.

  c Create a table showing marital status and website. Calculate the percentages by cell. What percentage of the whole sample lives together and heard of the website through an advert?

15 Study Figure 8.15: the chart about poverty. Interpret the chart in the light of the text in Textbox 8.14. Is the journalist right? Discuss.

16 Study Figure 8.21. It contains a box diagram showing the age of college students. Answer the following questions:

  a What is the minimum and what is the maximum age?

  b What age is the median? How can you tell?

  c Explain the extraordinary position of 'case 403'.

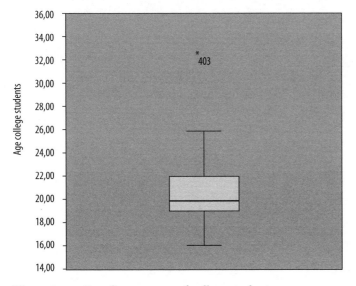

Figure 8.21   Box diagram age of college students

In the section 'Chapter 8' (tab Assignment solutions) you will find the solutions to the assignments in Section 8.7. You will find information about the design cases under tab 'Design cases' in the section 'Chapter 8'.

Qualitative Analysis

Qualitative research is coming into its own. In Chapter 5 we saw how qualitative research is used in combination with quantitative methods, in a *triangulated* approach. In this way the problem is tackled from various angles and the reliability of the results is enhanced. Open interviews are conducted in advance of the survey, to make an inventory of all the various concepts involved, or to investigate all the issues that play a role for the people, departments or organizations being researched. This approach means that your survey will get much closer to the issues at hand than would be the case if your knowledge of the situation was purely theoretical.

Qualitative research is an important prerequisite for establishing the reliability of your quantitative research results. But it also has an important role to play as stand-alone research in applied studies. For this reason, it is crucial to know about qualitative analysis methods.

In this chapter we will deal with the principles of qualitative analysis and the instruments used for this method of research. Qualitative analysis is extremely broad in its scope, encompassing a wide range of methods. It rarely happens that there is one answer to a qualitative research question. While methodological principles are important, in qualitative research the main thing is the interpretation that the researcher gives to the analysis. Their interpretation lends the analysis a certain degree of subjectivity, giving the perception of the situation extra depth. Important advantages that qualitative research has is its open approach, and the opportunity that the researcher has to react to situations, organizations and people. This does depend on the organization, the research questions, developments during the research and so on. In this chapter we'll discuss the theoretical basis of qualitative research, which will be the basis of your analyses.

Don't take qualitative analysis too lightly. Because not all the basic assumptions are fixed prior to the research starting, it may seem as though it is a 'free for all' and that the results are determined purely on the basis of how they are interpreted. But this is far from true. Qualitative research is a very in-depth and intensive process, encompassing several phases, and this guarantees that the results are reliable.

This chapter will introduce some qualitative analysis instruments as well as software packages that can be used to process and code data. We will demonstrate how these can be applied using examples.

Learning objectives

Once you've gone through this chapter, and on the basis of the aspects that we have dealt with, you will be able to summarize a text and describe it in terms of its concepts in such a way that you can answer your research question. You will also have insights into how the concepts are grouped and categorized, and you will be able to present these concepts in a diagram. You will also be able to list aspects of qualitative research in terms of reliability and validity.

Box 9.1

9.1   Qualitative Analysis of Texts

Qualitative research requires qualitative analysis. This may involve analysis of manuscripts and other texts (files), audiotapes, video, photographs, music and so on. You may choose to describe these texts, or summarize them, but you can go much further than that. For instance, you may decide to summarize the texts in codes or concepts. You can go on to interpret these concepts by sorting them into some kind of order, and, by doing so, give them structure. What happens is that, while you're analyzing the material in this way, you're creating a kind of model in your mind's eye. Handling texts like this is sometimes called *exploration*. In this section we'll discuss a few principles of qualitative analysis that we will illustrate using an interview text about 'glass ceilings'.

9.1.1   *Principles of Qualitative Analysis*

One of the objectives of qualitative analysis is to gain insight into a given domain and to develop theories about it. This chapter will show you that this definitely shares facets with conducting applied qualitative research. We will first discuss the theoretical principles of qualitative analysis. These principles are in line with the 'Grounded Theory' approach developed by Glaser and Strauss (1967), an approach that is still used for the analysis of qualitative material. Text box 9.2 shows an example of this method.

What veterans say

For an initiative set up by the Veterans Institute, a large-scale open interview project was set up that entailed interviewing veterans of war and peace missions that have taken place from the Second World War to date. This survey produced more than one thousand interview reports. These reports were re-analyzed recently, during which new research questions were addressed. The Grounded Theory approach was used for this. This analysis resulted in an extensive publication 'What veterans say' (see Chapter 5; Van den Berg et al., 2010)

Box 9.2

Qualitative research is not about collecting numerical data. It's about explor- *creating* ing the significance that people attach to certain situations and behavior. *meaning* Consider the difference between survey questionnaires and topic lists. In a quantitative survey you may ask the respondents about the political party that they intend voting for, that's it. Should you ask that question during an in-depth interview, on the other hand, then you'll be far more interested in how the respondents arrive at their choice of party, which arguments they base their choice on, to what extent the various aspects influence their choice and why. The respondents don't choose their answer from a prescribed list; their response is based on their own frame of reference, their own perceptions of the issue. This approach produces a perception of reality as put forward by the interviewees themselves. This approach is known as *symbolic interaction* (Boeije, 2005; Wester, 1991). It is an interpretative, i.e., open, approach to research (see Section 1.3 as well). What it means is that the perceptions of the research elements (often respondents) are the focus of the research. In this respect, you have to be flexible as the researcher, and respond to the situation as it unfolds.

The qualitative research process is not straightforward. Obviously your *iterative* research plan will consist of phases, but during the analysis you may dis- *process* cover that you don't have all the facts that you need. For this reason you may decide to carry out a second, or even a third round, after your initial round, using the results that you got from the previous rounds. In other words, you repeat the research process until you feel that you have a reliable answer to the research question, i.e., the problem formulation, (see Text box

9.3). This cycle is also known as *iteration*, or the *constant comparative* method. The advantage is that this method increases the reliability of your results because it allows you to check whether your previous findings are correct with the 'new' data.

9.3).

Microcredit

In 2010, Lim researched the microcredit system in Pondicherry, India (Lim, 2010). Alongside observations, he carried out a series of interviews. After each round, he checked to see whether he could answer his research questions, and then used the results from the previous cycle in a new round of interviews.

Box 9.3

---

inductive character Qualitative research, particularly the Grounded Theory approach, is inductive. This means that during the research we look for a theory that suits the data that has been collected (Swanborn, 2010). In other words, we look for structure in the data, we don't test preconceived theories. If we did that, we would be doing deductive research, i.e., hypotheses would be deduced and we would be testing those theories. With qualitative research, it is possible to develop new theories.

According to some scientists, the fact the qualitative research is inductive is a drawback. Why? Because deriving a good theoretical structure from your data, without having any principle or basis from which to work, is a time-consuming, expensive and labor intensive business, one that is only accomplished by very few researchers. For this reason, the Grounded Theory approach has been toned down over the years to a somewhat less stringent (more flexible) approach. By this we mean that in actual fact theoretical bases for the research are developed before analysis begins. Despite this, the approach to your analysis does remain inductive: creating a theoretical structure from the material to hand.

sensitizing concepts If you want to gain insights or develop a theory using qualitative research, then the first thing you do is look at your central question. Your central question will contain general concepts that you intend to research or explore. In the Grounded Theory approach, this is known as *sensitizing concepts* or 'orientating concepts' (see Wester, 1991; Wester, Smaling & Mulder, 2000; Baarda et al., 2001; Boeije, 2005, p.81). These concepts will only *orientate* your research; they are not fixed. The demarcation, discovering what they mean, will take place during the research.

Generally speaking, applied research is not used to develop theories; instead *using theory* it is used to answer practical questions. Theoretical principles may, however, *in applied* serve as a basis for the research and for the analysis (see Chapter 1). *qualitative*

Often qualitative methods are only used for parts of applied research. They *research* would be used *before* a survey, during pilot studies, when interviews are organized (or document analysis is done) to explore the field and to demarcate the subject. Those interviewed may give information about the subject, about key terms and concepts that will be used, and the meanings that are attached to them within the organization.

It may be that qualitative research is organized *after* a survey, as a way of further exploring the subject. This could be done using open interviews or focus groups. Sometimes those called during a telephone survey are asked whether they would be prepared to take part in exploratory research into the subject to hand. If they agree, then the responses they gave during the telephone interview will be further explored. In this way the respondent is given the opportunity to throw light on the subject and to put forward issues that were not dealt with during the telephone interview, but that are relevant to the research.

The information that you gather during applied research can be analyzed using the same methods as those described in more 'theory oriented' problem formulations. Also, for qualitative analysis you can opt for an inductive approach in which you can use 'orientating concepts'. You may not be using theory explicitly, but implicitly the theories will be there.

9.1.2   Qualitative Processing of Data

How do you process the information you have gathered? How do you ana- *unravel,* lyze it? You do this by deconstructing the information and then giving it *code and* structure. How do you do this exactly? We'll show you how using the fol- *construct* lowing 8 steps:

Step 1
Read all the information carefully. Divide the information (texts, interview reports and so on) into small pieces that you can summarize in one key term (*unraveling*). Don't take this step too lightly: think carefully about why you selected that particular piece of information.

Step 2
Evaluate all the terms you have used. What *value* do the research elements (respondents) attach to that term? This means interpreting the meaning. Are the terms negative in their tone, or positive?

Step 3
Now you come up with the word that best describes each piece of information, you *code* it. Normally the researcher would write the code in the margin of the text, or generate a code in the software program that will be used for analysis. Preferably, use one code (word) to describe that piece of information; one of the things you will be doing with it is summarizing the material (Boeije, 2005, p. 89). This kind of coding is known as *open coding*. It is done at the start of the analysis process and it is the step in defining the concepts that have been found. It is still very exploratory at this stage.

Step 4
The next step is to *group* the terms. What belongs with what? This is where you start the sorting process.

Step 5
Now you sort the coded terms and form a *hierarchy*: what is the most important code, what's next, and so on.

Step 6
Now you start looking for *relationships* between the concepts, such as associations and/or combinations. You make main groups and subgroups by checking to see which codes belong together and how they can be sorted. Think carefully about the reasons you have for grouping concepts, look for evidence for this in the text. At this stage in the coding process you may decide to split codes up. This stage in the process is called *axial coding* (Wester, 1991; Boeije, 2005). It is much less exploratory compared to the open coding process that we mentioned earlier.

Step 7
Now you give the concepts a structure, you look for relationships between them and address the question as to why you have discovered certain concepts and certain rankings in the concepts. You bring these relationships and rankings together in a *model*, or *diagram*.

Step 8
You discuss the model that has emerged in terms of the central question:
- Does it answer the question?
- Does it raise more questions?
- Is more information needed? If so, then you need to go back to collecting information until such time as you can formulate a complete answer to the central question.

If you read through these steps, it may seem fairly easy. In reality, though, analyzing qualitative information is a complicated, intensive and protracted process that takes place in various data collection and analysis phases, phases that are repeated several times. In other words, it's a process of ongoing comparison.

Giving structure to the findings is an aspect that plays a role throughout the research process. The process of coding that we have described, for example, resembles *mind mapping* in a way. This is a method that involves giving structure to your ideas about all kinds of aspects, by putting them down on paper in the form of key words, then grouping, evaluating, coding and structuring them. You can also use this method in your analysis. *mind mapping*

To organize your thoughts, you can take a piece of paper and use it as a 'landscape'. Start in the middle of the paper and use different colored markers, pens or pencils. The aim of the exercise is to make a vague subject more specific. The way you organize your thoughts on a subject is to give them each a key word and write them down. You then think about which thoughts are connected to each other and you indicate this by drawing a line between them; the lines may be thick or thin depending on the strength of the connection. In the end you will have a diagram like the one in Figure 9.1, which will show your ideas in a diagrammatic form.

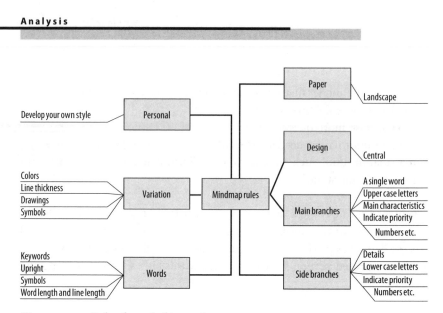

Figure 9.1   Rules for mind mapping

Figure 9.3 gives an example of a diagram showing the results of qualitative analysis of the 'glass ceiling'. It is more or less the same as a mind mapping diagram. We will discuss it further in 9.2.

9.1.3   Tools for Qualitative Analysis

There are several tools that you can use illustrate the results of your analysis:

1   As we have already mentioned, you can use a *schematic representation* of the results in a diagram or chart, which is usually the case with mind maps. You can also design a tree diagram for this (for example on your computer).

2   You can make a *card index* by writing down the terms on cards and then sorting them. For this kind of system, you can also use the famous yellow 'Post-it' notes by sticking them to a board and then giving them structure.

Figure 9.2   Example of a diagram using stickers (source: dreamstime.com)

3 An important tool is your *logbook*. This is where you keep all the notes to do with your analysis, the decisions you made, and your reasons for doing so. It is also important to note why you did not choose something, or why something did not work out. You may need it for your report. A tip: date your logbook and use a numbering system. You can introduce levels in your numbering system, for instance 4.3.1 (phase, section, type). Afterwards you'll easily be able to trace the phase in your research that you made the note. This is especially important to keep some kind of ordering in your notes if you go back to collecting data more than once.

4 Using *software* for qualitative analysis is very easy. These programs can be divided into two groups:

a In Section 9.3 we'll be discussing how you can use special software (such as Kwalitan and MAXqda) for your *text analysis*. If you don't have these software packages then you always use Word, PowerPoint or other standard software programs. In many of these programs it's possible to make charts. Memos and logbooks can be made using ordinary word processors. Using a system of 'index words' (can be done in Word) you can reduce the time spent searching.

b A useful tool for *mind mapping* is the software package *Mindmanager9*. You can create diagrams, work together in real time with other researchers and you can use it to sort your research information. The same goes for the planning program, Inspiration. It is ideal for mind mapping and for creating tree diagrams. You can also use this program for designing your research plan, schedules, organograms and so on. You can download a trial version of Inspiration from the Internet. Both programs are available on Surfspot.

You can also use MAXqda (for qualitative data analysis) to create diagrams. Of course if you want to design your own charts and diagrams you can fall back on standard programs such as Word, PowerPoint and Excel.

5 If you are analyzing using standard text processors (i.e., not specialized software), you can use the options that these programs offer to ensure that your analysis goes smoothly. We'll mention a few options here:

- Sections of text that don't seem relevant can be removed from your 'main text'. Don't delete them altogether, but rather save them in a separate file under a different name (for example: 'non-relevant texts'). Using 'cut and paste' is essential here.
- To find a piece of text easily you can number the lines or the selected text. In Word you can do this using document settings in the Format menu. You can choose from several types of numbering: by line, by text section or section (that is for a piece of text that has a different format to the standard formatting).
- There are also other ways to number the text. You could use a numbering system per respondent and subdivide the text that belongs to each respondent into pieces. For instance, the first number could indicate the person and the second the piece of text: '1/3'. This could then be followed by concepts from the pieces of text, for example '1/3/ unequal/criteria/domination'.
- If you want to save the text as a whole and then code the pieces separately, you can move them to another document using 'cut and paste' (Baarda et al., 2001, p. 234 onwards) and then code it. This will leave the original text intact.

This is how to use a text processor to help you analyze texts. You don't really need any other tools, although they are available in the form of specialized software packages for qualitative analysis. We will now discuss a few in the next section.

9.2   Content Analysis: the Case of the 'Glass Ceiling'

There is a lot of debate about whether or not the glass ceiling that prevents women from moving up to higher positions actually exists. Marijke Stellinga, for instance, talks about _The myth of the glass ceiling_ [_De mythe van het gla-zen plafond_] (2009; see also Morrison, 1994). Is it a question of women not being able to move up, or not wanting to move up, the corporate ladder? Suppose you carry out a content analysis of the current state of affairs of the so-called 'glass ceiling'. By this we mean the situation that prevents women from moving to higher positions within organizations. During your preliminary research you map out the current state of affairs in Michigan and California by studying scientific and newspaper articles. You carry out a content analysis looking for concepts that you could use for a number of in-depth interviews with women.

What do women think of the glass ceiling? What is their opinion on the subject according to newspaper and magazine articles? In Text box 9.4 we have gathered a few statements that women have made on the subject of the glass ceiling. We will go on to analyze them.

Statements from women about the glass ceiling

- 'That women have not broken through to the top of the business world also has to do with them. It's all in the mind. Women _think_ that they can't manage other people and not only that, they are less _ambitious_. Apart from anything else they have a different management style to men. They are more lenient, they work on their relationships more than on their own careers.'

- 'It's perfectly possible for women to climb the corporate ladder. They just don't want to. They're happy with their part-time jobs. Leave them alone!'

- 'Have you seen our annual report? There's not a single photo of a woman. In our company the balance is not good. It's all to do with the demands of the positions higher up, such as mobility, over time, experi-ence in working abroad. Women often don't meet these require-ments. What is more, the average age of our staff is not very high.'

- 'In our business, the arts, the posi-tions for men and women are the same. Both men and women can achieve things in the arts, it's talent that counts, not dominance. What annoys me is that people still look at a woman's appearance. It's not the same for men. Which is why I go to the hairdresser every four weeks and I watch my weight closely.'

- 'The percentage of women in man-agerial positions in our organization is 25, which is much too low obviously. Women often feel that they are not accepted and they behave accordingly; they're much less inclined to apply for a senior position.'

Continued

'In our company, if you have a senior position you are only allowed to work part-time for four days or more. For many women (those with children for example) it is too much. This is why they don't move up easily.'

'Women are still treated differently to men. Women have to behave like men if they want to be accepted in banking. It can be done, but the pressure not to climb the ladder is heavy. I cannot tell you how often I've had to prove that I can combine my work with my family, especially in the position I am now, it's not funny anymore. This social pressure will stop a lot of women from even trying.'

'You want to know what it's like these days? Should we push for more emancipation, or shouldn't we? We've come a long way but there's room for improvement. There are too few women in managerial positions. In some industries it's acceptable to work part-time, in others you have to justify it or it's out of the question.'

'On the one hand I'm a supporter of positive discrimination. If there are discrepancies in the percentage of men and women at the top, then all things being equal, you should choose the woman. On the other hand, women often have different qualities to men. When general objective criteria are used, women don't get the job. Selection committees should learn to assess these qualities differently.'

'Do you know what I think is unfair? The fact that men often earn more than women for the same job. That is a sort of "glass ceiling", I think. Women reach those positions but then don't get the same salary.'

'The most common type of division of labor among men and women is the "one and a half earner". The traditional division of labor between men and women is still being kept in place. Women still have less important positions and this means that they are financially dependent on their partners.'

Women are more likely to feel obligated to think of their families than men are. They question whether they can work more, do overtime, take on busy managerial positions. It's different for men. They do all of that for their family, it earns more (both in terms of income and status). To them being away from home is all part of the deal. Women don't think that way.'

Adapted from: Kohlmann, 2003; Stellinga, 2009

Box 9.4

We'll do the analysis of this text about the glass ceiling using the step-by-step procedure that we mentioned in Section 9.1.2. First you read the whole text again, a few times and carefully, so that you have a good idea of what the subject is about. It is important that you select all the information that is *relevant* to your subject. The subject is 'glass ceiling'. You must make sure that the texts that you select are on the subject. A remark like 'What is more, the average age of our staff is not very high' does not need to be included in the analysis. After you have read through it, you start the analysis:

text analysis *'Glass ceiling*

Step 1
You divide the text into relevant pieces, the deconstruction process. In the text we have chosen here, you can unravel the texts of each respondent separately. The text consists of various topics and sub-topics. This is what you can base your *classification* (grouping) on. For instance, you may think that the piece 'Have you seen our annual report? There's not a single photo of a woman. In our company the balance is not good' is a relevant fragment.

Step 2
This is when you interpret the meaning of the concepts that you've find, you carry out a so-called *evaluation*. In the fifth piece you'll find information about 'insecurity' and 'social pressure' among other things. These concepts have negative connotations in this context.

Step 3
In this analysis, it is important to *discover* concepts that you can use in your in-depth interviews as topics for discussion. That means that you must summarize each piece in one or more key words (open coding). In this example you don't use any pre-determined concepts in your analysis. You could summarize the second piece with the code 'gender inequality in organization'.

Steps 4, 5 and 6
This is when you *group*, *sort* and *evaluate* the concepts. You put the key words into *order* (hierarchy). Sometimes there's a lot of overlap and it's possible to combine keywords. You can also split codes. Look at the code 'gender inequality in organization'. 'Inequality' is in fact the main code that should be split into two subcategories, one of which would be 'characteristics of organization'.
You repeat this process several times during which time you review each piece and relate them to the others; it's called *axial coding*. You also look to see where each key word originates: from people, groups, organizations and

so on. You can note the evaluation of each key word in a table: is it seen as positive or negative? In Text box 9.4 they speak of 'acceptance' in a negative way, for example when they say that it is 'accepted' that you work part-time.

Steps 7 and 8
What is the cause, what is the effect? You can also do this so-called *causal ordering* with your key words, depending on your problem formulation and your research questions. You structure your codes, after which you put them in a *diagram*, in this case a tree diagram (see Figure 9.3). You go from the bottom up, from specific to general. If it is done properly then the most important concepts should be at the top. In this diagram it is the perception of inequality between men and women, followed by social pressure and at the bottom personal characteristics. You can then look for more information on the main concepts and repeat the analysis. The objective here is to check whether your findings also emerge from other analyses. In short, repetition enhances the reliability of your results.

Coding the text could produce a diagram like the one shown in Figure 9.3. This diagram is the result of one analysis by one researcher. It is therefore one of many possibilities: comparing it to new information or an analysis by another researcher could result in a totally different diagram. For instance, there may be a relationship between social pressure and inequality; in a new diagram you could indicate this relationship using lines. But equally the first findings may be confirmed. Using a more quantitative approach you may choose to count the number of times key words occur. The more these words are used by the respondents, the more significance they have and the more weight they have.

The concepts that you unveil in the analysis of the text about the 'glass ceiling' will be used as a basis for discussion in your in-depth interviews. You therefore analyze the text before you carry out your in-depth interviews. At a *lower level* in the diagram (i.e., on a level below the key concepts, see Figure 9.3) you may find a good operationalization of the terms. An example would be the operationalization of organization characteristics in the text in Text box 9.4 of the percentage of women in the organization. But of course you can always consult other literature for reference material and for operationalizations.

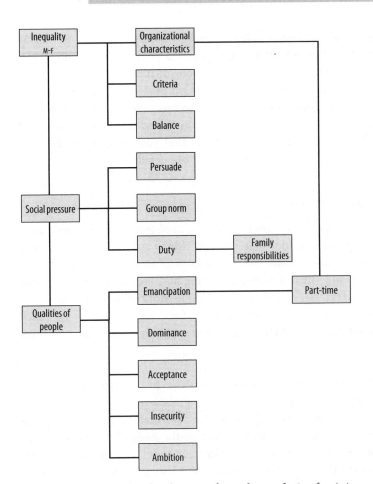

Figure 9.3   Example of a diagram from the analysis of opinions on the 'glass ceiling'

On the website under the tab Extra material in the section 'Chapter 9' you will find another extensive example of qualitative analysis.

9.3   Software as a Tool for Qualitative Analysis

More and more often these days computers are used to analyze texts or video and audio recordings. There are several computer programs on the market to support this kind of analysis. For instance you can analyze your observation data using The Observer™. You can use MAXqda, or Kwalitan to analyze your texts.

Many colleges and universities offer cheap software that you can use during your study. This often involves logging in with your student number and then downloading the program for use on your own computer.

Are your texts on paper and not electronic? No problem. You don't have to retype everything because most software programs these days can work with scanned material. You scan the text into something that can be processed digitally and then enter it into the package that you are going to use. We will now discuss one of these programs in more detail.

Kwalitan 5.0

Kwalitan is a software program that can be used in qualitative analysis of data. This program is a tool that you can use to analyze and order your data, but also to make memos for you logbook. You can also analyze texts, music, pictures and video material by coding and ordering, selecting, using search options (filters), and so on. Alongside 'normal' licenses, there are also special licenses that students can apply for. Student licenses are much cheaper but are valid for three months and can only be extended by three months.

There are two ways to use Kwalitan for analysis: by analyzing the text, i.e., by using the information given by *those being researched* as the input, or by analyzing the concepts, i.e., by using the information produced by the *researcher* as the input. Describing the text on the basis of concepts is called *coding*. Using this program you can order your codes, you can generate tree diagrams to rank them up to a maximum of 8 levels. If you base your analysis on the information given by the respondents (the words in the text), then you can do a word count of the different words used, and also rank them, or group them. Of course, you don't need a computer to code words and code concepts. But software has the huge advantage that you can make selections and do searches. You can use filter words as well as conduct searches using 'logical operators', which are symbols or words used to connect other words, such as 'and ... or' and 'not', that are used in searches.

matrix Frequencies of words, terms and concepts can be entered into a matrix: a table showing how often certain concepts occur. You can then enter this table into other programs to carry out analysis of a more quantitative nature.

memos It is important to make notes about all the decisions you make during your analysis, and the reasons you made these decisions. As a researcher you keep a logbook for this. Kwalitan offers you the option of making memos, and keeping them up to date. These memos are grouped into five subjects, including coding (concepts), theory and method. You can use titles and classifications to suit your needs.

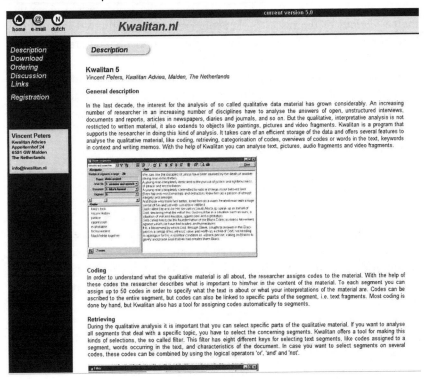

Figure 9.4   *A Kwalitan 5.0 demo screen*

9.4   Quality of the Results

Qualitative research always comes in for a lot of criticism when it comes to the quality of the results. Critics will tell you that qualitative research is not *reliable* and therefore it is not *valid* either. The first point of criticism, (reliability) is linked to the condition of being able to replicate qualitative research. Because qualitative research uses an open approach, often involving the development of models during the research, there is no demarcated setting for a study that will produce similar results when replicated. The condition of replicating a study is therefore at stake, according to critics. Because of this, it is difficult to assess the reliability.

The second point of criticism (validity) relates to both generalizability and construct validity of qualitative research. If a sample is not selected randomly or if it involves a small group of people, then the generalizability (the population validity) can be questioned. Furthermore, construct validity (are you measuring what you want to measure?) leaves a lot to be desired given that the *perceptions* of the research elements are central to the research. In this kind of research, it is the perceptions of the respondents that are paramount and not the concept or instrument being assessed.

The critics are wrong. In qualitative research these criteria are most certainly taken into account, but in a different way to quantitative research. We will now discuss the way in which reliability and validity are addressed in qualitative research and what we can do to ensure that the quality of the research is as high as it can be.

9.4.1   Reliability

The most important question you have to ask here is why you would apply the criterion of reliability to qualitative research. In fact, you are checking to what extent the requirement of reliability can be applied to your qualitative set up and what you can do to enhance reliability as far as possible. The example in Text box 9.5 shows that this is also possible in qualitative research.

Communication in the human resources department

Let's take a case study into internal and external communications of a human resources department in a company as an example. To get a taste of this, you are seconded as a researcher to work with the staff for four weeks during your vacation; you observe them in the work place by working with them, so it is participatory observation that you undertake. You also organize discussions with staff members in that department (and other departments), in which you talk about internal and external communications, their effects and how people view these aspects, the organizational structure, and so on. For this you use a recorder. You have close contact with one member of the client's staff. You carefully make a note of all your research activities in your logbook. Finally, you study the company's communications by analyzing internal and external communications, newsletters, press releases, and so on. You ask a colleague researcher to read and assess the result. The whole fieldwork phase takes about four months in all.

Box 9.5

Is this kind of research reliable? You may say it is not. This kind of qualitative research is difficult to repeat, and if you did, the chances that you would produce similar results are not good. You could put forward the following arguments to support this:

- Only one organization is being investigated, there is no material available to compare the results with.
- The perceptions of specific people are the focus of the research, these may change over time, or the people themselves may leave and be replaced with others.
- You work with the staff members in a given period. At a different point in time, say in December or during the following summer, things may be quite different.

Yet despite all of this you can ensure that your research is reliable and that the quality is high enough provided that you take the following rules into account, as much as you possibly can:

- Make sure that the argumentation that you use to support your problem definition and your research design is as elaborate and detailed as possible. Always bear in mind that it is these two aspects that form the backbone of your research.
- Make sure you have a good system to record the methods that you use and the steps that you take. As you go, write down your arguments and your reasons for choosing certain methods in your logbook. Make recordings of conversations. You can enhance the reliability of focus groups and observations by using more than one observer.
- Save your processed data in a separate file so that you always have access to the raw material in its original form (the discussion transcriptions and so on) in case you want to re-analyze it.
- Go through the analysis process as many times as necessary, collect additional information if required. Alternating data collection and analysis is a good thing for reliability because you are repeating your observations (Boeije, 2005, p. 148).
- Keep in close contact with your client about the design and progress of your research, preferably by using one contact person.
- Use 'peer evaluation' or 'peer consultation' which means showing fellow researchers your design, data collection methods and your analysis for reviewing and commentary.
- Use qualitative research as part of a triangulated research project if you can.

- Try to assess and evaluate your results as systematically (scientifically for want of a better word) as possible in terms of the analysis method you choose and the software you use. This (a somewhat more quantitative approach) reinforces the reliability of qualitative analysis. For instance, you can count the number of times a term occurs in a text or in the transcription of a conversations or focus groups and then use this to assess reliability between, say, different researchers (observers) using a specific method for your calculations. This is known as inter-rater reliability. So you see, you may well use math at some point. This method is used a lot in observational research.

What does this mean for the reliability of the example we gave in Text box 9.5? It means that it is good because several of the aspects we've just mentioned were taken into account during the research process: good research design, triangulation, intensive contact with one person, 'peer evaluation', using a logbook and a recorder.

9.4.2   *Validity*

Validity plays an important role in qualitative research. By validity we mean the extent to which research is free of systematic errors, in terms of both the measurement instruments used as the research population investigated.

generaliz- Generalizability (external or population validity) of the results based on the
ability population investigated is generally not the main objective of qualitative research for the simple reason that qualitative research often involves small groups of people and/or non-probability sampling. Apart from anything else, the information gathered is not quantitative.

For this kind of research, it is of no consequence whether the research findings are *statistically* generalizable or not (i.e., whether the sample is representative of the population). If generalizability has a role to play in qualitative research, then it involves *theoretical generalizability*, in other words: to what extent do the conclusions apply to similar situations (Baarda et al., 2001, p. 100). This can be achieved by leaving reality (the situation that you are investigating) intact as far as possible.

For example, it is not the objective at all to extrapolate the results of the case study involving the human resources department in Text box 9.5 to other organizations with a similar structure. The organization in question just wants to know what the state of play is regarding their internal and external communications, so that they can effect changes if and when it is necessary or preferable. A description of the situation in that organization will suffice.

E-cartoon of an assessment instrument

Example of an e-cartoon

E-cartoon is an assessment instrument that can be used for evaluations. Everyday situations are drawn in cartoon format, for example interactions with colleagues, management or clients. In each problem situation, several actions take place, as well as all the different ways that the candidate/test-subject can solve the problem. Animation is used to demonstrate the various social situations. After this, the candidate or test subject can use four responses to judge how effective each reaction is.

The final score is an indication of how effectively the person copes with social situations. This test is used for assessments, selection, but also in education (for example for internship placements). These so-called Situational Judgment Tests have a validity level that is comparable to the validity achieved by assessment centers and structured interviews (McDaniel, Morgeson, Finnegan, Campion & Bravermann, 2001).

Bron: www.vandermaesen.nl

Box 9.6

Construct validity comes in for a lot of criticism too in qualitative research. 'Are you actually measuring what you want to measure?' is a question often posed by critics of the method. It could be that the respondents say what they think is socially acceptable, things that would place them in a particular

measure what you intend to measure

group. People will always claim to be 'anti-discrimination' while in fact they are not. These responses are known as 'socially desirable'. Also, the answer to the question 'How often do you visit the dentist?' ('hardly ever') may not be a reflection of good dental hygiene, but more of fear of the dentist. Finally, it could be that the respondents know that you are conducting research. They may give you different responses to the ones they would give if they did not know that the information was for research. How can research avoid 'social acceptability' in their answers, for example?

On a more general note you have to ask the question of how researchers determine the method they will use to assess concepts. For this we should look at the example of the researcher as interviewer: if the researcher has mastered the art of interviewing and probing, then they will be able to get to the genuine response to the question. In qualitative research it is perfectly possible to take construct validity into account, for example by employing certain interviewing techniques when doing open interviews. You can also enhance the validity of your research by using systematic measurement and analysis techniques (see Text box 9.6).

internal   When we assess internal validity, we check to see whether the researcher has
validity   answered the question properly, in other words, whether the conclusions are *unbiased*. You are trying to prove a link between your findings and the central question. Qualitative researchers use the perceptions and interpretations that the respondent gives to a situation as the basis for internal validity, in other words the context in which the person being researched places the information. In doing so the researcher must ensure that their own background and opinions must not influence the research. Make sure you safeguard your objectivity as a researcher.

How can you restrict these 'systematic' errors in qualitative analysis to the absolute minimum?

- You can use tried and tested instruments for your data collection, i.e., systematic analysis methods. Consider, for example, the instruments that assessment centers use to assess the suitability of candidates for certain functions. You will find an example of this in Text box 9.6.
- Keep notes in your logbook; recording the information (for example using tape recorders) will prevent any distortion of what took place. It also improves the reliability of your results.
- You can use theories to base your analysis on, such as Grounded Theory approach that we discussed earlier. Look for interrelated concepts, or ones that aren't related at all, extreme cases, so that your description of the

phenomenon is as broad as possible. You can also look for cases that refute the information (i.e., negative cases).

- You can give your information to other people to read ('peer evaluation', audits, informants, and so on). This will also reinforce reliability.
- A triangulated research design works to the advantage of validity and reliability.
- The way you draw your sample must always be in line with your objective. Qualitative research (interviews, observations) often uses experts in its samples. The snowball method may help your research: ask the respondents whether they know of anyone else who would be suitable for the research (see Paragraph 7.5.1).

You can see that several of these criteria will have a positive influence on the reliability of your results.

9.5   Glossary of Most Important Terms and Their Meaning

Grounded Theory	Theoretical principle for qualitative analysis that is based on the perceptions that respondents, i.e., those being researched, have of reality.
Symbolic interactionism	Open approach of qualitative research in which the perceptions of the respondent are central.
Method of constant comparison	The repetition of the research steps (iteration) until a reliable answer to the research questions emerges.
Inductive research	Research in which theories are developed during the analysis.
Deductive research	Research in which existing theories are tested.
Sensitizing concepts	Orientating concepts from the research design that are expanded upon during the analysis.
Deconstruction	Dividing the text into small pieces that can be summarized in one word (code).
Open coding	Summarizing pieces of text in one or two words.

Axial coding	Analyzing the possible links between pieces of texts and codes.
Tree diagram	The results of the analysis summarized in a diagram.
Mind mapping	A method to give structure to ideas that resembles coding, structuring and evaluation of analyses.
Theoretical generalization	The extent to which conclusions are valid in similar situations.
Peer consultation/evaluation	An instrument to increase reliability that involves fellow researchers and colleagues reading the results and conclusions and giving their comments.

9.6   Assignments for Chapter 9

1 Describe the steps taken during text analysis on the basis of the following concepts:
   • deconstruction;
   • open coding;
   • axial coding;
   • diagram structure.
2 Have another look at the text about the glass ceiling (Text box 9.4).
   a Code and structure the text in your own way. Create two diagrams for this. For the first diagram, use 'level of organization' to order the information and for the second diagram use 'level of the individual'.
   b Do you come to a different conclusion? What is your conclusion?
   c Discuss the results with your study group.
3 On the website there is a sample interview with a patient who is suffering from Lyme's disease. Conduct an analysis on the basis of the Grounded Theory Approach. Code and structure the text. What are your conclusions?

WEBSITE
On the website, under the tab Extra material, in the section entitled 'Chapter 9', you will find an example of a qualitative analysis of interviews with people suffering from Lyme's disease.

4 Read the text in Text box 9.7. It *could be* an interview transcription of research that was conducted in 2002 among teenagers between the ages of 12 and 18 years.
   a Analyze the text.
   b Create a diagram using the concepts. The question we want to answer using this text is: what factors influence the way young people spend their leisure time?

Interview with a researcher who studied how children spend their time

People say that children are very busy these days. What do you think about this?

Being busy is not a problem! Children who have a full dance card are happier than those who have little or nothing to do in their free time. We studied how different groups of children spend their time, those from immigrant families and those from indigenous families. The results showed that the girls from immigrant families that were the least integrated were the ones who were the least satisfied with the way they spend their free time.

Why do you think this is?

The children who do lots of different things in their free time, the ones the papers are talking about, are generally 'white' children. Relatively speaking they are better educated and they have quite a lot of money to spend. Children who have nothing to do are jealous of them. They also want to do sports, go to the movies or the disco, but they don't have enough money.

Which groups don't have busy schedules?

The immigrant girls are the ones in particular who don't have busy schedules; they spend a lot of time, relatively speaking, on school work, homework and household chores if you compare them to the indigenous children. They would rather be busy, but because of their home situation and their financial circumstances, namely a lack of pocket money, it's not possible. Of these girls, the ones that don't feel integrated, 17% are unsatisfied with the way they spend their free time. This is compared to 4% of their indigenous counterparts who are unsatisfied.

So ... children are not too busy?

Well, I wouldn't put it like that. My conclusion is rather that children who are busy rarely complain about it. Those that aren't busy, those are the ones that are unhappy about how they spend their free time.

What is your opinion of the way that children spend their time? Is it one-sided? Varied?

Children are very good at combining their various activities. On average they spend about three hours a day at their computers, but they also spend time outdoors. Cycling, on the trampoline, roller-skating, playing ball. Children are good at keeping themselves occupied.

Don't children spend too much time at their computers or watching their own televisions?

No, I don't think they do. They are moving with the times but they still enjoy tinkering with things. Boys still play with Lego and girls like beading, drawing and playing with plasticine. These things have been popular for decades and their popularity hasn't flagged at all. But this also has a financial component: parents who don't have a lot of money can't afford these things for their children.

What can society do?

We should not focus on those busy children who have a wide range of things to do, they'll be fine. It's the children with nothing to do that should be getting the attention. They're at risk of missing the boat in society. They need help when it comes to building friendships and being more outgoing.

Box 9.7

5 What determines the reliability of qualitative research results?

6 Describe the aspects of internal and external validity for qualitative analysis.

7 Which aspects to do with the quality of research play a role in the following situations?

   a A researcher conducts interviews with couples who can't have children. The subject of the research is coping with the difficulty of their circumstance. The researcher herself has just suffered a miscarriage.

   b You interview people about the way they are addressing sustainability in their business operations. This means you have to elect people in their company that are involved with this issue.

   c For research into the procedures of micro credit, the researcher keeps in close contact with one person in the organization.

   d For the same micro credit study, the researcher opted for a multi-pronged approach: participatory observations, a study of the literature, focus focus groups and in-depth interviews with experts.

8 In this chapter and in Chapter 5, there are texts about the war veteran research. Discuss the reliability and the validity of this secondary qualitative analysis.

Part IV
Assessment and Evaluation

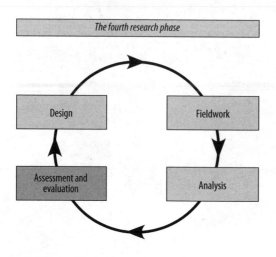

Part IV, the last part of the book, answers the question of how you can best go about evaluating, assessing and reporting on your findings.

In Chapter 10, we will discuss how to draw conclusions based on the results of your analysis, how to assess these conclusions and how to formulate discussion points. We'll talk about the pitfalls, but we will also discuss whether you have met your research objectives. When evaluating the research results, we'll be addressing questions such as:
- Which conclusions can I draw on the basis of my results?
- Has the central question been answered?
- Is my research reliable and valid?
- Which recommendations for the future can I propose (both in terms of the client and the research technique)?
- What can I learn from this research in terms of methodology and content?
- Which points for discussion has the research produced?

In Chapter 11, all the information is brought together in a research report. What should be included in the report and in which order, how to compile your reference list and how to present your conclusions will all be discussed in this chapter. You will also be given a few writing tips.

10

Conclusion and Discussion

The fieldwork is behind you now. The analysis is ready. You have a huge pile of results on your desk. Now you have to draw the correct conclusion from these results. This is a tough one. Apart from anything else, what are the 'correct conclusions'? By 'correct conclusions' we mean 'valid conclusions'. That is to say: you have found a valid answer to your central research question, i.e., an internally valid answer.

This chapter is all about drawing the correct conclusion. In terms of theory, you link the results of the core question, and in practical terms, you draw up recommendations for the organization, your client's organization that is. Evaluating the results will also be discussed, both for qualitative and quantitative research.

10.1 Drawing Conclusions

When you start thinking about your conclusion, the time has come once again to stop on your 'research road' (see Chapter 1) and look back. How did you tackle the research process? How did the design and the fieldwork go? What was the problem formulation (the central question and objective) again? Do you have a solution to the question based on the analysis? Will you achieve the research objective? What went well and what went wrong? For this you can consult the literature that you used in your research design. Are there any interesting links? You can also compare your own results to those of other research, which will not only enhance the reliability but also the validity of your own results.

definition   What does it mean exactly: to draw conclusions? When you draw conclusions you link the research results with the problem formulation and you answer the central question. You interpret the results on the basis of the problem formulation. You also address the question of whether you can achieve the research objective with this answer. Drawing conclusions is therefore not simply a matter of summarizing the results: there's more to it than that!

10.1.1   *Answering the Main Research Question*

central
formulation
revisited   The first thing you do is revisit the central question and the objective of the research (your problem formulation). You should have done this during the fieldwork and analysis as well. Normally you would have carried out much more analysis than is actually necessary to be able to formulate a good answer to the question. This is when you will need to make a selection from the analysis, and only refer to the most relevant results.

Even though drawing conclusions is not the same as giving a summary of the results, you do have to make a kind of synopsis. First you give a short sketch of the background to the research and you repeat the central question. Then you mention briefly your research design once again. The next step is to answer the sub-questions and after that the central question.

sentences,
no numbers!   Preferably, don't start the conclusion with the sentence: 'The answer to the central question is …'. That is way too brief. There's also no point in repeating the results, they should speak for themselves. The aim of the conclusion is to formulate a good and, preferably, to the point answer to the central question. You do this in your own words. Avoid using numerical results, you've already shown these. The conclusion should consist of sentences not numbers. It should not be a repetition of the results.

explaining
the conclu-
sions   There is one more thing. When you presented the results you only described them, without any interpretation. In the conclusion you interpret the results, or give a possible explanation for the findings. For instance, if you investigated the difference in the career paths of men and women, you may be able to find an explanation in the fact that many women interrupt their careers to have children, in failing emancipation policies or in the glass ceil-

ing. It could also be that your research findings confirm or refute those of another research. In your conclusion you discuss this comparison and explain why it is that you think these differences came about. We'll discuss this further in Section 10.2.1.

Normally you would first present the results of your research before you draw your conclusions. Articles about research in newspapers and magazines often deviate from this. In newspapers and magazines you often come across the conclusion first, for instance, that women, despite a growth in their participation in paid work, still lag behind men in terms of salary. Only then do they go on to explain this conclusion using research results to do so (see Text box 10.2). *newspaper articles*

Inequality in income still persists

For about the last ten years, the number of women taking on work outside the home has grown. Yet it is taking time for them to catch up to men in terms of income levels. Despite emancipation policies, the majority of women are still not financially independent. The average income of women in 2001 was just over half (53%) of that of the average income of men. That is an improvement of 3% in three years. For women, part-time work has become the norm. Seventy percent of working women work less than 35 hours a week. This is a trend that has emerged during recent years. In 1990, 40% of working women worked on a full-time basis.

Also, women still earn less than men for the same type of work. Their average hourly wage is 25% lower than the average hourly wage for men. This can partly be explained by differences in experience and education. But that still leaves an unexplained difference of 7%.

Source: *de Volkskrant*, March 5, 2003

Box 10.2

In the article in Text box 10.2, an analysis of incomes and working hours of men and women is described. The journalist starts with the conclusion: women have not yet caught up to men in terms of income equality. She then goes on to describe the results using numerical information. The sequence of the research project as it is described in the article is different to the sequence in the research report. In this case, presenting the findings first has a purpose: the journalist uses this to grab attention before elaborating on the research later.

Text boxes 10.3 and 10.4 show two more examples of conclusions in which the central question is answered.

Emeriti

In their research into the activities of retired professors, Becker and Verhoeven (2000) address the question: 'Which activity patterns do retired professors display, particularly in terms of their field of interest?' This central question was divided into a number of sub-questions, such as:

- How did they prepare for their retirement?
- How has their retirement been?

In their conclusion, Becker and Verhoeven answer these questions by repeating them and then formulating short and concise answers that are derived from their analyses:

- Of the professors who participated, 30% prepared for their retirement, in a variety of ways, between their 50th birthdays and the end of their employment.
- The emeriti reported that during their retirement they mainly occupied themselves with publishing scientific articles and mentoring PhD students.

Box 10.3

Highlands Sports Club

Research was conducted among participants of a cross country meet organized by Highlands Sports Club into satisfaction with the organization. In the conclusion, the question was answered as follows: 'The answer to the question "What are the perceptions of the organization and the way the cross country event progressed?" is: "Good". With an average of 8+, the organizers of the cross country meet can be extremely satisfied. This figure of 8+ showed little variation in the results, indicating that most of the respondents have similar thoughts on the subject.'

Box 10.4

The information in all three text boxes show that a conclusion consists of more than a mere summary of the results. The examples also show that conclusions can be presented in various ways and with various aims in mind.

1 In the research among retired professors, the sub-questions are first repeated before the answer is given: the conclusion is preceded by an iteration.

2 The conclusion about the field event is short and succinct: 'Good'. A concise conclusion that is evaluative in its content, which for the client this is a sign of appreciation.

3 Putting the conclusion at the beginning of the newspaper article, such as the one about women's incomes lagging behind those of men, can be an

indication of how important the writer considers this conclusion to be. This article also puts forward a possible explanation for this inequality: differences in experience and education. However, there is still an unexplained difference of 7%. The reader is left to give their own interpretation of this.

10.1.2 Presenting the Conclusion: An Example

Late 2002, the article in box 10.5 appears in a national newspaper. Panic strikes the nation! Talk shows summons experts to the studio, it's the headline item in the 8 o'clock news. Documentary shows sift through the archives for old information and interview patients on TV.

Increased chances of breast cancer through alcohol

Research shows that every glass of alcohol increases the risk by seven percent

Alcohol increases the chance of breast cancer among women. This has emerged from a large-scale international study in which several leading epidemiologists took part. Scientists compared the data from 58,000 breast cancer patients with more than 95,000 women who don't suffer from breast cancer.

Those who drink one glass of alcohol per day increase their risk of cancer by seven to eight percent. When this increases to two, three or four glasses their risk goes up by the same factor. Women who drink on average four glasses of alcohol per day, have an increased risk of between 28 to 32% of contracting the disease when compared to their counterparts who stick to mineral water.

According to Prof. Dr P. van den Brandt, professor of epidemiology at Maastricht University and a member of the research team, at least 4% of all breast cancer cases can be blamed on alcohol consumption. 'This translates to around four hundred cases per year in the Netherlands.'

Van den Brandt recognizes that drinking alcohol also has positive side-effects. 'Women are confronted with the difficulties of weighing the pros and cons of moderate alcohol consumption. It has often been shown that drinking one or two alcoholic drinks lowers the chances of heart disease. Not to forget that other factors also prevent cardiovascular disease, such as stopping smoking, exercising and avoiding obesity.'

Apart from alcohol, there are several other factors that play a role in the chances of contracting breast cancer. Earlier research shows that women who take the pill for long periods of time are at least twice as likely to contract breast cancers than those who don't. Other factors are the age of starting menstruation (the sooner it starts, the greater the risk), the number of chil-

dren (the more children you have, the lower the risk) and breast cancer in the family.

The research results were presented in the *British Journal of Cancer*.

Source: Van Vliet, 2002

Box 10.5

What is the story? The newspaper article presents the results of recent research that (according to the journalist) claims that for every glass of alcohol that a woman drinks, the risk of breast cancer increases by between 7 and 8%. Disappointed, many women abandoned their glass of red wine. No more good times. Excited, the journalists quickly work out that a night on the tiles increases the risks of breast cancer by almost 50% (6 glasses times 8% is 48%, isn't it?). What now?

The best way to check the results of this research is to refer to the original article from the *British Journal of Cancer* (Collaborative Group on Hormonal Factors in Breast Cancer, 2002). What is the case? Quantitative research was carried out into factors that influence the likelihood of contracting breast cancer. In other words they researched the factors that contribute to the risk of contracting breast cancer and the extent to which this happens. This included investigating whether alcohol consumption and/or smoking increased the risk of breast cancer. The researchers conducted a secondary analysis on existing data from 53 earlier studies (also known as meta-analysis) on the subject and compared the behavior patterns of 58,000 women suffering from breast cancer with more than 95,000 women without the disease. They analyzed a model which included a number of factors that may influence the chances of contracting the disease. These factors included alcohol consumption, smoking, doing sport, hereditary aspects, number of children, age (of first menstruation), breastfeeding, education and country of origin.

The study went on to assess the 'relative risk' of contracting breast cancer and the effects of alcohol (and smoking) *in addition to* this risk. The chances of preventing cancer among women who do not drink alcohol (as a reference category) were compared to the chances of cancer among women who do drink alcohol. It will be clear that every woman, on the basis of a number of factors, runs the risk of contracting breast cancer. Based on this, they then looked at the percentage increase in risk of cancer for each glass of alcohol drunk per day. It emerged that the average consumption of one glass extra per day increases the risk of contracting the disease by 7.1% *above the existing risk*.

Results of Dutch studies show that the risk of breast cancer among women under 75 years of age is about 8.8%. Consuming one glass of alcohol per day increases that risk to about 9.4% (7% of the basic risk of 8.8% is 0.6%). So you don't look at the risk of cancer in terms of absolute percentages, but at the *relative* increase: i.e., in relation to the general risk of breast cancer based on other factors. In other words: the risk of breast cancer for women in the developed world increases by 0.7 per 100 women upon the consumption of one extra glass of alcohol per day.

Because the media based their calculation on the absolute effect, they caused panic. Television journalists calculated that drinking five glasses of alcohol increased the risk of cancer by a third. This is a classic example of what misinterpreting research results can lead to. You have to drink large quantities of wine to dramatically increase your chances of breast cancer. The chances of succumbing to alcohol poisoning, however, are much greater (Van Vliet, 2002).

Recent research into breast cancer

Incidentally, recently more research has been carried out into the effect of alcohol on, among other things, breast cancer. It turns out that alcohol does increase the risk of breast cancer, but this applies to alcohol in general and not just to wine. Moderate alcohol consumption does increase the risk of cancer among some women, but the risk is not high (Allen et al., 2009). Always be careful when interpreting an 'effect' when you can only be referring to one 'correlation'.

Box 10.6

10.2 Discussion and Evaluation

Your research doesn't end with the presentation of your results and drawing your conclusions. In many cases you will have to give the client recommendations based on the research objectives. These recommendations consist of advice for improvements or changes to the client's situation. This is the last part of your research and it takes place after you have drawn your conclusions.

There is also an opportunity to discuss the results. A discussion? Yes: often at the end of their research, the researchers give their own personal view of the issues, they mention what they have learnt from a methodological and content point of view (i.e., they give their own evaluation) and they may even give their own opinion of the subject. Not all research reports contain a discussion section. You'll come across it more often in theoretical research than in practical research. Your research objective will normally determine whether or not to include a discussion section in the research report. If this discussion is relevant to your research objective, then you include it. If not, then you restrict the text to practical aspects, i.e., by giving the client useful and usable recommendations. We will discuss how to do this in Section 10.2.2.

10.2.1 Conclusions from a Broader Perspective

the rele- In your discussion, you primarily talk about the conclusions in light of the
vance of problem formulation. What, for example, do these research results mean for
your society? You talk about this in the discussion section. You can also give you
conclusion own personal opinion about the conclusions in this section. You could, for example, link the conclusions to a broader political context; you could juxtapose it to other opinions and perhaps discuss it in the light of other literature. What do the research results mean for the client, for practical goals, but also for the research objectives from an information point of view? For instance, you could put the research into employment participation and income levels of women (see Text box 10.2 and 10.7) into a different context. You could add a political discussion point to your research report by including statements about the current emancipation policies and how political parties view them. You could argue that women themselves play a role in the fact that they lag behind men in terms of employment because of the choices they make to do with their families and children. Other researchers may respond to this.

Low employment participation by women

In response to research into low employment participation by Nyfer (*de Volkskrant*, June 2, 2003), the researcher put forward women's own, independent decisions as a factor. A policy consultant reacted to this by saying that women's choice not to participate in the employment market is for a reason, and not just for the sake of it. Their decision is based on their 'given situation', such as leave options, pressure from their environment, the wishes of their male partners or their ideas about motherhood.

Another part of your discussion is an evaluation of the research process. *evaluating* What went well? What went wrong? Did you learn anything from the pro- *the process* cess? If so, what did you learn? Text box 10.8 gives you an example of such an evaluation. For example, during the fieldwork recruiting of respondents may not have gone according to plan. The discussion section is the place for you to elaborate on this and to indicate how it may be improved in follow-up research. You can also clarify why the response rate was too low, how communications with the client or staff at the organization went and similar aspects when you evaluate the process.

Learning moments

One researcher learned from his mistakes when he discovered that the response codes were incorrectly printed on fifty copies of the questionnaire. He didn't notice the mistake himself. If he'd given it to someone else to check, then the mistake would have been picked up. A serious mistake like this undermines the concept validity of the questionnaire. In his discussion about data collection, the researcher mentioned that an extra external check would have been the correct thing to do. The responses given on the questionnaires that were printed wrongly were not included in the analysis.

During your research, you assessed its quality at several points along the *quality of* way. *the results*
- During the operationalization you took into account the validity of the instruments, which should be as high as possible.
- When you draw the sample, you take into account the generalizability of the results (and your conclusion).
- During the analysis you test the reliability of your data and you check whether your instruments are valid.

methodolo-
gical justifi-
cation

When you evaluate your product, you come back to aspects of quality once again. Are your research results reliable? Can you generalize the results to the population? In other words, was the sample externally valid? How valid are your instruments? Did you actually measure what you intended to measure? How 'socially desirable' were the answers? How *internally valid* are the results? Did anything happen that may have jeopardized this validity? Did any untoward selection, growth or situations occur? Do these results give you a good answer to the research question? (See Boeije et al., 2009). In short, how good is your research in terms of its *methodological quality*? See Text box 10.9 for an example.

Independence and care for the elderly

During research among the elderly, a researcher was confronted with the problem that the methodological quality of the research results was undermined because the respondents were giving socially desirable answers.
The problem was 'To what extent is it possible to put "demand for care" by the elderly at the center of their service policy in a nursing home?' The objective of this applied research was to investigate whether *demand* for care should be the basis of the service they offered, as opposed to the *supply* of care (i.e., a care package that comes standard in nursing homes for the elderly). If 'demand for care' remained central to their policy, it would mean that the basic philosophy at the nursing home would remain the same, i.e., the elderly would still be independent and

responsible for their own decisions. To find an answer to this question, the researchers set up a qualitative research project based on semi-structured interviews with a number of residents.
The researchers scrutinized the results of this study. An investigation of the literature (Van den Heuvel, 1987) showed that the elderly are inclined to give socially desirable responses and are 'easy' to please. According to the author, they have never learned to be critical. The researchers tried to overcome this problem by organizing more than one round of interviews and by asking open questions, so that they could glean a more nuanced picture of the situation. Even in subsequent interviews, social desirability was detected in the responses (Wester et al., 2000, p. 59).

Box 10.9

Often the validity (and along with it, the reliability) of your results will not be very high. There may be several reasons for this. For example: a high respondent refusal rate (respondents refusing to take part because they have 'survey fatigue'), a non-generalizable sample, 'politically motivated' answers or random errors during the fieldwork, which in turn put pressure on the reliability. What can you do with the results? Throw them away? No, alongside methodological quality, you also have to look at the *usability* of your results.

Research results can also be used indirectly, to prompt a debate over a specific subject for example. This is what is known as *conceptual use*. Research into the effects of integrating immigrants could, for instance, be used to prompt a discussion about shaping and changing immigration policies. A consequence could be that the concept 'newcomers' (asylum seekers, families who reunite in a new country, refugees) could be revisited. Even if the results can't be generalized to a broader group, they are often seen as *indicative*, as a suggestion to use the results. *conceptual usability*

Research results can also have very direct applications. They can be set up to steer and support change. This kind of research is mostly very practical in its approach. While the validity and reliability have to be as high as possible, the usability of the results is sufficient reason for the client to consider the research a success. In cases like this, the results are *used instrumentally* (Boeije et al., 2009; 't Hart et al., 1998, p. 188-191). *instrumental usability*

During your evaluation, you look back over the research. What indications can you find to prove that the usability of your research was adequate? What expectations, as the researcher, did you have of the contribution by experts from the organization? Were their contributions useful? Could you use the information that you got from the organization in your research? What did you think of the co-operation you were given by the organization? Did they implement all the changes? What has the organization done with the research information?

It often happens that aspects of the research in themselves contribute to change in the organization. The *Hawthorne effect* is one of these. As we mentioned in Chapters 4 and 6, people in organizations are sometimes influenced if they know that research is taking place. In this way the research process itself, not only the results, affects the organization (Arnold, Cooper & Robertson, 1998, p. 43). This effect influences the internal validity. Just by presenting the results the process of change is started. *Hawthorne*

The fact that research can be extremely useful, even if the results are not generalizable to a wider population, is proven by case studies. The quality of case studies is sometimes doubted. We saw how case studies only have one research element: N = 1. Those who criticize case studies say that you are *case study* only describing one situation: that of the 'case' itself. This is why the results are not generalizable. Also, you can't do a re-test to increase the reliability. And so it goes on: plenty of aspects to criticize.

All of this criticism is based on criteria that are required of quantitative research. But case studies are qualitative by nature. Of course it is not going to be possible to generalize the results to 'a population'. That population doesn't exist. But this does not mean that the results are not extremely valuable and useful for the organization (that is often the subject of the case study).

Incidentally, the reliability and validity of case studies can be assessed through, for instance, aspects of the report process, triangulation, peer evaluation, contact with the client, comparison to other case studies, systematic analysis and so on.

In Text box 10.10 an example of instrumental usability is described. It is about research held in 2003 into the use of General Practitioners Information System by the ATLAS users club.

ATLAS members consultation

ATLAS is an association that uses two GP information systems, i.e., communication systems in which patient information is exchanged between doctors, pharmacies, and other medical services that are members. The systems they use are developing all the time and the association was keen to get opinions and suggestions from their members to develop policies. The results are not generalizable to the whole population of GPs because only the members of the association were asked for their input. The research was set up to support decisions about changes that were taking place and to get as much input as possible from the users' association of this GP information system. This approach increased the instrumental usability of the research.

Source: Verhoeven, 2003

Box 10.10

10.2.2 Making Recommendations

Finally, it is important to make recommendations. Broadly speaking, recommendations can be divided into two groups: those for the organization and those for future research. Recommendations for future research often have to do with suggestions for broadening the sample, for measuring other factors and so on.

If the research results are to be used to steer and evaluate change, then they will extend to suggestions for optimizing these changes and include reflections on the future. In this you can indicate which measures can be used to achieve the objectives of the research (for example, improvements to services).

Recommendations for an organization include practical suggestions for changes or improvements in relation to the research subject. Make sure that these recommendations stem from the research results. The objectives that organizations have when they commission research are often twofold. Firstly they are looking for suggestions for change; secondly they want to be able to use the research results to muster support within the organization for the changes that they want to implement.

recommendations for the organization

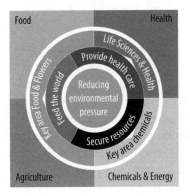

Figure 10.1   Recommendations for developing life sciences studies in diagram form

This sometimes leads to a situation in which you as the researcher are confronted with the client's hidden agenda: they may want to push through a measure using your research results to support it. Make sure you stay in charge of your results and don't be put under pressure when it comes to making recommendations. Figure 10.1 illustrates the recommendations for developing life sciences studies using four pillars: health, food, agriculture and chemicals. Text box 10.11 gives an example of recommendations.

The Healthy Weight Monitor

The Quality of Life section of the TNO (Netherlands Organization for Applied Scientific Research) investigated factors that influence exercise and eating habits. For this they use a sample of the population from the following age groups: 4 to 11 years, 12 to 17 years and 18 years and above. Based on the results, the following recommendations were put forward:

- develop policies so that a fitness norm for adults and children is worked out;

- ensure that there is good information about healthy exercise;
- ensure that there is good information about healthy diets, for example about eating vegetables and fruit;
- ensure that publicity campaigns appeal to the youth;
- promote exercise programs at companies (Van Keulen, Chorus & Verheijden, 2010).

recommendations for future research In the scientific world, research is considered 'good' if it raises more questions than it answers. In itself, this is correct. The results should raise new questions. You can include these 'new' research questions in a recommendation for further research (see Text box 10.12).

There could, however, be other reasons for recommending further research. Perhaps the sampling was not good, perhaps the non-response was high, or the research design did not lead to good answers to the research question (due to unforeseen circumstances). If this is the case then you can recommend repeating the research using a different design, sample or method of analysis. Needless to say you don't use this opportunity to fish for another project. Becker and Verhoeven (2000), for instance, suggested conducting the emeriti research at other universities (see Text box 10.3). They pointed out that this research should pay attention to the comparability of the results. They also recommended that the universities should keep each other informed about any research that they carry out on the subject.

Social networks of men and women in the labor market

In the report on their secondary analysis of the social contacts that help men and women to get better jobs, Verhoeven et al., (2000) concluded that these studies did not investigate the influence

that can be expected from partners. The three researchers themselves also didn't investigate the role that partners play in getting a better position in the labor market and which network con-

Continued	
tacts they bring to the relationship. In their recommendation for further research they therefore suggest that	future studies should investigate the role of partners and their networks.

Box 10.12

10.2.3   *Conclusion and Discussion Summed Up*

Finally we present what the conclusion and discussion should cover, in point form and based on questions.

Conclusions and discussion in question format	
Conclusion	**Discussion**
Repeat the central question.	Is there a link with other research results?
Repeat the research objectives.	If so, which results and how are they linked? Can you expand your conclusions? If so, how?
Summarize:	
What are the reasons and the intention of the research?	Are there points for discussion? If so, which ones?
What are the answers to the questions and sub-questions?	What did you learn from your research?
How can you explain these answers?	What went well and what went wrong?
	How good is the reliability and validity of the study?
	What threatened the validity and reliability and how did you solve the issues?
	What are the recommendations:
	– for further research;
	– for policy;
	– for improvements or changes?

Box 10.13

10.3   Glossary of Most Important Terms and Their
         Meaning

Conclusion	Summary of the main findings and answer to the problem formulation.
Discussion and evaluation	You evaluate your conclusion and give your own opinion of it; you also discuss the quality of your results and give recommendations.
Methodological quality	Quality of your research design.
Conceptual usage	The research results are used indirectly (for example to start a discussion).
Instrumental usage	The research results are used directly (for example to implement changes).
Recommendations	Suggestions for changes (for example in an organization) or for future research.

10.4   Assignments for Chapter 10

1   Write in your own words what you consider to be important when it comes to determining the quality of your research conclusions.
    a   Describe the reliability and the validity.
    b   Mention things that threaten the validity.
    c   What can you say about the validity and the reliability of the results of a case study?
2   Several subjects take part in research into the effects of nicotine patches on their smoking habits. The subjects respond to an advert and are put into experimental and control groups using random selection. Due to a shortage of time and money, no pre-testing took place. One of the subjects drops out during the experiment: it turns out that he has an acute form of cancer and dies shortly afterwards. Also, a relatively large proportion of the group stop smoking early on in the research, very successfully. Enquiries show that the subjects highly appreciate the counseling that the researcher offers. The researcher concludes that the nicotine patches work. What kind of threat to the internal validity of his research should he mention in his conclusion?
3   Read the article about lower incomes among women in Text boxes 10.2 and 10.7.
    a   What function does the conclusion have here? Why have they chosen to present the conclusions like this?

b Put forward a few policy recommendations of your own.

c What recommendations for research would you propose?

4 TNO's Healthy Weight Monitor (Text box 10.11) contained the following sentence in the conclusion: 'These results are based on self-reporting. Self-reported information does not always reflect true eating and exercise behavior; it often stems from socially desirable answers and an exaggeration of healthy behavior (…)' (Van Keulen et al., 2010). The same thing occurred in the research among the elderly described in Text box 10.9 (Independence and care for the elderly). Describe the aspects of quality that the researchers are talking about. What could be a solution for this problem in both these research projects?

5 Read the results of the study into 'study duration' in Text box 10.14 carefully. Discuss the following in small groups:

a What do you think the objective was of the CBS research?

b Propose a good problem formulation for the research. Tip: it is policy research!

c What is the most important conclusion?

d What recommendations would you give to the government, based on these results?

e Would separate recommendations for men and women be useful here? Motivate your answer.

Study duration has hardly dropped

All the measures put in place during the past decades to encourage students to study faster have so far not lead to students graduating younger. On average, students are 25.1 years old by the time they finish their master's degrees. That was the case in 1995 too, according to CBS figures. The government has been trying to limit the duration of studies for a long time because the costs of a university education per student are high ($18,000 per student in 2003). The implementation of the two-phase structure, intended to limit many studies to four years, a rise in tuition fees and achievement bursaries have not had much impact at all.

Women do tend to finish their studies faster than men. While men on average took 67 months to complete their studies in 2004, the women took 61 months to graduate. (…) Household expenditure on university education has gone up considerably during the last 8 years: from $1.3 million in 1995 to $1.97 million in 2003. This increase is linked to the voluntary contribution from parents, the cost of excursions and particularly the rise in costs for books and educational tools.

Source: Robin Gerrits, *de Volkskrant*, January 7, 2006

Box 10.14

6 Read the results of the study into reading abilities in Text box 10.15. As a consequence of these results, the minister for education intends to implement far-reaching education reforms.

a Discuss the reliability of the research.

b Can the results be generalized? If so, to which population?

c Which recommendations would you give the minister?

Reading abilities among children

PISA (Programme for International Student Assessment) is a research program undertaken by Organisation for Economic Co-operation and Development, OECD. PISA investigates the practical knowledge and skills of 15 year old pupils. This research is carried out in 65 countries based on a representative sample in each country. In the Netherlands, a sample of 4,760 pupils was drawn from a population of 204,019 15 year olds. In 2009 research was conducted into the reading abilities of 15 year olds and, to a lesser extent, into their mathematics and science abilities. In 2003 the focus was on mathematics and in 2006 on science.

The following emerged from the results: 'In each of the three areas investigated, the Netherlands scores well above the average for OECD member states. For reading skills, the Netherlands comes tenth on average in the list of all the participating countries. For mathematics and science, the Netherlands comes eleventh out of all the participating countries. Dutch pupils achieve higher scores for these skills than pupils in neighboring countries of Belgium and Germany (...). Reading skills have not dropped significantly in the Netherlands over the past 10 years; however low literacy does occur among the less educated. Knowledge of the sciences has also not dropped significantly. Knowledge of mathematics has dropped significantly.'

Source: Gille, Loijens, Noijons & Zwister, 2010

Box 10.15

WEBSITE   In the section 'Chapter 10' (tab Assignment solutions) you will find the solutions to the assignments in Section 10.4. You will find information about the design cases under tab 'Design cases' in the section 'Chapter 10'.

11

Compiling a Research Report

In Chapter 10 we discussed how you draw conclusions and formulate recommendations; in Chapter 11 we'll be talking about how you put all this information together into a good research report.

During the research project you will have gathered together a lot of text: your research design, your preliminary report, the data you've collected, a mountain of results, your conclusions and recommendations – and last but not least – your logbook. Now you are going to use this information to write your research report. Writing a coherent research report is no easy feat. How to tackle it, the order it should be in and the scientific requirements that it must meet will all be dealt with in this chapter. We will show you how best to present your results and how you can put together an executive summary. We will also discuss specific aspects of qualitative and quantitative research. We will be paying attention not only to the content of the report but also to aspects of form and style, with some writing tips that will help you to write a clear, readable report. We will close with a section on assessing reports.

Before we give you a step-by-step breakdown about the structure of a research report, we'd like to draw your attention to a few general points:

- When you first set up your research, you start on the report, we mentioned this in Chapter 3; you work on the report throughout the whole research project. You do this not only by making notes in your logbook, but also by setting up a table of contents so that you know what you're working towards. You then use this list of contents when you start writing the report.
- When you write the report, you make decisions about each target group. You do this by anticipating the way the results will be used within the organization, but also by bearing in mind the various people that will be using the report.

- You will be 'handing over' various versions of your report before it is finalized. Bear this in mind so that you plan enough time! If your schedule is too tight, then you are bound to run out of time.
- Reports are often published to inform as wide a group of people as possible about the results of the research, but also to make so-called critical assessments possible. Publishing the results of research may initiate a series of research projects if the results are tested in new analysis. You may therefore also be invited to judge the research reports of other researchers and colleagues.

Learning objectives

By the end of this chapter, you will know about the design and structure of a good research report, as well as about planning the time schedule and the objectives of your research report (and its possible publication). You will also know about the criteria that scientific reports (for publication) and executive reports must meet and how you must present the list of references for the literature that you have consulted.

Box 11.1

11.1   The Structure of a Research Report

We can be brief about the structure of your research report: you write it like you did it! It sounds really easy, but actually it's not. Report writing is almost an art in itself; you have to do it a lot before you get good at it. Some people are inclined to give a short summary of their research in their report, which means that they overlook all kinds of important things. Reports like this are not easy to follow. Other researchers digress so much that it becomes full of unnecessary information and repetition. That won't do either.

So what should you do? That depends on a lot of things, which seems facetious but it is true. Generally speaking, though, there is a format for research reports. If it is a scientific report, then the most important requirement is that you can replicate the research independently based on the research report. That means that it must contain all the relevant information, but not too much and in the right order!

When you write a research report it is essential to stick to a certain structure. In many cases (in fact, in most cases), it needs to have a specific layout or order. Figure 11.1 shows an example of a prescribed order. If you stick to this order when you are writing, you will notice that the research will start to take shape as you go along. This means that report writing can be fun, despite all the requirements that you have to meet.

```
Cover page
Summary
Introduction
Method
Results
Conclusion en discussion
References
Appendices
```

Figure 11.1   Overview of prescribed order

11.2   The Main Content of a Research Report

In the previous section, we gave you an overview of the structure of a research report. In this section and the next, we'll indicate what the content of each part should comprise. Besides the design of the cover page, we'll discuss how to write an abstract, and what information should be in the introduction, method, results, conclusions and discussion.

11.2.1   Title Page

On the title page, big surprise, you put the title. Think about the title carefully. It should 'say it all'. In brief, in one sentence it should be clear what the report is about. The relationships between the important parts of your research must be described in one sentence. Because of this requirement, some titles can be very convoluted which is why some people choose a short, catchy title followed a subtitle that elaborates on the research relationships.

Two examples of titles are shown in Text box 11.2. Generally speaking, these titles are easy to understand, but they are not all easy to read. The third title, for instance, would have been more informative if it had mentioned the period during which the research took place. From the first title it is not clear whose perceptions of discrimination are being investigated: members of staff or clients. If it had mentioned whether it was the staff or the clients, it too would have been more informative.

Titles of research reports

Discrimination in the workplace
A study of perceptions of discrimination
at nursing organization 'Carius'

What the veterans have to say
Various perspectives of stories about
experiences during military operations

From Deltaworks to dialect
A study of Zeeuws identity as experi-
enced by the residents of cities and
towns in Zeeland

Along with the title, and subtitle where relevant, you mention the following on the title page:

- your name;
- date and place (for example, the name of the college if that is where you submitted your report);
- the name of your tutor/examiner;
- the institute or college for which/at which you made the report;
- (sometimes the word count of the main text).

11.2.2 Abstract

Your report always starts with an abstract (summary). This is a piece comprising (normally) a *maximum* or 250 words (about half a page) in which you describe the research project (design, central question and objectives, sample and methodology) and the main findings. Most readers are interested in a short overview of the research, so everything should be mentioned. On the basis of the abstract, the reader will decide whether the report is relevant for them, and whether they will read it, borrow it from the library, ask for additional information, and so on. This will probably be the most difficult part of the report. You have to describe the entire research project in a couple of short paragraphs, and you must not leave anything out, so you have to be able separate the main issues from the minor issues. For this reason you write the abstract once the entire report is finished and you have a good overview. In Section 11.4, we'll be discussing another kind of summary: the executive report (or summary).

Sometimes you come across a personal note before the summary, a word of *preface*
thanks from the researcher or something similar. The summary is not the *(acknowl-*
place for this. You put your personal acknowledgements in a preface. You'll *edgements)*
find an example in Text box 11.3.

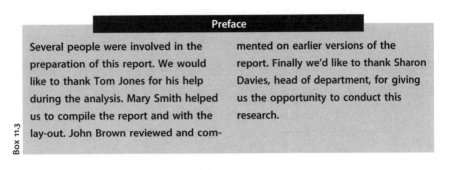

Box 11.3

Preface

Several people were involved in the preparation of this report. We would like to thank Tom Jones for his help during the analysis. Mary Smith helped us to compile the report and with the lay-out. John Brown reviewed and com-mented on earlier versions of the report. Finally we'd like to thank Sharon Davies, head of department, for giving us the opportunity to conduct this research.

11.2.3 Background and Introduction

In the *introduction* of your report you describe the *problem and objectives.*
Before this you describe the *background* to (the *reason for)* the research,
along with a short sketch of the situation. In applied research, it is often a
problem situation in an organization or among a group of people that is the
reason for conducting research. This is the immediate cause for deciding to
start research (in an organization). In Text box 11.4 we give two short examples of the reasons for launching an applied research project.

Background to applied research

Profiles of web visitors Deltaworks online

'Since its launch, the website "www.del-taworks.com" has enjoyed a growing number of visitors, up to 1,000 per day. The website designers would like to fine-tune the information they make available on the website – but also their product information – to suit the needs of these visitors: their target market. However, they have no information about the profile of these visitors. For this reason, they will conduct a web survey in which the background infor-mation of the visitors, their reasons for visiting and their interests will be assessed.'

Source: www.deltawerken.com

Home Affairs Committee announces a new enquiry into Firearms Control

The tragic shootings in Cumbria and in Northumberland have urged the Home Affairs committee to examine the legislation governing firearms. They exam- ined whether or not there is a need for changes to the way in which firearms certificates are issued, monitored or reviewed as a means of preventing gun violence.

Source: www.parliament.uk

Box 11.4

If you are reporting on empirical research, then you give an overview of any previous research into the subject in the theoretical introduction. You also mention the underlying theory upon which the assumptions about the results can be formed. By doing so you indicate the *relevance* of the subject, in other words why it is important to conduct research into this topic.

The main aim of the introduction (for both applied and theoretical research) is to interest the readers in the subject and to give an account in terms of the scientific importance and/or practical importance of the research (see Text box 11.5).

Branding

If you sell a particular brand of sports shoes, then it's not just quality that you take into account. The image of the brand plays an increasingly important role. This was the reason why a young manufacturer of sports shoes wanted to carry out brand imaging research for his sports brand. The practical interest was that the manufacturer wanted to effect any recommendations that the research may have for targeted marketing.

Box 11.5

Demarcation or model design? Not every client is interested in an elaborate theoretical explanation. If the research is mainly about practical issues, then you can keep the theoretical underpinning to a minimum. But it is always important to include a good demarcation of the concepts in your report. For example: 'By ... we mean ...' (the *stipulative* definition, you remember, don't you?). If you want to inform your fellow researchers about the theoretical foundations, then you can include a section on the theory alongside the more practically oriented version. Referring to previous research into the subject will increase the reliability of your own research.

After you have demarcated the subject, you formulate the problem and with it the research objectives. The central question normally includes a number of sub-questions, the more concrete research questions that you used during the research. You list these under the main question.

Together the central question and objective form the problem description of your research. For example, the objective of the parliamentary enquiry into firearms legislation includes examining 'The extent to which legally-held guns are used in criminal activity and the relationship between gun control and gun crime, including the impact of the Firearms (Amendment) Acts 1997' (www.parliament.uk).

11.2.4 Method Section

One of the most important scientific requirements that a research report must meet is that the research can be replicated exactly using the information contained in the report. The section in which you describe the research method must therefore be structured accurately and precisely. Those who read the report, including other researchers, must be able to assess, on the basis of this section, whether your research design is methodologically sound. Often in applied research this is considered to be less important. Clients want short and concise information about the design, sample and analysis method. Research quality is a side issue to them because they are primarily interested in the conclusion and recommendations that emerge from the report.

Below we have listed the most important parts of the section about method.

Participants or subjects
In this section you describe the (operational) population, the sample frame and the sampling method you used (random or non-probability, which method specifically). This is where you can give a description of the population in terms of relevant background characteristics. If you're describing the research group for qualitative research, you basically go about it in the same way. If you've conducted interviews, then you describe the group from which the respondents were chosen and how you recruited them.

Research design
When you give an account of your research design, the first thing you do is describe which data collection method you chose and the reasons you had for doing so. Is it qualitative or quantitative or a combination of both? Did

you conduct a survey, in-depth interviews, an observation or an experiment? Or was it desk research? List all the limitations and possibilities of the method or methods you chose; don't stick to the methodological aspects only; mention other factors as well, such as time, money, available research facilities and research elements.

Measurement instruments

Which instruments did you use to test your theory and to answer your research question? By 'instrument' or 'tools' we mean the technique you used to assess a concept. It could be a question, an observational category or a discussion topic. You demonstrate how you translated the concepts in the introduction into so-called 'measurable units'.

operationa-
lization

This is when you describe how you *operationalized* the concepts. For quantitative research, describing the operationalization is a painstaking business, for qualitative research less so. You also describe the topic list that you used and the way you derived your topics from the concepts. The perceptions of the respondent are the focal point of in-depth interviews, so you can't really give a precise operationalization of your discussion guide. The topics lists or questionnaires that you used are attached to the report in the form of appendices. Text box 11.6 and 11.7 show examples of measurement instruments.

Highlands Sports Club

A survey was organized for Highlands Sports Club which took the form of a self-completion postal survey among *all* the volunteers. So a sample was not drawn from the population because there were not enough people to do so. The survey included some questions about motivation for doing voluntary work for Highlands Sports Club. Under concept demarcation in the research report, the researcher mentions a few goals in voluntary work: its social relations, it's stimulating, an investment and it means caring for other people (Lindeman 1996). In the method section the research mentions under 'instruments' the operationalization in the

form of statements (items) that the respondent must rate on a five point scale from 'completely applicable' to 'not at all applicable'. A few of these items are as follows:

- 'A sports organization cannot do without volunteers.'
- 'A social organization cannot do without volunteers.'
- 'It is nice to be able to interact with other volunteers.'
- 'It's good to help others.'
- 'Voluntary work is relaxing.'
- 'When you do voluntary work you learn about new things and you learn new skills.'

Box 11.6

Box 11.7

Evaluation study for the youth orchestra

The report of the evaluation study into the organization of the board of the youth orchestra indicated that the respondents' experiences, opinions and suggestions formed the most important basis for the in-depth interviews. The justification of these 'instruments' in the report was kept very general: a small group of research elements, an open approach and the perceptions of the respondents as the basis. The aim of the in-depth interviews was to gather opinions, concepts and topics that could be used in follow-up research. The subjects that were discussed involved information about the current organization, the significance those involved gave to this, their experiences of and ideas about the organization and what they would like in the future. A topic list was appended to the report as information.

Analysis procedure

The next step is to discuss which analysis procedure you used to process, describe and assess the data. This is where your logbook is very useful: you can see exactly which methods you used, and now you describe them in this part of the text. In quantitative research it is usually very clear which analyses are necessary to answer the question. You also mention the hypotheses that you are testing (plus your statistical predictions).

Qualitative analysis is often based on a specific analysis method, such as the Grounded Theory Approach of Glaser and Strauss (1967) or Wester's symbolic interactionism (1991). These are the theoretical principles for the *analysis*. This is why they should *not* be discussed with model building (concept demarcation, theoretical introduction) unless they are used as a basis in the content part of the research.

11.2.5 Results

The research findings in your report give an objective and independent picture of the material you have gathered, be it quantitative or qualitative. Here you describe the response and the results of your analysis. You don't mention the conclusions yet, even if it is difficult not to!

Before you present the results of your analysis, you describe the fieldwork process. If you carried out a survey, you mention the response rate. An example of how to show the response rate in your report is given in Table 11.1. Did you organize in-depth interviews? Did you use the snowball method *data collection process and response* for this to find people to talk to (i.e., respondents)? How did it go? Did you use the telephone, letters, through a network of contacts? What was the result?

Table 11.1   Example of response rate for suburb survey

Suburb	Response rate per suburb % (n)	Distribution of questionnaires by suburb %
Highlands	82.0 (123)	26.7
Eastlea	73.3 (110)	23.9
Avondale	72.0 (108)	23.4
Alexandra	80.0 (120)	26.0
Total	76.8 (461)	100.0

In Table 11.1 you can see the response rate for a survey carried out in four suburbs in a medium sized city. The response rate is high, the distribution per suburb is about the same. In practice, you will seldom come across such prime examples of response rates.

quantitative results For quantitative analysis results, the results section comprises numerical information and test results accompanied by an explanation. The *most important* tables and graphs are also given. If there are lots of tables and graphs, then most of them (the least relevant) are presented in an appendix. More about this later.

significant? In this part of the report you also indicate whether certain assumptions were confirmed ('are significant') or not: i.e., or whether your hypotheses were refuted. At this point, you don't address the issue of why this is or what the answer to the central question should be. You save this for the conclusion.

qualitative results The same goes for qualitative analysis results: you report on all the steps you took and you describe the information that you found. Sometimes you can present your results using a diagram. (Have another look at Figure 9.3!)

11.2.6 Conclusion and Discussion

In the last part of your report the most important thing is that you look back: what were the questions being researched? How did the research project go? The point here is not to rewrite the whole research process all over again. You repeat the problem and objective and after that you 'simply' answer the central question. That is to say, the time has come to draw conclusions from your results and interpret them, without mentioning figures.

In the discussion, you are also 'allowed' to give your opinion on the matter. Go and have another look at what we said about this in Chapter 10. In the discussion section, the one that follows the conclusion, you give a grounded interpretation of the results and you try to persuade the reader that you are correct in this interpretation. You can fall back on (newly discovered) literature if necessary. This is also the right place to evaluate the methods that you used: what went well and what went wrong? What could be done differently in follow-up research? Are the results valid? And reliable?

In the discussion you indicated the extent to which the client's objectives *recommen-* were met and what should happen next: you put forward some recommen- *dations in* dations. This is the most important part of the project as far as the client is *applied* concerned. The recommendations must be good. So don't say: 'Do more *research* research' because that is way too vague and, not only that, it is going to look like you're fishing for more work. Good recommendations are clear, unambiguous, results orientated and focus on the research subject (see Text box 11.8). They should make suggestions for improvement that are achievable. Recommendations that cannot be implemented will end up in the bin. Also, recommendations should be achievable within a reasonably short space of time. There is no point at all in making recommendations about an as yet unknown situation at some point in the distant future.

Recommendation for promoting an informative website

A government agency commissions 'O & O' research bureau to investigate awareness and usage of a website containing information about and background to the government's emancipation policy. This website is regularly updated and is intended for politicians and policy-makers. It contains background information as well as statistical information, articles and news reports. The results show that not everyone knows about the existence of the website, that the information about the website does not reach all the stakeholders (the target group is too narrow) and that people sometimes prefer to have information 'on paper'. Those who are aware of the website and those who visit it regularly rate its content highly. On the basis of these results, 'O & O' research bureau make the following recommendations:

• Appoint someone to update the website on a daily basis.

• Develop a good search option for the site.

- Make it easy and quick to access the site by putting the correct information in the right place and in a good, easily understood and readable format.
- Make sure there are print options (for example by making pdf files available or by offering so-called 'print versions' of the information).
- Make sure there is an e-mail option (the option of sending the message from the site to the visitor's own e-mail address).
- Start a PR campaign to promote the website and increase awareness with the aim of extending the target group.
- Alongside the website, publish a regular newsletter (on paper and by e-mail) containing the latest information about the updated site.

Box 11.8

11.3   List of References and Appendices

The main body of your report contains all the necessary information: the theory, the research design, the results and the conclusion. You have stuck to the main points, but sometimes there is additional information that is not directly pertinent for the main text but is worth mentioning. You put this kind of information in the appendices. In this section we will tell you how to do this. We will first show you how to refer to literature that you have consulted and how you make a list of references. We will also give you some examples of references that conform to the method used by the *American Psychological Association* (APA). You will find more information about this in Section 11.3.2.

referring to   During your research, and therefore also when you are writing your report,
sources   you will often refer to literature and the results of other researchers. It is essential that you do this correctly. Why? Because then the reader can see where this information came from and where they can find additional information on the subject. It also improves the reliability of your text. You can use it to support the information you have mentioned.

plagiarism   Not only that, it is the decent thing to do: mention where you got the information from. After all, you have 'borrowed' it from its original source. If you pretend that it is yours, then you are committing *plagiarism*. It is not permitted; within their study students may be punished by failing the course and, in extreme cases, students may be expelled.

11.3.1 *Referring to Literature in the Text*

In the body of the text, you generally refer to the publication by mentioning *references in* the author's surname followed by the year in which the work was published *the text* and the page on which you found the information. You can do this in sev- *(citations)* eral ways. In Text box 11.9 we show you a few examples, in accordance with the APA guidelines. We'll talk about this in the next section.

Mentioning sources in the text

- (Jansen, 2006) → A reference to the author and his work. If you are referring to his work in general, then you don't need to mention page numbers.
- (Jansen, 2006, p. 35-39) → This is a reference to the author Jansen and the specific piece of text to which your reference refers, for example: a quote.
- 'Jansen claims in his thesis (2006) (...)' Because you mentioned the author's name in the text, you don't have to mention it again between the brackets.

- 'Verhoeven, Jansen and Tazelaar (2000) describe the social capital of men and women in light of their positions in the labor market. (...) The contacts that women have at their disposal are generally not as good as those of their male counterparts (Verhoeven et al., 2000).' → This is an example of a double reference in one article. The first time you mention all the authors, the second time you don't need to anymore, you use the first author's name and 'et al.', which means *et alii* or 'and others'.

References to the Internet must also be mentioned in the text. In Chapter 2 *referring to* we spoke about Google's enormous popularity, to the extent that a new word *works on* has been coined 'to google'. A warning at this point is called for: anyone can *the Internet* put anything onto the web. This does not mean that it is reliable; the source of the information is often difficult to verify and because of this, it is difficult to ascertain how authentic it is. Not only that, there is a lot of so-called 'gray literature' on the Internet, i.e., publications of limited edition, for a restricted audience, such as research reports, records, theses and so on. When you look for sources on the Internet, make sure you find out the origin of the information. Where did it come from? Is it from a respected scientific journal, a newspaper, an online encyclopedia? Even that does not guarantee that the information is reliable.

Take, for instance, Wikipedia, the freely available encyclopedia. On its home *Wikipedia* page it states that everyone is free to search for, add or adjust information.

This means that Wikipedia cannot guarantee the accuracy of the information (Wikipedia, 2006). Be on the safe side. If you want to use the Internet to find research sources that are more reliable, then look for information in Google Scholar, the search engine for scientific information. Alternatively you can visit Scopus (www.scopus.com).

The Internet has a wealth of sources: web pages, online magazines, newspapers, downloads, PDF files, databases and so on. You can cite websites in various ways. If the website contains an independent (electronic) document, it will have an author. Then you can use the normal reference in the text (see Text box 11.9) accompanied by the year in which the text was created on the website. Often it will suffice if you mention the URL.

11.3.2 APA Guidelines for Reference Lists

The sources that you refer to in your text are listed in the reference list straight after the main text. It is important that you actually refer to these sources in the main text. Reference lists are compiled according to the guidelines of one institute for standardizing texts in the United States: the American Psychological Association (APA). In social and other scientific articles and reports these guidelines are strictly adhered to. The aim of these rules is to arrive at one 'standard' for writing articles and reports. The APA has guidelines for articles and research reports:

- structure;
- lay-out;
- references in the text for various sources;
- the list of references.

New versions of these guidelines appear regularly, adjusted to conform to new and amended views, Internet developments and so on. At the moment (2011), Version 6 is the latest version. Most social science research institutes follow these APA guidelines, which in practice boils down articles being rejected for publication if they do not adhere to them.

APA as a guideline The APA requirements are very strict. Since this book is about applied research, we have chosen to view these rules more as *guidelines* and to apply them somewhat less stringently than is usual in the world of scientific research (see Text box 11.10 too). For instance, in scientific articles it is not common practice to put tables and graphs in the main body of the text, all figures and charts are put in the appendices. This is different in applied research where it is common practice to illustrate the results with tables and graphs.

Bear in mind that these rules are just something that someone at some point made up. You are free to question whether they are either useful or necessary. Regardless of what you may think of them, you have to acknowledge them for the simple reason that you will come across books and articles that follow APA guidelines. You have to be able to recognize the various formats and make use of them. With this in mind, using them yourself is the sensible thing to do.

All books have ISBNs, short for International Standard Book number. There *ISBN or* are also unique numbers for digital articles: Digital Object Identifiers. These *DOI* are very useful numbers if you are looking for things on the Internet. The system was invented to improve locating material in a digital environment; it comprises a publisher's number, a magazine number and a unique article number. It makes it very easy to trace things on the Internet, even if you don't know the title or who the author is. When you refer to articles, also on Internet pages, it's advisable to mention this number (see Text box 11.10).

APA List of references

The list of references at the end of this book has been compiled to conform to the APA guidelines. Note that in English the list of references is entitled 'References' not 'Literature'. We will give you some examples.

Books

Ajzen, I., & Fishbein, M. (1980). *Understanding attitudes and predicting social behavior.* Englewood Cliffs, NJ: Prentice Hall.

Swanborn, P.G. (2009). *Research Methods: The Basics.* The Hague: Boom Lemma.

Article in a scientific journal

Allen, N.E., Beral, V., Casabonne, D., Kan, S.W., Reeves, G.K., Brown, A., & Green, J. (2009). Moderate alcohol intake and cancer incidence in women. *Journal of the National Cancer Institute, 101*(5), 296-305.

Article with a DOI number

Cashin, S.E., & Elmore, P.B. (2005). The survey of attitudes toward statistics scale: A concept validity study. *Educational and Psychological Measurement, 65*(3), 509-524. DOI: 10.1177/0013164404272488.

Continued

Chapter in a book

Ajzen, I. (1987). Attitudes, traits, and actions: Dispositional prediction of behavior in personality and social psychology. In: L. Berkowitz (ed.), *Advances in experimental social psychology*, 20 (pp. 1-63). New York: Academic Press.

Research report

Verhoeven, P.S. (2004). *NIP-HRM ledenraadpleging 2004. Vragenlijstonderzoek naar tevredenheid met en verwachtingen ten aanzien van de HRM-sectie van het Nederlands Instituut voor Psychologen* [NIP-HRM-member survey. A survey into the satisfaction with and expectations with regard to the HRM-section of the Dutch Institute for Psychology]. Middelburg: Bureau voor Onderzoek & Statistiek.

Internet – an online document

Wikipedia. (2006). *Over Wikipedia*. Retrieved on 27 February 2011 via www.wikipedia.org/wiki/wikipedia.

Internet – online document with DOI number

Schiraldi, G.R. (2001). *The post-traumatic stress disorder sourcebook: A guide to healing, recovery, and growth* [Adobe Digital Editions version]. DOI: 10.1036/0071393722.

Internet – website

Verhoeven, N. (2010). *Onderzoeken doe je zo!* [This is how you do research!] Den Haag: Boom Lemma uitgevers. Retrieved on December 12, 2010 via www.onderzoekendoejezo.nl.

Internet – online magazine

Nelson, F. (2011). After Bin Laden. *The Spectator*. Retrieved May 11, 2011, from www.spectator.co.uk/spectator/all/6919163/after-bin-laden.thtml.

The first example is about a book by Ajzen and Fishbein. It was published in 2009 by Prentice Hall in Englewood Cliffs, New Jersey. Initials follow surnames to facilitate putting the list into alphabetical order. The placement and use of punctuation marks (commas, periods, semi-colons) is prescribed, so don't deviate, down to the last space and comma!

The second entry is from P.G. Swanborn, published in 2009 by Boom Lemma in The Hague. The title is *Research Methods: The Basics*. Titles of books, publications that are not included in magazines, journals or books, as well as the names of magazines are all written in italics, always. The next entry is an article worked on by a string of authors, seven in total. Whereas you would normally have to mention all the authors' names in the text the first time round, in this case you put et al., after Brown because you only ever have to mention the first six. This is an example of a publication (an article) that is included in a magazine, therefore its title is not in italics, whereas the name of the magazine is: *Journal of the National Cancer Institute*. This information follows the title:

- the *volume* (101);
- the *issue* (week, month, quarter etc.);
- the *page numbers* of the article itself (296-305).

Verhoeven's research report dating from 2004 looks a lot like the references to Azjen and Fishbein, and Swanborn, except that it is not the publisher that gets a mention, but rather the institute where the report was compiled. The translation is usually added in square brackets.

References to Internet sites contain not only the year in which the page or arti-

cle appeared, but also the day on which the information was retrieved from the web, and the DOI. Websites are updated regularly and it is perfectly possible that you might visit the site and find that the information has disappeared. All references to Internet sites should mention the URL or the DOI so that everyone can refer to the information. As we have already mentioned, the DOI is a unique number that is assigned to an article. Even if you don't have the title of the article and don't know who the authors are, if you use a DOI you can still find the article. Internet pages don't always have all the information you need. Sometimes there's no mention of the authors name, or no indication of when the information was put on the web. If the author is unknown, then you leave it blank. If the year is unknown then put (n.d.), which means no date.

Box 11.10

Reference software

Working on your reference list is a nit picking business. If you don't do it properly, there's a chance that your report will be rejected, your article won't get accepted for publication or you will be given a low mark. This should not be allowed to happen. For this reason, there are software programs available that make it all a lot easier.

Two such programs are Endnote® (www.endnote.com) and Reference Manager® (www.refman.com). Once you've installed them, you can use them as you go along in Word. User friendliness sometimes leaves a lot to be desired. On the one hand you can easily enter sources and import them into Word. On the other hand your document becomes peppered with 'fields' that make it difficult to lay out your final report. Both software packages are quite expensive.

software for references

managing   There is a simple way to manage your references via the Internet, for exam-
references   ple via citationmachine.net. On this website you can select the reference style
using the   you want (Modern Language Association (MLA), a language and literature
Internet   style or APA 6). You then indicate what kind of publication it is (book, article, Internet site, and so on). You enter the information and then you get the
reference list in the correct style.

online   A good way of doing it is by using online reference databases that you can
subscrip-   subscribe to. A lot of colleges and universities have these services for staff
tions   and students. RefWorks™ (www.refworks.com) is an example of this. You
open the program on the Internet. RefWorks is on while you're searching
for articles and books. If you find something then you import the source
into the database. If you are busy writing your report, then as you go along
you import references into your document and at the end you will have a
correctly compiled references list. You can't make any mistakes and at the
end you have a perfect, alphabetical listing that conforms to the APA guidelines.

references in   Finally, if you are using Word 7 or a more recent version, it is possible to
Word   create a bibliography, which is another word for a literature list. You do
have to keep a record of citations in a specific field, from the beginning. If
you do it properly, then you can create a bibliography using 'gallery', and
once again it will conform to the APA guidelines.

Figure 11.2   *Reference software*

11.3.3 Appendices

The appendices only contain additional information that is not needed when
reading the text but that can be used for reference work, for example (provided it is clearly numbered, see Text box 11.11). There is not always room
for certain tables and overviews in the text, simply because they are too

long. Also, they don't always help the reader get a better understanding of the text. These overviews and tables belong to the report but as appendices. Some people may find additional analysis results riveting, but not everyone does. You can also put that information in the appendices. Depending on who is going to read the report, you can also put an overview of the response rate, some tables and more technical calculations of your tests and assessments in the appendices. There is room in the appendices for the following things:

- topic lists;
- example(s) of the questionnaire(s) used;
- invitations and recommendation letters;
- technical explanations, for example about web survey design;
- additional results;
- long tables;
- information that is not immediately relevant to the text;
- information about the response, tables and technical text calculations (depending on who the report is intended for).

Numbering the appendices

For clarity, you must number your appendices and give them titles. For example:

Appendix A.1 Invitation letter

Appendix A.2 Example of questionnaire

Appendix A.3 Tables of demographics

Appendix A.4 Tables of the results

The text you refer to the appendices as follows: '(…) In the appendix (A.2) you will find an example of the questionnaire (…)' and '(…) For a full overview of respondent demographics we refer you to Appendix B.1 (…).'

Box 11.11

11.3.4 Criteria for the Contents of a Research Report

What exactly should a research report contain? Which parts belong where? In Table 11.2 you will find an overview of all the parts of a research report. For each part there is a summary of the most important criteria in terms of content.

Table 11.2   *Criteria for writing a research report or article*

Title page	– Full title and subtitle.
	– Name of researcher(s)/authors(s).
	– Date and place.
	– Institute.
	– Name of coordinator/supervisor.
Abstract	– Not more than about half an A4 page ($\pm$ 250 words).
	– Problem and objective.
	– Design, results and main findings.
	– Relevant information!
	– Short and concise.
List of contents	– Research reports should always have a list of contents.
	– In articles, a list of contents is not always necessary.
Introduction	– Background and reasons for research.
	– Objective (research – objective and project objective).
	– Central question and sub-questions.
	– Concept demarcation.
	– Theoretical introduction (model).
Method	– Population and sample.
	– Data collection method and description of fieldwork undertaken.
	– Measurement instruments (operationalization).
	– Analysis procedures used.
Results	– Sample demographics.
	– Quantitative and qualitative results.
	– Tables, diagrams, graphs and overviews.
	– Unbiased and independent review of the results.
	– Definitely no conclusion!
Conclusion and discussion	– Reiteration of the central question and objective.
	– Linking of results to problem.
	– Answer to the central question.
	– Other conclusions.
	– Recommendations.
	– Methodological evaluation of the results.
	– Discussion of the findings.
	– Your own opinion maybe, argumentation definitely.

Table 11.2   *Criteria voor het schrijven van een onderzoeksrapport of artikel (vervolg)*

References	– In alphabetical order.
	– Conform industry standards (APA).
	– Be comprehensive and exact.
	– All references in the main body of the text are mentioned in the list of references. Don't mention works you didn't cite!
Appendices	– Tables for reference purposes.
	– Additional and supplementary information.
	– Tables and overviews that are too big to fit in the main text.
	– Invitation letters, questionnaires, discussion guides.
	– Clearly numbered.
	– Clear and *comprehensive* references in the main text.
General remarks	– Is the text clear, properly organized and coherent?
	– Can anyone read it? Don't use jargon!
	– Put quotes in quotation marks.
	– Check spelling and grammar.
	– Be consistent in your choice of spelling, i.e., UK or US language settings, don't spell it organise one minute and organize the next.
	– Check your text for style.
	– Use a simple, consistent section numbering.
	– Check that your section titles are clear and that they cover the content.
	– Stick to one format.

11.4   Writing an Executive Summary

Research reports often contain very technical language, tables that are difficult to read and complicated explanations. Clients want reports they can read, one that can get sent straight to the board, without convoluted explanations and boring presentations. It's a problem. Because if you want to safeguard your results you have to write down exactly what you researched, how, when, where and the rest. This excludes the research report from being the 'readable' report that the client longs for. Not only that, the client wants to get on with implementing your recommendations; they'll need to see them first though. In short, what they're interested in is an explanation of the results, the implications for the organization and your recommendations.

Fortunately there's a solution. You can write an executive summary or executive report. These are extended abstracts (or an overview) of the research, accompanied by an explanation of the results and a clear overview of the recommendations. In applied research, this is the most read part of report. It contains – in a nutshell – the most important, usable and useful information for the organization or target audience. With it, they can get to work straight away.

You may ask why you can't simply use the abstract for this. That's because it is much too short for this and it does not contain the recommendations and a proper explanation of the results. This means you have to make a short, readable version of the research report, one that can be used as is.

Contents of an executive summary

- Reasons for the research.
- Short introduction with background and definitions.
- Central question and objective.
- Description of methods and procedures, timeline.
- Short description and explanation of results.
- Lists of conclusions and recommendations.

Box 11.12

It is difficult to say how long an executive summary or report should be but it should not exceed four A4 pages, even if it is a really extensive summary. If you opt instead for a short executive report, then it should be about eight to ten pages. The most important criteria are that it contains all the important findings and all the recommendations, and that the client can use it as it is. The criteria for the contents are given in Text box 11.12.

11.5 Writing Tips

People often find that writing a research report is an arduous task. It has to be finished by a certain date, the client (or supervisor) may not be happy with it, you get writer's block. These are the downsides of the writing process. Look on the bright side: as we have already mentioned, research often comes to life in your hands. It's just like a film is made up of rushes, normally not in chronological order, once you've edited it all and put it all together the story comes alive. It becomes a whole.

We would rather not give you a ready-made recipe for writing a report. Having said that, it may be helpful to bear the following tips in mind once you start writing your report.

A good tool for all your writing activities is to keep a detailed list of contents in your logbook. Start compiling it from the beginning: this is what your report is going to look like. You can use the APA guidelines for this. Each chapter has sections and sub-sections, with an indication of what is going to go into each section. A detailed list of contents is a very flexible instrument. During the research – and the report writing process – you can change sections or move them around. Things may come to mind about the contents of these sections. You can jot them down in the list of contents. It's also an easy way to see how far you are and what you still need to cover. *detailed list of contents*

The best advice you can get on this subject is that you give yourself as much time as you can for writing the report. This is because it takes a long time to write a report, to confer about it and then to rewrite it! It's not always easy to give yourself lots of time in practice, as much as you may want to, because there simply isn't much to go round. Clients are always impatient to see the results; your study project or your research report for your final paper often have to be handed in by 'week 20' or whatever. Time often runs out for this important part of the project. Not only that, the report writing is normally left to the end when you're busy catching up all the other time you've lost. All the more reason to plan your available time properly. Prioritize! *planning*

Text box 11.13 gives a general sketch of the milestones you'll come across when you're writing. Use these to help you divide your time well. Remember that everything depends on how easily writing comes to you, how much preparation you've put into it, other things you have to do, what the rest of your day looks like and so on.

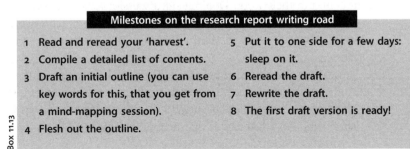

Milestones on the research report writing road

Box 11.13

1 Read and reread your 'harvest'.
2 Compile a detailed list of contents.
3 Draft an initial outline (you can use key words for this, that you get from a mind-mapping session).
4 Flesh out the outline.

5 Put it to one side for a few days: sleep on it.
6 Reread the draft.
7 Rewrite the draft.
8 The first draft version is ready!

After you've passed these 8 milestones, you can present your draft to your supervisor or client. Taking their comments into account, you redo steps 6 to 8 until everyone is happy.

Remember that most of your time will be spent thinking about and putting together an outline of your report, including going through all the information you have 'harvested', i.e., milestones 1 to 3. Use your detailed list of contents when you make your outline. Fleshing out your outline will take less time, relatively speaking. Reading it, rereading it and rewriting it, on the other hand, takes a lot of time.

managing your drafts — Final research reports are never written in one go. Various drafts will go back and forth between the researcher and the client, the student and the supervisor. Make sure you manage your versions as well as possible, for example by giving them a document name that includes the version number. Another way to do it is to put the date, or version number in the header or footer.

Google Docs — If you're working on the project with other people, then Google Docs is an option. If you have an account, you can up- or download the latest version of your document at any time. You can work on the document online, using all kinds of formats, and together with other people (all at the same time!). You can invite people to look at the document, you can put documents online or send them as attachments. Each group member has access to all the documents, in the latest version. Finally, managing the versions is easy because you can always see who was the last person to work on it. You can also reinstall older versions.

peer assessment and peer consultation — Try to think of your first version as a draft; you can expect to get comments. If you're part of a study group, then find people to assess it for you (*peer assessment*). This does *not* imply that you're free to tear each other's work apart. When you're compiling a report, this is not helpful! Give your fellow students useful tips, constructive criticism and additional information when it comes to their work. Don't avoid discussions about the content. Organize a discussion session about your work with a group of fellow students or colleagues. This is a way to learn a lot about one another's progress (and mistakes)!

Researchers use this method a lot to support one another in their work. This kind of collegial co-operation is often called *peer consultation* instead of 'peer assessment'. It's what colleagues do for each other, no strings attached and objectively. An advantage is that it improves the reliability of your research.

Your final report may be published in various versions. This is the case if there are various target audiences: management, participants and researchers. This may mean that you will be presenting the information in various ways, in terms of style, information and complexity. For example:

- to suit the level of knowledge among the target audience (they may not be familiar with research jargon);
- a short and concise summary, with recommendations for the management;
- with an emphasis on the research being replicable, on the theoretical model and the methodological aspects; in brief, this is a version suitable for your fellow researchers because it is one of the conditions for being able to assess reliability.

11.6   Assessing Publications

Some reports are for internal use only, but often they are published in journals, scientific or otherwise, as theses (for doctoral research) or in book form. You can judge these publications in several ways. The first thing you can look at is how useful the results are, or you can judge the report on the basis of the methods and the theory it uses. The way to do this depends on your intention. If you're working for the policy department of a municipal organization and you want to use the report to develop a new policy plan, then the emphasis will be on the usability of the results. If as the researcher you are interested in a particular theory or you want to test a hypothesis, then you will look at the concept demarcation and the theoretical foundations or the methodological aspects of the report. In brief, the way you look at a report depends on the function that the research report has for you.

The way you judge a research article depends on its objective. But how do you know what the writer's objectives are? You can assess this by looking at the interpretation given in the article. Articles can be intended for various audiences: *target audiences for publication*

1 *Researchers*. This target group normally has their own journal. The objective here may be to explain a theory or test a method.
2 *Students*. The aim here is to clarify a research set up, the way the research was conducted. You have to pay attention to the way the information is presented to the students. Is it explained clearly? Does the article have a clear structure?
3 *Managers/policy makers*. The objectives of articles and reports that target this group often have to do with using the results to develop policies. A

summary of the research will normally suffice; the emphasis should be on evaluating the recommendations.

4 *Implementation.* Are the research results important to those who have to implement things in organizations? Then you need to take into account what the target audience know about the subject. When you judge the report, you assess the suitability for the audience. If, for instance, it is about safety regulations for forklift operators, then the recommendations for those implementing the regulations need to be formulated in such as way that they can be implemented.

5 *General public.* Often you'll see short articles in national and regional newspapers about research and its results. The aim is to disseminate the information to a very broad public on all levels. This is difficult. How do you decide what should be included and what should not?

Social services doing a good job

The social services are doing a good job; this is according to research that an independent research bureau carried out among their clients. More than half of 800 questionnaires that were sent out were completed and returned.

The research results showed that clients are satisfied with the treatment they received from civil servants. Other aspects that were rated highly included supply of information, the care with which queries were handled and the speed with which decisions were made. Despite this, there were a few aspects that clients were dissatisfied about.

Telephone access to the social services is not what it should be. Waiting times are long because the service is only accessible by telephone during the mornings. Also, respondents felt that social services are not transparent enough in how they deal with appeals and complaints; they are dissatisfied with the difficult language used in correspondence and council orders; and they would prefer to have more privacy at the counter.

Social services would like to repeat the client satisfaction research in two years time so that they can safeguard the quality of the service they offer.

Box 11.14

Text box 11.14 shows an article about research carried out by the Social Services. On assessing the article's content, the first thing you notice is that the article starts by referring to the response rate: 'More than half of 800 questionnaires that were sent out were completed and returned.' For the rest, the article is mainly about what aspects of their service clients are satisfied with, followed by four areas that came in for criticism. Finally, we're told that they want to repeat the research in two years time 'so that they can safeguard the quality of the service they offer'. With the knowledge that you have gained about setting up and carrying out research, you are now able to do a critical assessment of this article, which is what the newspaper reporter did (see Text box 11.14). Text box 11.15 contains a response to this article. According to the writer, the research conclusions as reflected in the article were drawn a little too 'quickly'; they're a lot less straightforward for those who are aware of the restrictions that the research was subjected to. The reader is misled because too much information has been left out.

Letter in response to the article about Social Services research

Jumping to conclusions

Recently I read an article in your newspaper that claimed that the Social Services function adequately. Apparently, this was the conclusion of a survey. Despite having not read the research report in question, a few critical comments seem to me to be in order. Firstly the article reports that a large section of the respondents failed to return the questionnaire. The fact that 'more than half' of the potential participants actually took part in the research leads to the conclusion that almost as many cast the questionnaire aside. A non-response of almost 50 percent is considerable for a survey. A very real possibility exists that among this group of non-participants there are clients who felt disinclined to take part in a survey commissioned by the Social Services. The notion that their contribution is unlikely to be used to find a solution to the problems that they experience at Social Services may well have played a role in their decision.

Furthermore, during the survey I was also a client of the Social Services. As such I took part in this research. I noticed that the questions focused to a large extent on practical issues, such as accessibility and the intelligibility of the language they use. Obviously these are important indicators of the adequate functioning of a government department. The opportunities to express criticism of the functioning of the service in the research concerned were, however, extremely limited. For this reason the research suffered from obvious shortcomings in this respect as well. Finally, from my own experience and conversations that I have had with members of the People on Social Security Association and those representing clients on the board, the experience is that social services occasionally make mistakes. Apart from criticism of the way some officers treat people, there is dissatisfaction with the bureaucratic strictness with which the social services apply rules and regulations. Their stringent interpretations give rise to personal frustration. Clients are expected to apply for jobs that they hardly stand a chance of getting. There are also complaints about the relatively high incidence of fines and disciplinary actions. It has been my own experience that a member of the social services' legal staff based his response to a complaint

of mine solely on the insights of my former officer. Clearly he did not consider it necessary to apply the principle of listening to both parties: plainly a characteristic of amateurism.

Bob Bouhuis, Laag-Soeren
College lecturer in research methods

Box 11.15

In Text box 11.16 we give a few critical remarks about the article.

Evaluation of the Article about the Social Services

1   We will never find out what the actual response rate was. The term 'more than half' could mean so many things. Bob Bouhuis is right in his claim that the response was still quite decent. Suppose the non-response actually was 45%. That means that a large portion of the questionnaires were not completed. What do these people in particular think of social services? Why haven't they filled in the questionnaire? We don't know. In any event the population validation of the research leaves a lot to be desired – and in turn the reliability of the results. On the basis of the information contained in that research, it is not possible to draw conclusions about the opinions of the whole population (all social services clients).

2   The pronouncement that the clients are happy about their treatment at the hands of civil servants is not very specific. You don't know what treatment by officers it is that they are talking about. You also don't know how they measured this 'satisfaction'. What response options were the people given? And from how many could they choose?

3   The phrase 'the speed at which decisions were taken' needs elucidation. How fast is 'fast': a week, a month? What was this response time compared to? Other social services? Social desirability is a step away because clients that take part in research are perhaps the ones who are least likely to be critical, even if they are assured that the research is anonymous.

Continued	

Box 11.16

4 It would also have been more informative if the article had mentioned why it was considered necessary to repeat the research in two years time. Are interventions about to be implemented? Do they want to measure the effect of certain measures? Are they having to justify themselves to the ministry? Are cutbacks or a reorganization looming?

5 The objective is: to safeguard the quality of service. Agreed. To safe-

guard means 'to preserve'. What if the general quality of service was not rated well in this assessment? The article is not clear about this. Are people looking for improvement? Or do they want to improve the quality of service anyway? Which aspect of 'quality' of service are they talking about? First you establish what is meant by 'quality' and how this should be evaluated.

If research is published as a book or article, you are given the opportunity to *status and* scrutinize it. Publications in well-known and prestigious scientific and pro- *quality* fessional journals are the ones most highly esteemed (especially among the scientific community). But even if publications in some journals are highly esteemed, this is no guarantee of quality (Dassen & Keuning, 2008).

Before an article is accepted for publication in a journal, an intensive phase of so-called *peer review* takes place. Fellow researchers, often but not always scientists, who work as editors for the journal, review your report and comment on it. Sometimes you may get asked to make recommended changes that you don't agree with at all. Do not change your article for the sake of getting it published. Publishing an article may be a political or strategic decision too, more so than one based on the content of the report. And not all 'peer reviews' are good either. A consequence is that the quality of the articles may vary, despite the fact that the journal itself is highly regarded (for instance by its impact factor). For this reason the recommended thing to do is to read reports, articles, and books as well, critically and compare them with material from other sources.

11.7 Glossary of Most Important Terms and Their Meaning

APA guidelines   American Psychological Association's report and reference styles.

References   Citations of sources used.

ISBN	International standard book number.
DOI	Digital object identifier, unique number of a written source.
Plagiarism	Intellectual property theft: using text from another author without quoting the source.
Milestone	Sub-objective during research, measured in time.
Peer review	Evaluation of articles, before publication, by fellow researchers.
Peer assessment/consultation	Fellow students or colleagues read the various versions of your report and comment on it.

11.8 Assignments for Chapter 11

1 The list of references in the back of the book is very long. The following references are in it. Indicate what types of documents they are. How do you know?

a Ajzen, I. (1987). Attitudes, traits, and actions: Dispositional prediction of behavior in personality and social psychology. In: L. Berkowitz (ed.), *Advances in Experimental Social Psychology*, 20, pp. 1-63. New York: Academic Press.

b Arnold, J., Cooper, C.L., & Robertson, I.T. (1998). *Work psychology. Understanding human behavior in the workplace*. London/Harlow: Prentice Hall.

c Canning, A.B. (2002). *An introduction: Big6™ information problem-solving with technology*. Retrieved on November 21, 2002, from www.Big6.com.

d Crok, S., Slot, J., Trip, D., & Klein Wolt, K. (2002). *Vrijetijdsbesteding jongeren in Amsterdam*. Amsterdam: Bureau voor O + S.

2   Study the following references and give (where possible) their title, author, year, type of document and page numbers.

  a   Allen, N.E., Beral, V., Casabonne, D., Kan, S.W., Reeves, G.K., Brown, A., & Green, J. (2009). Moderate alcohol intake and cancer incidence in women. *Journal of the National Cancer Institute, 101*(5), 296-305.

  b   Glaser, B.G., & Strauss A.L. (1967). *The discovery of Grounded Theory.* Chicago: Aldine.

  c   NIBUD (2010). Students' borrowing behavior. A preliminary study into studyloans, debts and other financial matters. Utrecht: National Institute for Family Finance Information.

  d   Canning, A.B. (2002). *An introduction: Big6™ information problem-solving with technology.* Retrievedsolving with technology. Retrieved on November 21, 2002, from www.Big6.com.

3   Below are some research subjects. Discuss possible objectives and target groups for these projects in your group.

  a   A large high school commissions research into 'safety at school' among the pupils.

  b   A web shop wants to know about the profile of its visitors and what their perceptions are of the range and quality of their products.

  c   A new medicine is tested among a group of specially selected subjects. The client is the manufacturer of the medicine.

  d   The provincial library wants to know about visitor numbers over the previous five years, the reasons behind these numbers and what can be done to get visitor numbers up.

4   Read the article about the study on the social services in Text box 11.4 again.

  a   What could be the problem and objective for this research?

  b   Put forward a proposal for the sample structure.

  c   Which data collection method has been used?

  d   What conclusions does the journalist draw?

  e   Discuss the quality of the research. Base your discussion on the response in Text box 11.15.

5   Read the article about parents opting to have two children in Text box 11.17.

  a   The article is in fact about two research projects. Where is the turning point in the text?

  b   What is the journalist's objective in the second piece of research that he describes here? Discuss your answer.

  c   What method is used in the research that the journalist first describes? What were the research elements?

d Formulate a problem and objective for both research projects.

e Put forward a discussion point based on the conclusions and discuss it in your study group.

Most parents prefer to have two children

Families in Europe are standardizing. Figures from the Central Bureau for Statistics (CBS) show that parents in a majority of cases prefer to have two children. The CBS studied family composition among nearly a million families in which the youngest child is between 8 and 12 years old. More than half the children have one sibling.

One out of eleven children have it all to themselves. The number of families with one child is slightly less than those with three children. One out of twenty families has four children, while a family comprising five or more children is an exception.

The research undertaken by the CBS is purely numerical. According to family sociologist Kees de Hoog, standard families are usually the product of a compromise between the man and the woman. Six years ago, De Hoog, who is affiliated with Wageningen University, worked on research for the National Family Council. He thinks that the developments detected by CBS started in the sixties.

De Hoog gives a rough sketch of the standard family. The woman takes the initiative, but her wish to have children is seldom greeted with enthusiasm. The husband is anxious about the impact on the family income and who will take on childcare but eventually gives in. The step from one child to two is much smaller than from none to one. Once again it will be the woman who brings up the subject and once again the man will object. But it has already become apparent that the combination of work and childcare is possible and so his resistance is less obstinate. However, if the standard woman carries on pushing, then the standard man digs his heels in. Two children are enough for a family.

The increase in age at which children are conceived also plays a small role. De Hoog: 'A woman who has her second child at the age of 38 can't see herself doing the diaper thing once she's in her forties.'

The CBS calculations also include immigrant families where generally speaking families are larger. De Hoog signaled a drop in the number of children among immigrant families from an average of seven to three or four. 'Integration has not failed altogether.'

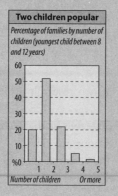

Two children popular

Percentage of families by number of children (youngest child between 8 and 12 years)

Number of children   Or more

Box 11.17

6 Refer to Text box 11.17 about choosing to have two children.

   a How would you make a short summary of the results?

   b What would you change if you were to turn the short summary into an executive summary?

   c The research described is 'purely numerical'. What do you think De Hoog means by this? What criticisms does he make?

   d Produce an alternative research proposal that addresses this point of criticism.

In the section 'Chapter 11' (tab Assignment solutions) you will find the solutions to the assignments in Section 11.8. You will find information about the design cases under tab 'Design cases' in the section 'Chapter 11'.

Appendix Sources

Introduction

When writing this book, the author chose only to refer to literature in the main text where it concerned literal quotes. For these you will find references in the text. This appendix contains an overview of the literature that was consulted. It also contains a list of the websites used for developing the text, for examples and sometimes for figures. This book is an *introduction* to methods and techniques. This means that not every subject has been thoroughly explored. For those who would like to know more about the subjects mentioned in this book, there are tips and suggestions for further reading, websites and other information, on the companion website.

References

Achterstand inkomen is hardnekkig [Arrears in income stubborn]. (5 March 2003). *de Volkskrant.*

Docent Nederlands vindt favoriete schrijvers leerling helemaal niets [English teachers don't like pupils' favorite writers]. (1 November 2002). *de Volkskrant.*

Hoe verschillende peilingen de vier grootste partijen inschatten [How the various polls assess the four largest parties]. (18 January 2003). *de Volkskrant.*

Opiniepeilers ondermijnen democratie met gebakken lucht [Opinion polls undermine democracy with hot air]. (3 June 2010). *NRC Handelsblad.*

Loonkosten top stijgen met 20% [Wage costs increase by 20%]. (24 May 2003). *de Volkskrant.*

Peilingen hebben veel kwaad gedaan [Polls have done damage]. (10 June 2010). *NRC Handelsblad.*

Proefpersonen voor psychologisch onderzoek [Subjects for psychological research]. (2006). Retrieved on February 19, 2006, from www.aanbodpagina.nl.

Tussen kakkers en normalo's [About preppies and normalos]. (November 24, 2005). *de Volkskrant.*

Twee kinderen populair [Having two children is popular]. (February 24, 1993). *de Volkskrant.*

Veel kinderen zijn arm [Many children are poor]. (October 5, 2010). *BN DeStem.*

Zwangere vrouw vaker opgenomen [Pregnant women admitted more frequently]. (November 24, 2005). *de Volkskrant.*

Abma, T., Nierse, C., Griendt, J. van de, Schipper, K., & Zadelhoff, E. van (2007). *Leren over lijf en leven. Een agenda voor sociaal-wetenschappelijk onderzoek door nierpatiënten* [Learning about body and life. An agenda for social science research by kidney patients] (research report). University of Maastricht.

Ajzen, I. (1987). Attitudes, traits, and actions: Dispositional prediction of behavior in personality and social psychology. In: L. Berkowitz (ed.), *Advances in experimental social psychology*, 20 (pp. 1-63). New York: Academic Press.

Ajzen, I., & Fishbein, M. (1980). *Understanding attitudes and predicting social behavior*. Englewood Cliffs, NJ: Prentice Hall.

Allen, N.E., Beral, V., Casabonne, D., Kan, S.W., Reeves, G.K., Brown, A., & Green, J. (2009). Moderate alcohol intake and cancer incidence in women. *Journal of the National Cancer Institute, 101*(5), 296-305.

Arnold, J., Cooper, C.L., & Robertson, I.T. (1998). *Work psychology. Understanding human behaviour in the workplace*. London/Harlow: Prentice Hall.

Baarda, D.B., & Goede, M.P.M. de (2001). *Basisboek methoden en technieken* [Introduction to methods and techniques]. Houten/Groningen: Stenfert Kroese.

Baarda, D.B., Goede, M.P.M. de, & Kalmijn, M. (2000). *Enquêteren en gestructureerd interviewen. Praktische handleiding voor het maken van een vragenlijst en het voorbereiden en afnemen van gestructureerde interviews* [Conducting surveys and interviews. Practical guide for designing questionnaires and preparing and conducting structured interviews]. Houten: EPN.

Baarda, D.B., Goede, M.P.M. de, & Meer-Middelburg, A.G.E. van der (1998). *Basisboek open interviewen. Praktische handleiding voor het voorbereiden en afnemen van open interviews* [Introduction to open interviews. Practical guide for preparing and conducting open interviews]. Houten: Educatieve Partners, Stenfert Kroese.

Baarda, D.B., Goede, M.P.M. de, & Teunissen, J. (2001). *Basisboek kwalitatief onderzoek. Praktische handleiding voor het opzetten en uitvoeren van kwalitatief onderzoek* [Introduction to qualitative research. Practical guide for designing and conducting qualitative research]. Groningen: Stenfert Kroese.

Babbie, E., R. (2005). *The Basics of Social Research*. Belmont, CA: Thomson Wadsworth.

Ball, Karlene *Recognition of Excellence in Aging Research Committee Report*. (n.d.) Retrieved on April 11, 2011, from http://aging.senate.gov/award/nih22.pdf.

Becker, H., & Verhoeven, N. (2000). *Utrechtse emeriti; een sociologische verkenning* [Utrecht emeriti: a sociological exploration] (research paper). Utrecht: University of Utrecht.

Bensing, J.M., & Lindert, H. van (2003). Vermoeider dan ooit [More exhausted than ever]. *Medisch Contact, 58.*

Berg, H. van den, Stagliola, S., & Wester, F. (ed.) (2010). *Wat veteranen vertellen. Verschillende perspectieven op biografische interviews over ervaringen tijdens militaire operaties* [What veterans say. Various perspectives on biographical interviews about experiences during military operations]. Amsterdam: Pallas Publications.

Boeije, H. (2005). *Analyseren in kwalitatief onderzoek. Denken en doen* [Analysing qualitative research. Thinking and doing]. Amsterdam: Boom Onderwijs.

Boeije, H., 't Hart, H., & Hox, J. (2009). *Onderzoeksmethoden* [Research methods] (8th edition). Den Haag: Boom Lemma uitgevers.

Borstkankervereniging (2005). *Rapport doorlooptijden borstkankerzorg* [Report on treatment times for breast cancer]. Nederland: Borstkankervereniging.

Brinkman, J. (2001). *Cijfers spreken. Statistiek en methodologie voor het hoger onderwijs* [Numbers talk. Statistics and methodology for higher education]. Groningen: Wolters-Noordhoff.

Bruin, R. de., & Molenbroek, J.F.M. (2001). RSI bij studenten [RSI among students]. *Tijdschrift voor Ergonomie, 26*(4), 17-28.

Buuren, H. van, & Hummel, H. (1997). *Onderzoek, de basis* [Research, the basis]. Groningen: Wolters-Noordhoff.

Canning, A.B. (2002). *An introduction: Big6™ information problem-solving with technology.* Retrieved on November 21, 2002, from www.Big6.com.

Chalmers, A.F. (1987). *Wat heet wetenschap* [What is research]. Amsterdam/Meppel: Boom.

Checkit Search engine Mediabureau (2010). *Checkit nationale Search Engine Monitor* [Checkit national Search Engine Monitor]. Retrieved on October 2010, from www.checkit.nl/nationalesearchengine-monitor.html.

Collaborative Group on Hormonal Factors in Breast Cancer (2002). Alcohol, tobacco and breast cancer – Collaborative reanalysis of individual data from 53 epidemiological studies, including 58,515 women with breast cancer and 95,067 women without the disease. *British Journal of Cancer, 87*(11), 1234-1245.

Crok, S. (2003). *Gelukkig druk* [Happy to be busy]. Retrieved on February 6, 2003, from www.onstat.amsterdam.nl.

Crok, S., Slot, J., Trip, D., & Klein Wolt, K. (2002). *Vrijetijdsbesteding Jongeren in Amsterdam* [Leisure time activities among the youth in Amsterdam] (research report). Amsterdam: Bureau voor O + S.

Dassen, T., & Keuning, F. (2008). *Lezen en beoordelen van onderzoekspublicaties. Een handleiding voor studenten hbo- en wo-gezondheidszorg, geneeskunde en gezondheidswetenschappen* [Reading and assessing research publications. A guide for college and university students of health care, medicine and health sciences]. Amersfoort: Thieme Meulenhoff.

Dekker, P. (ed.) (1999). *Vrijwilligerswerk vergeleken. Nederland in internationaal en historisch perspectief* [Voluntary work compared. The Netherlands from an international and historical perspective]. Sociaal en Cultureel Planbureau.

Dekker, W., & Teeffelen, G.J. van (2003). Loonkosten top stijgen 20% [Top salaries rise 20%]. (24 May 2003). *de Volkskrant.*

Delnooz, P. (1996). *Onderzoekspraktijken* [Research practices]. Amsterdam: Boom.

Dijk, J. van (1984). *Westers marxisme als sociale wetenschap: object, methode en praktijk van een onderzoekstraditie* [Western Marxism as social science: objective, method and practice of a research tradition]. Nijmegen: SUB.

Eisenberg, M.B., & Berkowitz, R.E. (1992). Information problem-solving: The big six skills approach. *School Library Media Activities Monthly, 8*(5), 27-29, 37 & 42.

Emans, B. (1990). *Open interviewen. Theorie, techniek en training* [Open interviews. Theory, technique and training]. Groningen: Wolters-Noordhoff.

Engbersen, G. (1991). Moderne armoede [Modern poverty]. *Sociologische Gids, 38*(1), 7-24.

Enquiry into Firearms Control. (n.d.) Retrieved on July 15, 2010, from www.parlement.com.

ESDS longitudinal studies. (n.d.) Retrieved on April 25, 2011, from www.esds.ac.uk/longitudinal/resources/international.asp.

Ess, H. van (2002). Dresseer uw zoekmachine. Zeven zoektips voor betere resultaten [Train your search engine. Seven searching tips for better results]. *Computertotaal, september,* 52-54.

Families spending less, third of children tell survey. (2011). Retrieved on April 13, 2011, from www.bbc.co.uk/news/education-12829746

Gaag, N. van der (2002). Waar wonen wij? De geografische verdeling van de bevolking in Nederland [Where do we live? The geographical spread of the population in the Netherlands]. *DEMOS, 18*(7), 56-60.

Gageldonk, A. van, & Rigter, H. (1998). *Preventie van psychische en gedragsproblemen: een beknopt overzicht van de stand van wetenschap* [Preventing psychological and behavioral problems: a concise overview of the state of science]. Den Haag: ZON. Retrieved on December 23, 2002, from www.trimbos.nl.

Gerrits, R. (7 January 2006). Studieduur nauwelijks afgenomen [Study duration has hardly decreased]. *de Volkskrant.*

Gille, E., Loijens, C., Noijons, J., & Zwitser, R. (2010). *Resultaten PISA-2009; praktische kennis en vaardigheden van 15-jarigen. Nederlandse uitkomsten van het Programme for International Student Assessment (PISA) op het gebied van leesvaardigheid, wiskunde en natuurwetenschappen in het jaar 2009* [Results of PISA 2009: the practical knowledge and skills of 15 year olds. Dutch results of the Programme for International Student Assessment (PISA) for reading skills, mathematics and science in 2009]. Arnhem: Cito.

Glaser, B.G., & Strauss A.L. (1967). *The discovery of Grounded Theory.* Chicago: Aldine. Nederlandse vertaling (1968). *De ontwikkeling van de gefundeerde theorie.* Alphen aan den Rijn: Samsom.

Gootjes-Klamer, L. (2009). *Over smaak valt te twisten; onderzoek naar waardering van beeldende kunst bij Pabo studenten* [There's no accounting for taste: research into art appreciation by college students]. Poster presented at the 'Research in cultural education' conference held on June 22, 2009 in Zwolle. Retrieved on September 9, 2010, from www.cultuurnetwerk.nl.

Greyhound Mystery Traveler. (n.d.) Retrieved on April 25, 2011, from www.ibiblio.org/hhalpin/homepage/notes/survey.pdf.

Hart, H. 't, Dijk, J. van, Goede, M. de, Jansen, W., & Teunissen, J. (1998). *Onderzoeksmethoden* [Research methods]. Amsterdam: Boom.

Heuvel, W.J.A. van den (1987). De mening van ouderen: tevreden? [The opinions of the elderly: satisfied?] In C.W. Aakster (ed.), *'Oud'. Beeld van ouderen en ouderenzorg* ['Old'. An image of the elderly and care for the elderly]. Groningen: Wolters-Noordhoff.

Hogendoorn, M. (1999). *Communicatieonderzoek. Een strategisch instrument* [Communications research. A strategic instrument]. Bussum: Coutinho.

Hopstaken, L.E.M. (1994). *Willens en wetens. Ziekmelden als beredeneerd gedrag* [Knowing full well. Reporting sick intentionally]. Universiteit Groningen.

Huff, D. (1991). *How to lie with statistics.* London: Penguin Books.

Huizing, L., Ossenbruggen, R. van, Muller, M., Wal, C. van der, & Lensvelt-Mulders, G. (2007). *Improving panel sampling: Embedding propensity scores & response behavior in sampling frames* (research report). Amsterdam: Motivaction.

Huizingh, E. (2008). *Inleiding SPSS 16.0 voor Windows en Data Entry* [Introduction to SPSS 16.0 for Windows and Data Entry]. Den Haag: Sdu Uitgevers.

Jadad, A. (1998). *Randomised controlled trials.* London: BMJ Books.

Janssen-Noordman, A., & Merrienboer, J.J.G. van (2002). *Innovatief onderwijs ontwerpen. Via leertaken naar complexe vaardigheden* [Designing innovative education. Using learning tasks to acquire complex skills]. Groningen: Wolters-Noordhoff.

Janssen-Noordman, A., Nelissen-de Vos, Y., & Ummels, N. (2002). Aanleren van complexe vaardigheden [Acquiring complex skills]. *Onderwijs Innovatie* (3), 17-26.

Jong, R. de (2010). *Onderzoek onder deelnemers Fietschallenge 2009* [Research among participants of the Cycling Challenge 2009]. Retrieved on November 17, 2010, from http://cyclobenelux.com.

Keeter, S., Kennedy, C. (2006). *The cell phone challenge to Survey Research* (research report). Washington: The Pew Research Center.

Kenter, E.G.H. (2002). Willekeur en leeftijdsdiscriminatie [Arbitrariness and age discrimination]. *Medisch Contact, 57*(43), 1577.

Keulen, H.M. van, Chorus, A.M.J., & Verheijden, M.W. (2010). *Monitor Convenant Gezond Gewicht: nulmeting (determinanten van) beweeg- en eetgedrag* [Monitor Covenant Healthy Weight: zero measurements (determinants of) exercise and eating habits]. Leiden: TNO Gezond en leven (TNO-rapportKvL/GB 2010.074).

Kohlmann, C. (2 June 2003). Vrouw werkt niet zomaar weinig [There's a reason why women work less]. *de Volkskrant.*

Lampert, M., Haveman, D., Zuur, K., & Sahin, H. (2005). *Young mentality.* Amsterdam: Motivaction/ Samona Uitgevers/Young Works.

Lim, B. (2010). *Academic internship at prime educational and social trust Pondicherry, India. To what extent might certain participant self-help groups default on their loans or encounter late payments on accounts?* (research report). Middelburg: Roosevelt Academy.

Lindeman, E. (1996). *Participatie in vrijwilligerswerk* [Participating in voluntary work]. Amsterdam: Thesis Publishers.

Maso, I., & Smaling, A. (1998). *Kwalitatief onderzoek: praktijk en theorie* [Qualitative research: practice and theory]. Amsterdam: Boom.

Mayer, B. (2000). *Do unconscious threats give us the shivers? A critical inquiry of Ohman's hypotheses about the pre-attentive elicitation of phobic fear.* Heerlen: Open Universiteit.

McDaniel, M.A., Morgeson, F.P., Finnegan, E.B., Campion, M.A., & Bravermann, E.P. (2001). Use of situational judgment tests to predict job performance. *Journal of Applied Psychology, 86*(4), 730-740.

Meel-Jansen, A.Th. van (1998). *Veelzijdig zien. Het pentagram model voor kunstwaardering* [From several points of view. The pentagram model for appreciating art]. Rijksuniversiteit Leiden.

Meeren, W. Vander, & Gerrichhauzen, J. (ed.) (1993). *Selectie en assessment. Theorie en praktijk* [Selection and assessment. Theory and practice]. Utrecht: Uitgeverij Lemma.

Meulen, D. van der (2002). *Multatuli. Leven en werk van Eduard Douwes Dekker* [Multatuli. The life and work of Eduard Douwes Dekker]. Amsterdam: SUN.

Migchelbrink, F. (2002). *Praktijkgericht onderzoek in zorg en welzijn* [Practical research in healthcare and well-being]. Amsterdam: SWP uitgeverij.

Morrison, A.M., White, R.P., & Velsor Van, E. (1994). *Can Women Reach The Top Of America's Largest Corporations?* New York: Perseus Publishing.

Mueller, T.E., Gavin, L.E. & Kulkarni, A. (2008). The Association Between Sex Education and Youth's Engagement in Sexual Intercourse, Age at First Intercourse, and Birth Control Use at First Sex. *Journal of adolescent health, 42*(1), 89-96.

Mulders, R. (2002). *Interview-NSS gaat mobiel interviewen* [Interview-NSS will conduct mobile interviews]. Retrieved on January 15, 2003, from www.emerce.nl.

National Survey of Family Growth (n.d.) Retrieved on April 25, 2011, from www.cdc.gov/nchs/nsfg.htm.

NIBUD (1998). Het NIBUD-onderzoek. *TUDELTA, 30*(26). Retrieved on March 30, 2006, from www.delta.tudelft.nl.

NIBUD (2010). *Leengedrag van studenten. Een vooronderzoek naar studieleningen, schulden en overige geldzaken* [Student borrowing habits. A preliminary research into study loans, debts and other money matters]. Utrecht: Nationaal Instituut voor Budgetvoorlichting.

Nicis Institute (2010). *De Veiligheidsmonitor* [The Security Monitor]. Retrieved on October 26, 2010, from www.veiligheidsmonitor.nl.

Nijdam, B. (2003). *Statistiek in onderzoek. Beschrijvende technieken 1* [Statistics in research. Descriptive techniques 1]. Groningen: Wolters-Noordhoff.

Nijdam, B., & Buuren, H. van (1999a). *Statistiek voor de sociale wetenschappen. Deel 1 Beschrijvende statistiek* [Statistics for social sciences. Part 1 Descriptive statistics]. Groningen: Wolters-Noordhoff.

Nijdam, B., & Buuren, H. van (1999b). *Statistiek voor de sociale wetenschappen. Deel 2 Inleiding in de inductieve statistiek* [Statistics for social sciences. Part 2 Introduction to inductive statistics]. Groningen: Wolters-Noordhoff.

Nijhof, G. (2000). *Levensverhalen. Over de methode van autobiografisch onderzoek in de sociologie* [Life stories. On autobiographical research methods in sociology]. Den Haag: Boom.

Oomkes, F.R. (2000). *Communicatieleer. Een inleiding* [Communication science. An introduction]. Den Haag: Boom Onderwijs.

Oost, H. (1999). *De kwaliteit van probleemstellingen in dissertaties* [The quality of problem formulation in dissertations]. Utrecht: IVLOS.

Oost, H. (2002a). *Een onderzoek rapporteren* [Research reporting]. Baarn: HB Uitgevers.

Oost, H. (2002b). *Een onderzoek voorbereiden* [Preparing research]. Baarn: HB Uitgevers.

Parlementair Documentatie Centrum (2005). *Parlementair onderzoek TBS-stelsel* [Parliamentary enquiry into the TBS scheme]. Retrieved on March 26, 2006, from www.parlement.com.

Pauchli, W. (2010). *Spijbelen in het MBO, praktijkgericht onderzoek* [Truancy at college: applied research]. Utrecht: IVLOS.

Pieters, J.M., & Jochems, W.M.G. (2003). Onderwijs en onderwijsonderzoek: and ever the twain shall meet? [Education and educational research]. *Pedagogische Studiën, 80,* 407-413.

Ponte, P. (2007). *Onderwijs van eigen makelij* [Home-grown education]. Den Haag: Uitgeverij Lemma.

Reijn, G. (November 5, 2002). Roddelbladen scoren niet alleen bij de kapper [Gossip magazines a hit, and not only at the dentist]. *de Volkskrant.*

Rooij, E. van, Pass, J., & Broek, A. van den (2010). *Geruisloos uit het onderwijs. Het verschil tussen klassieke en geruisloze risicofactoren van voortijdig schoolverlaten* [Silent drop outs. The difference between classic and silent risk factors for leaving school prematurely] (research report). Nijmegen: ResearchNed. Retrieved on October 4, 2010, from www.voortijdigschoolverlaten.nl.

Roy, G., & Vanheuverzwyn, A. (2002). *Mobile phone in sample surveys.* Kopenhagen: ICIS.

Salary Survey. (n.d.) Retrieved May 16, 2011, from www.robertwalters.com/resources/salarysurvey2010/ USA_Salary_Survey_2010.pdf.

Sande, J.P. van de (1999). *Gedragsobservatie. Een inleiding tot systematisch observeren* [Behavioral observation. An introduction to systematic observation]. Groningen: Wolters-Noordhoff.

Saunders, M., Lewis, P., & Thornhill, A. (2003). *Research methods for business students.* Harlow: Prentice Hall.

Sayer, R.A. (2000). *Realism and Social Science.* London: Sage.

Slotboom, A. (2008). *Statistiek in woorden* [Statistics in words] (4th edition). Groningen: Wolters-Noordhoff.

Smith, N. (2002) *American Empire: Roosevelt's Geographer and the Prelude to Globalization.* California: University of California Press.

Spangenberg, F., & Lampert, M. (2010). *De grenzeloze generatie* [Generation without boundaries]. Amsterdam: Uitgeverij Nieuw Amsterdam.

Stellinga, M. (2009). *De mythe van het glazen plafond* [The myth of the glass ceiling]. Amsterdam: Uitgeverij Balans.

Strien, P. van (1975). Naar een methodologie van het praktijkdenken in de sociale wetenschappen [Towards a method for practical thinking in the social sciences]. *Nederlands Tijdschrift voor de Psychologie, 30,* 601-619.

Strien, P. van (1986). *Praktijk als wetenschap, methodologie van het sociaal-wetenschappelijk handelen* [Practice as science: methodology for social science approaches]. Assen, Maastricht: Van Gorcum.

SURFnet. (2006). *Het SURFnet-netwerk.* Retrieved on October 21, 2006, from www.surfnet.nl/info/net-werk/nationaal/home.jsp.

Swanborn, P.G. (1987). *Methoden van sociaal-wetenschappelijk onderzoek* [Methods for social science research]. Amsterdam: Boom.

Swanborn, P.G. (1998). *Schaaltechnieken. Theorie en praktijk van acht eenvoudige procedures* [Scale techniques. Theory and practice of eight simple procedures]. Amsterdam: Boom.

Swanborn, P.G. (2000). *Case-study's. Wat, wanneer en hoe* [Case studies. What, when and how]. Den Haag: Boom Onderwijs.

Swanborn, P.G. (2002). *Evalueren* [Evaluating]. Den Haag: Boom Onderwijs.

Swanborn, P.G. (2010). *Basisboek sociaal onderzoek* [Introduction to social research]. Den Haag: Boom Lemma uitgevers.

Trochim, W.M.K. (2006). *Research methods knowledge base.* Retrieved on December 19, 2010, from www.socialresearchmethods.net.

Tweevoeter (2005). *Nordic Walking ontlast de gewrichten nauwelijks* [Nordic Walking barely relieves strain on the joints]. Retrieved on January 27, 2006, from www.tweevoeter.nl.

Ultee, W., Arts, W., & Flap, H. (1992). *Sociologie. Vragen, uitspraken, bevindingen* [Sociology. Questions, statements, findings]. Groningen: Wolters-Noordhoff.

Verhoeven, N. (1998). *Dienstencentra in de gemeente Soest. Een inventarisatie van de behoeften en wensen ten aanzien van het gebruik van dienstencentra, door 55-plussers in Soest en Soesterberg* [Service center in Soest Municipality. An inventory of the needs and wishes regarding the use of the service center by those above the age of 55 in Soest and Soesterberg]. Soest: Bureau voor Onderzoek & Statistiek.

Verhoeven, P.S. (2002a). *AJO, een jeugdorkest in beweging* [AYO, a youth orchestra on the move]. Soest: Bureau voor Onderzoek & Statistiek.

Verhoeven, P.S. (2002b). *De deelnemers aan het woord. Evaluatieonderzoek onder deelnemers aan de Sylvestercross 2001* [Participants' opinions. Evaluation research among participants of the Sylvester Cross 2001] (research report). Soest: Bureau voor Onderzoek & Statistiek.

Verhoeven, P.S. (2002c). *De medewerkers aan het woord. Evaluatieonderzoek onder medewerkers aan de Sylvestercross 2002* [Staff opinions. Evaluation research among staff of the Sylvester Cross 2001]. Soest: Bureau voor Onderzoek & Statistiek.

Verhoeven, P.S. (2002d). *Gebruik van het Milieucompendium 2001. Verslag van het evaluatieonderzoek onder (mogelijke) gebruikers van het Milieucompendium 2001* [Using the Environment compendium 2001. Report on the evaluation research among users of the Environment compendium 2001] (research report). Soest: Bureau voor Onderzoek & Statistiek.

Verhoeven, N. (2003). *ATLAS Ledenraadpleging 2003. Vragenlijstonderzoek naar tevredenheid van de leden van de HIS-gebruikersvereniging met de ontwikkelingen op het gebied van Promedico en Arcos* [ATLAS members consultation 2003. Survey into the satisfaction of HIS users into the developments in Promedico and Arcos] (research report). Soest: Bureau voor Onderzoek & Statistiek.

Verhoeven, P.S. (2009). *Quality in statistics education. Determinants of student outcomes in methods & statistics education at universities and colleges* (diss.). Den Haag: Boom Academic.

Verhoeven, N. (2010). *Onderzoeken doe je zo!* [This is how you do research!]. Den Haag: Boom Lemma uitgevers.

Verhoeven, N., Jansen, W., & Tazelaar, F. (2000). Sociaal kapitaal van mannen en vrouwen op de arbeidsmarkt [Social capital of men and women in the labour market]. *Tijdschrift voor Arbeidsvraagstukken, 16*(1), 49-67.

Vermeulen, M. (5 February 2003). Kinderen met een lege agenda zijn pas sneu [Children with nothing to do are the sad cases]. *de Volkskrant.*

Verschuren, P.J.M. (1999). *De probleemstelling voor een onderzoek* [Problem formulation for research]. Utrecht: Het Spectrum.

Verschuren, P., & Doorewaard, H. (2007). *Het ontwerpen van een onderzoek* [Designing a research project] (4th edition). Den Haag: Boom Lemma uitgevers.

Verster, J.C., Bekker, E.M., Roos, M. de, Minova, A., Eijken, E.J.E., Kooij, J.J.S., Buitelaar, J.K., Kenemans, J.L., Verbaten, M.N., Olivier, B., & Volkerts, E.R. (2008). Methylphenidate significantly improves driving performance of adults with attention-deficit hyperactivity disorder: A randomized crossover trial. *Journal of Psychopharmacology, 22*, 230-237.

Visser, E. de (5 April 2003). Met Ritalin had ik minder haast [When I was on Ritalin, I was in less of a hurry]. *de Volkskrant.*

Vliet, D. van (13 november 2002). Alcohol verhoogt de kans op borstkanker bij vrouwen [Alcohol increases the risk of breast cancer among women]. *Algemeen Dagblad.*

Vrolijk, A., Dijkema, M.F., & Timmerman, G. (1972). *Gespreksmodellen* [Discussion models]. Alphen aan den Rijn: Samsom.

VU Medisch Centrum (2010). *Universitair Netwerk Ouderenzorg* [University network for care of the elderly]. Retrieved on December 19, 2010, from www.vumc.nl/afdelingen/UNO/.

Wester, F. (1991). *Strategieën voor kwalitatief onderzoek.* [Strategies for qualitative research]. Muiderberg: Coutinho.

Wester, F., Smaling, A., & Mulder, L. (ed.) (2000). *Praktijkgericht kwalitatief onderzoek.* [Applied qualitative research]. Bussum: Uitgeverij Coutinho.

Wikipedia. (2006). *About Wikipedia.* Retrieved on February 27, 2011, from www.wikipedia.org/wiki/wikipedia.

Websites Consulted

www.aging.senate.gov

Buurtwinkels.ahm.nl

Citationmachine.net

Docs.google.com

Dreamstime.com

isiwebofknowledge.com

mediatheek.thinkquest.nl

medischcontact.artsennet.nl

nl.surveymonkey.com

scholar.google.com

scholar.google.nl

www.aanbodpagina.nl

www.aging.senate.gov

www.amstat.org/publications

www.archeon.nl

www.bbc.co.uk

www.bedreigdedemocratie.nl

www.Big6.com

www.borstborst.nl/leven-met-borstkanker.php

www.bovenaan.nl

www.cbs.nl

www.cdc.gov

www.coe.usu.edu

www.communicatieonderzoek.nl

www.computertotaal.nl

www.delta.tudelft.nl

www.deltawerken.com

www.endnote.com

www.ergonomie.nl

www.esds.ac.uk

www.europarl.europa.eu

www.fi.uu.nl

www.franklin-square.com

www.geheugenvannederland.nl

www.huygensinstituut.knaw.nl

www.ict-onderwijsmonitor.nl

www.ibiblio.org

www.ir.ub.rug.nl

www.knaw.dans.nl

www.kwalitan.nl

www.kwfkankerbestrijding.nl

www.learningsolutionsgroup.com

www.library.uu.nl

www.lifesciences2020.nl

www.maxqda.de

www.minvws.nl

www.motivaction.nl

www.netq.nl

www.nownederland.nl

www.nrc.nl/W2/Lab/Profiel/Provincies/enquête.html

www.parlement.com

www.picarta.nl

www.qualiteit.nl

www.refman.com

www.refworks.com

www.robertwalters.com

www.sanford-artedventures.com

www.scopus.com

www.socialresearchmethods.net

www.surfspot.nl

www.trimbos.nl

www.tweevoeter.nl

www.unicef.kpnis.nl

www.vandermaesen.nl

www.wikipedia.nl

Index

About the Author

In 1997, Nel Verhoeven graduated in sociology from the University of Utrecht. Since then she has accumulated a great deal of experience as a sociological researcher and statistician. This included working as an independent social science researcher for several years, during which time she acted as a statistics consultant, advising business and institutions in these matters. She has also developed curricula and taught at colleges and universities.

Nel Verhoeven is currently working for the Roosevelt Academy in Middelburg, the Netherlands. She is Associate Professor of Methodology and Statistics. She is also Head of the Eleanor Institute for Undergraduate Research, a project bureau of the Roosevelt Academy. In 2009, Nel Verhoeven completed her doctoral study in statistics attitudes and teaching at universities and colleges. Nel Verhoeven is also the author of *Sterk in je werk* [Strength in the workplace] (Boom Education, 2006) and *Onderzoeken doe je zo!* [This is how to do research!] (Boom Lemma uitgevers, 2010). She also develops digital courses about research and statistics.